REPUBLIC
ON TRIAL

REPUBLIC ON TRIAL

The Case for
Representative Democracy

Alan Rosenthal , 1932-
Eagleton Institute of Politics
Rutgers University

Burdett A. Loomis
University of Kansas

John R. Hibbing
University of Nebraska, Lincoln

Karl T. Kurtz
National Conference of State Legislatures

CQ PRESS

Washington, D.C.

CQ Press
1255 22nd St. N.W., Suite 400
Washington, D.C. 20037

(202) 729-1900; toll-free, 1-866-4CQ-PRESS (1-866-427-7737)

www.cqpress.com

Printed and bound in the United States of America

06 05 04 03 02   5 4 3 2 1

♾ The paper used in this publication meets the minimum requirements of the American National Standard for Information Sciences—
Permanence of Paper for Printed Library Materials, ANSI Z39.48-1992.

Cover: Auburn Incorporated

Library of Congress Cataloging-in-Publication Data

Rosenthal, Alan
    Republic on trial : the case for representative democracy / Alan
Rosenthal, Burdett A. Loomis, John R. Hibbing.
        p.   cm.
Includes bibliographical references and index.
        ISBN 1-56802-652-8 (alk. paper)
        1. Democracy—United States. 2. Representative government and
representation—United States. 3. Legislators—United States.
4. Political participation—United States. 5. United States—Politics and
government—Public opinion. 6. Public opinion—United States. I.
Loomis, Burdett A. II. Hibbing, John R. III. Title.
    JK1726 .R73 2003
    320.973—dc21

                                                    2002008193

To our twenty-one children and grandchildren

(and those yet to come), that they might

better appreciate representative democracy

Contents

Tables and Figures

Preface

The four of us are intrigued and amazed by how the American political system operates, and that it works as well as it does. It is a complex, human, and unpredictable process that we have spent our careers as political scientists trying to understand and explain. We think we have made progress, but we have yet to nail it down.

Republic on Trial: The Case for Representative Democracy was a pleasure to write. It enabled us to take stock, compare ideas, and learn from each other in a collaborative effort to capture and communicate the essence of the American system of representative democracy.

To many readers, perhaps, it will provide a new perspective on an old subject. Indeed, it was written with multiple purposes and audiences in mind: as a basic orientation for college students beginning their study of American government; as a useful framework for more advanced students in courses on Congress, state legislatures, interest groups, and lobbying; and, finally, as an argument on behalf of representative democracy that elected public officials and other practitioners themselves ought to be making.

The basic ideas contained in this book were first tested in *A New Public Perspective on Representative Democracy: A Guide for Legislative Interns*, a monograph that deals only with state legislatures and that was published in 2000 by the National Conference of State Legislatures (NCSL) and cosponsored by the American Political Science Association (APSA) and the Center for Civic Education. After a year's trial with college-age legislative interns, the monograph was revised to incorporate Congress as well as state legislatures and published, again by NCSL, as *The Case for Representative Democracy: What Americans Should Know about Their Legislatures* (2001). The Center on Congress at Indiana University joined NCSL and the other two organizations as partners in the publication of this volume. *Republic on Trial* represents a significant expansion of both the case for and the case against our system of representative democracy, and it is aimed at a wider market.

We are grateful to William Pound, NCSL's executive director, whose dedication to America's legislatures led to the creation of NCSL's Trust for Representative Democracy and provided the forum for these ideas. We appreciate the support and encouragement provided by Sheilah Mann of APSA, Charles Quigley and Michael Fischer of the Center for Civic Education, and, especially, Lee Hamilton of the Center on Congress. Our discovery that Hamilton, a former member of Congress from Indiana, was making arguments about Congress that were nearly identical to ours about state legislatures inspired us to expand the scope of our work.

Brenda Carter of CQ Press saw the potential of this book and with Charisse Kiino, Ann Davies, and Joanne Ainsworth helped us convey our ideas and polish our writing. K. Robert Keiser of San Diego State University, Brian Fife of Indiana University—Purdue University, Fort Wayne, and Terry Jones of the University of Missouri, St. Louis, reviewed the manuscript. Bruce Holdeman of 601 Design in Denver provided drawings that illustrate the good and the bad of the "legislative stew" far better than do the more traditional "how a bill becomes a law" cartoons. Karen Hansen of NCSL provided valuable editorial and design advice. Joanne Pfeiffer of the Eagleton Institute of Politics at Rutgers University and Joyce Johnson of NCSL assisted us in the production of the book.

Above all, thanks to James Madison for his enduring vision and justification of the American republic in the Constitution and *The Federalist Papers*. This book would not have been written without the benefit of his writings.

Alan Rosenthal
Burdett A. Loomis
John R. Hibbing
Karl T. Kurtz

Introduction

AFTER THE CONSTITU-
tional Convention, Ben-
jamin Franklin was
asked what kind of gov-
ernment the framers had
produced. "A republic, if
you can keep it," he
replied. The American
republic is synonymous
with representative
democracy, the political
system through which
citizens govern them-
selves. Representative
democracy is *democratic*
in that the people have
the power to choose
those who govern; it is

representative in that the people themselves do not govern but leave governance to the agents they elect. The engines of representative democracy are
Congress at the national level and legislatures at the state level, with the executive and judicial branches playing important supporting roles.

Congress and the state legislatures have proved to be enduring and re-
silient institutions. Fashioned more than 200 years ago, they have managed
to adapt to different challenges and environments. Together with presidents and governors (and to some extent the courts as well), they make
laws, enact budgets, and raise revenues. They engage in activities that

constitute critical government functions affecting the health, welfare, education, and economy of the nation and the states.

Today, however, representative democracy, as practiced in the nation and the states, is under fire. The critics are many, the supporters relatively few. Indeed, it would appear that the American republic is on trial. The case against political people, political institutions, and political processes is frequently heard. The case for representative democracy also must be heard, and making the case that representative democracy works—not without flaws but better than any conceivable alternative—is a principal purpose of this book.

Problems of Democracy

Any political system can be expected to encounter problems, and representative democracy in the United States has its share. The system and its institutions have encountered military aggression, as in the Second World War; internal strife, as in the Civil War; domestic crisis, as during the Great Depression of the 1930s; and periods of populist and progressive reform. The system has weathered storms and less tempestuous waters as well. Currently, American democracy is engaged in warfare of a distinctive kind, as it attempts to root out terrorists at home and abroad and repel an ugly threat to its people.

In a period of national crisis Americans normally rally around the flag as they did following September 11, 2001. The aftermath of the terrorist attacks on the World Trade Center and the Pentagon saw unparalleled unity in the country. Support for the president rose to stratospheric levels, and even Congress received extraordinary job performance ratings in public opinion polls. But beneath the national mood there persists a distrust and cynicism toward the practices and workings of the system. It is as if Americans separated the exceptional situation, where politics are of no matter, from the normal situation, where politics count all too much in the mind of the public.

Americans have always had an uneasy relationship with their political institutions and elected officials. Their ideal images of democracy don't allow for the rough and tumble of democratic practices. The latter are referred to derogatorily as "just politics"—the way the system unfortunately works but not the way it ought to work. Few people believe that it actually works pretty much as it should. Understanding of the processes of politics is limited, partly because people have little time or incentive to try to understand, and partly because the processes are extraordinarily difficult to comprehend. The costs in sheer effort of trying to understand are higher than all but a few of the most motivated are willing to pay.

There is a common expression in legislative circles that is attributed to Germany's late-nineteenth-century chancellor Otto von Bismarck: "There are two things you don't want to see being made—sausage and legislation." The saying likens the legislative process pejoratively to a sausage factory, where the ingredients, manufacturing processes, and final product all are unattractive and untrustworthy. Sausage making is no longer what it was in Bismarck's time, or even in the novelist Upton Sinclair's time, as described in his muckraking book on the meat-packing industry, *The Jungle*. The sausage-making process has been completely reformed. It is tightly regulated by the government, focused on quality control, and quite comprehensible to anyone who wants to understand it. Legislation and lawmaking are very different—more diverse, broader in scope, and much more indeterminate. The legislative process, whether in Congress or in the states, is unique, incomparable, not like anything else in people's experience—and no longer, if ever, like sausage making.

Another ubiquitous image of the legislative process is the cartoon board game of "how a bill becomes a law" in which a bill moves from introduction to first reading to referral to committee and on through many steps ending with the governor signing a measure into law. However technically accurate these cartoons may be, they are not really how a bill becomes a law. Nor is it important that anyone outside a capitol building understand the details of first reading, second reading, conference committees, enrollment, or engrossment. The flaw of these legislative board game illustrations is that they leave out the dynamics of disagreement, public input, deliberation, negotiation, and compromise that are much more vital to the public's understanding of what Congress and state legislatures do.

We believe the cartoon of the "legislative stew" presented in this introduction more accurately describes how a bill *really* becomes a law. It

A Bill Becomes a Law: Revised Version

suggests how ideas that appear straightforward at the outset become complicated as they draw more attention from different "cooks"—other legislators, the public and their lobbyists, the media, and political parties—and more ideas are tossed into the pot of legislation. Whether it is stew or legislation, the results of this collaboration among many different cooks are usually a far cry from the original recipe and have been watered down somewhat to finish the job. How a bill goes from introduction to enactment can be a messy and mysterious process. But in the legislature, unlike in the kitchen, too many cooks do not spoil the broth.

Perhaps its incomprehensibility is one reason that the legislative process is so difficult to appreciate. Before the searing experiences of Watergate, which resulted in the impeachment and resignation of President Richard M. Nixon, and the Vietnam War in the 1960s and 1970s, Americans may not have appreciated the day-to-day operations of their system, but they maintained a basic trust. That basic trust is much diminished today, replaced by a pervasive cynicism toward and distrust of the political people, institutions, and processes that govern the nation and the states. As we will explain in Chapter 1, this perspective has developed and flourished because of the unrelenting negative environment in which politics is conducted.

Dangers of Distrust and Cynicism

Today's distrust and cynicism on the part of Americans is practically taken for granted. People live with it, and politics appears to adjust to this perpetual condition. But the adjustment has serious consequences. Public distrust and cynicism toward representative democracy has an erosive effect on the public sphere, making the challenge of self-government more difficult than it would otherwise be. And self-government is no easy matter under the best conditions.

First, *distrust and cynicism are demoralizing* to those who make a commitment to public service. Elected public officials are sensitive to the negative mood. It disturbs them, and they feel frustrated in not knowing what to do about it. For example, at the 2001 annual meeting of the National

Conference of State Legislatures, public opinion consultant Frank Luntz conducted an interactive session attended by about 1,000 state legislators from around the country. He polled a sample of 250 of them on what they liked least about being a legislator. He offered the following items from among which they could choose:

- Constant fund-raising
- Constant campaigning
- Lack of financial compensation
- Media scrutiny
- Partisanship
- Personal family sacrifices
- Lobbyists
- Public cynicism

All are considered burdens of legislative office. But the sample of legislators ranked public cynicism highest. They feel it.

The happiness of legislators might not be of concern in itself. However, able people are being discouraged from holding public office. Some who are already serving decide to leave rather than to have to put up with such a mean climate. For instance, during Walter Baker's term in the Kentucky General Assembly, some of his colleagues were convicted of corrupt practices in connection with a Federal Bureau of Investigation sting known as Boptrot. The media vehemently assailed the entire legislature and called into question the integrity of every member, even though only a few were guilty. Baker, a man of great integrity and the fourth generation of his family to serve in the Kentucky legislature, announced his retirement soon after. He had had enough. Baker's son was unwilling in such a climate to continue the family tradition of legislative service, and Baker did not try to persuade him otherwise.

More numerous than those who drop out because of public distrust and cynicism are those who never even get into politics because of such a nasty climate. Years ago, the men and women who ran for and were elected to state legislatures had to sacrifice personal income, outside careers, and family life in order to engage in legislative politics. Some of those who did so subsequently went on to Congress and had full-time careers in public office. Today, many otherwise eligible candidates—like Walter Baker's son—are not willing to make the sacrifices required by political life. Sacrificing income, an outside career, and one's family may be tolerable for those who feel strongly about making a difference, but additionally risking one's reputation because of public cynicism and distrust may not be worth it—at least for many people who might be well suited for public service. If the fire doesn't burn in their bellies, they are likely to pursue paths that are not so heavily mined.

Second, *distrust and cynicism help weaken legislative institutions,* thus making the job of governing more problematic than it would otherwise be. Look, for example, at what has happened to legislatures in California and Colorado.

A quarter of a century ago the California Legislature was the nation's model legislature, almost as sophisticated as Congress. In a 1970 study of all fifty legislatures, which was conducted by the Citizens Conference on State Legislatures and funded by the Ford Foundation, California ranked first. Everyone looked up to California's legislature, a professional body whose members were able and creative lawmakers and whose staff was highly skilled. Like Congress and the president, the California Legislature played a role coequal to that of the governor and the executive branch of state government. No longer is the California Legislature a model, let alone *the* model. Legislators here, as well as in sixteen other states, are term-limited. Members of the California Assembly are permitted to serve only six years and members of the California Senate are permitted only eight years before having to move on. The expertise of their predecessors is gone, and leadership, especially in the assembly, is inexperienced and short-lived. Term limits, reductions and controls on the size of the legislature's budget, and other blows to the legislature as an institution have been inflicted not by the governor, lobbyists, or legislators themselves. They have been imposed by the California electorate, which initiated and ratified many institutionally damaging amendments over the past twenty years. Today's legislature in the largest state of the nation is straitjacketed in tax and budget policy and restricted in other domains as well.

In most respects the part-time, citizen legislature of Colorado contrasts sharply with the full-time, professional legislature of California. In recent times, Republicans have controlled the Colorado legislature and Democrats the California Legislature. Regardless of these differences, both are hamstrung. Even more than in California, the legislature in Colorado has had a reputation for being the dominant branch of state government. Today it is only a shadow of its former self, because of the citizen initiatives that have limited the terms of members, reshaped internal procedures, and curtailed the legislature's tax and budget authority. The Colorado legislature, for instance, has lost one of the most fundamental powers in a representative democracy, the power to tax. A voter-initiated constitutional amendment requires that any change in Colorado tax laws be approved by a vote of the people.

Other legislatures, North, South, and East as well as West, and the U.S. Congress find themselves in similar circumstances. Most of them are weaker political institutions than they were in the 1970s. In large part, this stems from the climate in which they operate nowadays. The outlet for this public antagonism in California, Colorado, and twenty-two other states has been voter initiatives that circumscribe legislative authority to make law. Although legislative authority has not been as directly challenged in the twenty-six states where there is no voter initiative, their legislatures still suffer from lack of support and understanding—but no lack of distrust. One consequence is that just about everywhere the process of consensus building is adversely affected, and reaching agreement becomes even more difficult than it normally is.

Third, *distrust and cynicism are undermining our system of government while facilitating alternatives.* One alternative to representative democracy is *executive dominance*, whereby presidents and governors work their will and legislatures act as rubber stamps. Another alternative is *direct democracy*, whereby the study, deliberation, and negotiation of representative assemblies is supplanted by public initiatives or referenda that vote major issues up or down.

Although Americans have not made a deliberate choice to reject representative democracy in favor of an alternative system, their negative mood has serious consequences for governance. It affects the types of people who run and serve, whether and how consensus gets built, the policies that are enacted, and the degree to which the policies work. If people were to give some thought to how and how well the political system actually works and whether an alternative would work better, they would opt for the system they already have. Perhaps not. But after some deliberation, their choice at least would be more informed, more considered, and more conscious. The republic is on trial, and Americans have to choose now because it may be too late to choose later.

Examining Whether Representative Democracy Works

A fundamental question for the citizens of any political system is, Does it work? That entails an examination of how it works and whether it meets the standards or conditions by which its effectiveness can be assessed. Our objective in this book is to help readers make a judgment as to the effectiveness of their political system. In the interests of full disclosure, we shall leave no doubt as to what we think. Representative democracy works. It does not work perfectly, it has its problems, but on balance it operates along the lines the founders of our nation had in mind and is a good fit for a democratic society such as ours. And it is constantly undergoing change and adaptation.

Admittedly, we, the authors, are closer than most to the phenomena about which we are writing. The four of us are political scientists who have devoted considerable time and energy to the study of Congress and state legislatures. Thus, we have come to know the subject pretty well. Some might say that we know it too well, have gotten too close to legislators and legislatures, and—like some cultural anthropologists—have gone native. Familiarity with a subject can interfere with the objectivity that we as scholars try to bring to our work. We try to guard against that, but there is no denying our backgrounds. One of us has observed state legislatures close-up for more than thirty years and has worked with legislators in more than thirty states. Another has written about Congress, state legislatures, and interest groups. A third, who has studied Congress extensively, recently explored through national surveys and focus groups the public's view of the principles and practices of democracy. And one of us has worked for thirty years on the staff of the National Conference of State Legislatures, an organization that serves the legislators and legislative staff in the fifty states.

We try to give due consideration to the problems of representative democracy—partisanship, negative political campaigns, campaign contributions, and the unequal power of interest groups. But our principal thrust, as readers can see, is to make the case for representative democracy, despite its problems. Indeed, a major justification for this book is that the discussion has been one-sided, and we hope to redress the imbalance.

Nowadays praise in any form is rarely given the political system or political institutions, although individual practitioners manage to win plaudits from time to time (not infrequently for their criticism of the system of which they are a part). Academics, by temperament and training, come naturally to the role of critic. So do journalists, reformers, and students. It is easy to engage in the discussion of what's wrong with American politics. Negative campaigns, with which critics take issue, are not restricted to the electoral arena; they go on in the broader arenas of governance. But in these skirmishes there are few defenders of the political system. Hardly anyone makes the case for the system we have, whereas many critics make the case against it. Indeed, the environment is so filled with the negative that a disservice is done not only to the nation's political institutions and processes but also to the nation's citizens. If the republic is to receive a fair trial, people have a right to hear not only the case *against*, which they hear all the time, but also the case *for*. By offering an alternative perspective on representative democracy, perhaps we can furnish necessary balance.

Before we examine the central issues of this book, it is necessary in Chapter 1 to review not only what people think about the system but, more important, why they think what they do. The picture of distrust and cynicism is not a pretty one. But, in view of the environment for politics over the past thirty years, it is to be expected because the dice are so negatively loaded. In Chapter 2 we contrast the way people feel today to how the framers of the U.S. Constitution felt in the eighteenth century. Despite the reservations that the framers had about human nature and political power, they were engaged in the positive work of creating a political system of balanced powers and fashioning legislative bodies designed to represent the states and the people.

Chapter 3 addresses the question of whether there is a need for representative democracy. If the public stood in agreement on most policy issues, there would be no need for a legislature, that is, a body to represent the differing views of society. Americans tend to think, "we all agree, so why are those people down at the capitol always disagreeing?" But if the people are wrong and there is no public will and less consensus than is commonly believed, then legislatures are necessary to represent the differing points of view and translate them into policy.

In Chapters 4 through 8 we examine the conditions that have to be met if representative democracy can be said to work. None of these conditions can be expected to be satisfied fully, but each has to be met in large part. It is up to the reader to judge from the analysis advanced in these chapters whether the processes and practices of the system pass the test.

The first condition, addressed in Chapter 4, pertains to the character and motivations of legislators themselves—the people who serve as representatives in a representative democracy. In order for the system to work, these elected officials must be people of basic integrity, motivated to promote what they consider to be the public interest. This allows for some who are corrupt, some who are unethical, and some who are self-absorbed (all of whom, after all, are elected by voters in their states and districts). But the vast majority have to be of a much better sort. Are they?

The second condition, explored in Chapter 5, requires that somehow representatives and constituencies be closely linked. Constituency interests and opinions have to be expressed, to some degree, by elected representatives. Moreover, the connection between legislators and constituents must extend beyond policy to the more nitty-gritty concerns of the people back home. If constituency counts as far as legislator behavior is concerned, then the linkage condition is satisfied.

The third condition, treated in Chapter 6, applies to the expression of people's values and interests through political organizations known as special interest groups. If such groups represent a large majority of the population, if they cover nearly all conceivable interests, and if they have access to the legislative process, then another condition is met. But if such groups have as members only a few people, if they cover only certain interests, and if only certain groups have access, then Americans ought to question how well representative democracy is working.

The fourth condition, the subject of Chapter 7, relates to the legislative process itself. If disagreement is a fundamental hallmark of public opinion, constituencies, and interest groups, then the process can be expected to be contentious. But the process should also include elements of study, deliberation, negotiation, and consensus building. And making policy must require a majority of votes. That is the way a democratic system is supposed to work. The public, unfortunately, does not adequately understand this principle.

The fifth and final condition, which is dealt with in Chapter 8, pertains to accountability. For representative democracy to work, individuals, political parties, and the institutions themselves must somehow be accountable to the citizenry. That is to say, voters have to be able to reward or punish their elected representatives for their actions. Thus, the electorate has to have ultimate control.

In Chapter 9 our perspective changes. Focusing on Congress and state legislatures, we ask how well they have been working, mainly by looking at their performance today as compared with that in the past. Are they more or less representative, capable, transparent, ethical, competitive, participatory, internally democratic, and responsive? We look for progress in achieving such values and characteristics.

Chapter 10 reprises and concludes by suggesting additional standards by which representative democracy can be judged and then asks how it compares with alternative systems—that of executive dominance and that of direct democracy. The comparison, as the reader might expect, demonstrates that the current system of representative democracy has significant advantages.

Perhaps there is a preferable political system out there, but we have not discovered it. The present system works. There are no guarantees, however, that it will continue to work, not without greater public understanding, appreciation, and support. We hope that this book contributes to that end—building understanding, appreciation, and even support to go along with continuing criticism and healthy skepticism, all of which are required for the health of a democracy.

1

What Does the Public Think?

FOR SOME TIME NOW Americans have been unhappy with their political institutions and the politicians they elect to govern. The terrorist attacks on September 11, 2001, changed the nation's mood, at least for a while. It changed how the public regarded government, the president, Congress, and perhaps others in public office as well. In the rally around the flag, all benefited from the more positive light being cast.

But Americans' cynicism and distrust, which have been in the making since the 1960s, are now rather deeply embedded. This does not mean that support for the nation or for democratic principles is lessened. At this emotional level, Americans continue their allegiance, especially in the face of the hateful threat to the United States and its democratic system. But the specific institutions and processes of representative democracy are in question and in jeopardy. However positive Americans feel at one level—that of nation and even government as a whole—during a time of crisis, at another level they feel negatively about just how the political system, its institutions, and its politicians work.

What People Think

Public opinion polls, and in particular the American National Election Studies survey—a biennial investigation of voting behavior and public opinion conducted by the University of Michigan—provide compelling evidence of public dissatisfaction with political institutions and political officeholders both in Washington, D.C., and the states.

For many years people's trust in government was in decline. When asked in the 1960s, "How much of the time do you think you can trust government in Washington to do what is right?" three out of four people responded "just about always" or "most of the time." By 2000 only two out of five people responded this way. Over the course of about thirty-five years the decline was gradual but steady, rebounding from time to time but not enough to change direction for very long.

The terrorist attacks on the United States on September 11, 2001, caused trust in government to increase markedly. A *Washington Post* poll found that almost two-thirds of Americans said that they trust the federal government to do the right thing "nearly always" or "most of the time." Whether such trust will continue for long is questionable, since it also increased during the Persian Gulf War but then receded. The context in which this trust-in-government question is asked, it would seem, heavily affects how it is answered. With the United States at war, not to trust the government to do the right thing verges on being unpatriotic. In more normal times dependence on government is diminished and trust is less vital.

Until the recent surge in support, public confidence in government institutions—specifically legislatures—had declined steadily. Congress has not fared well according to Gallup Polls, which have been taken from 1973 on. In that year, 42 percent of the public said it had "a great deal" or "quite a lot" of confidence in Congress. By mid-2001 the percentage was down to 26. Confidence in the presidency also dropped but was still much greater than confidence in Congress. Meanwhile, confidence in the Supreme Court has been reasonably high and stable over the years. Out of fifteen public and private institutions, Congress ranked last or next to last in public confidence in three recent years. After September 11 confidence in Congress rose, but by 2002 it was declining.

Public opinion data on confidence in state legislatures are elusive. Evaluations of legislative job performance range greatly from place to place and time to time. However, one indicator of citizen confidence in state legislatures has been the adoption through the initiative process in nineteen states of term limits for legislators. A variety of factors shaped the vote of state electorates, but one of them surely was dissatisfaction with the legislature and legislators. In two states, Mississippi and North Dakota, term limits were defeated on the ballot, perhaps suggesting that these electorates had more confidence in their legislatures.

People do not believe that government works in their interest, except for national defense. They feel alienated, in part because they do not believe that those who govern pay any attention to their views. Recently 56 percent agreed with the statement, "I don't think public officials care much what people like me think," whereas in 1964 only 36 percent agreed. In one survey, people were asked whether they thought their elected representatives, if contacted by them, would pay attention to what they said. About half the respondents thought members of Congress would pay very little or no attention. State legislators were not regarded much better; 41 percent thought they would pay very little or no attention if contacted by the people surveyed. In 1997 the Florida Annual Policy Survey asked Florida citizens how well they and others like them were represented in state government. A majority responded that they were represented very poorly or poorly, with three out of five between the ages of eighteen and thirty-four feeling that way.

If public officials are not listening to ordinary people, to whom are they listening? When asked in 2000, "Would you say the government is pretty much run by a few big interests looking out for themselves or that it is run for the benefit of all people," only one-third believed it was run for the benefit of all the people. In 1964, by contrast, almost two-thirds believed that it was.

One of the problems government faces, according to Americans, is corruption engaged in by dishonest politicians at the expense of the public. Fifty-five percent say that corruption is a "very important" problem and 34 percent a "somewhat important" problem. Government is corrupt, people believe, because those involved in running it are corrupt. In fact, more than one out of five Americans say that "quite a few" people running government are crooked. Even if those elected are essentially honest when they start out, a majority of Americans believe it is "almost impossible" for them to stay honest after going into politics. Only 12 percent rate congressmen and only 17 percent rate state officeholders as "very high" or "high" on honesty and ethical standards. At the state level, for example, New Jerseyans were asked recently how many politicians they thought were corrupt; half the respondents thought that anywhere from 50 to 100 percent were corrupt. In an earlier survey, New Jerseyans were asked what percentage of legislators in Trenton they believed took bribes. One-third of the respondents answered that some percentage between 50 and 100 took bribes.

Whatever Americans think about government per se, their views of politics and political institutions are basically negative. At best, they are cynical; at worst, contemptuous. Those in the younger generation are more tuned out and turned off than their elders. The Youth Civic Engagement Survey, conducted in early 2002, administered a number of questions about government, politics, and participation to 1,166 individuals, ranging in age from fifteen to twenty-five. One question in the survey asked respondents to check off "the words that come to mind when you hear the word POLITICS." Only 18 percent checked "interesting," whereas 47 percent checked "boring." On the positive side, "public service" came to the minds of 26 percent and "responsive" to the minds of 7 percent. On the negative side, "lying" came to the minds of 54 percent, "corrupt" to 48 percent, and "for the rich" to 40 percent.

Why People Think the Way They Do

Many explanations are offered for why people are as negative as they are and why they have become distrustful and cynical. In *Disaffected Democracies,* a book based on studies of public attitudes toward parliamentary institutions in other nations, Susan J. Pharr and Robert D. Putnam offer a general framework for interpreting public dissatisfaction. For them, public orientations are a function of the information to which citizens are exposed, the criteria by which the public evaluates government and politics, and the actual performance of representative institutions. Here we examine the first two explanations related to information and criteria, plus other factors that appear to account for the orientations Americans have toward government institutions. Later on, in Chapter 9, we explore the explanation that relates to the performance of representative institutions.

A Democratic Surge

One explanation of declining public trust places American discontent and disenchantment in a much larger context. The problem is one of governability, which confronts democracies not only in North America but also in western Europe and Japan. How can government function when demands and expectations are on the rise and authority is on the decline? In the American context, Samuel P. Huntington, a noted political scientist, calls this combination of increasing expectations and declining acceptance of government authority a "democratic surge," or an "excess of democracy."

The World Values Survey shows that between 1982 and 1997 respect for authority declined in twenty-eight of the thirty-six countries for which data were available. Two-thirds of these countries also evidenced declining confidence in the armed forces and police. In eleven out of fourteen advanced industrial democracies confidence in parliament has declined, even though citizens overwhelmingly support the idea of democracy.

The decline in the United States has been marked, Huntington argues, because democracy and governability have gotten out of balance. Demands for greater equality and participation, along with the polarization of political positions, have been accompanied by less loyalty to political parties and less deference to government. In a representative democracy, legislators are expected both to listen and lead. At present, the populace is less inclined to let them lead and more inclined to make them listen.

The contemporary "culture wars," in which people insist that their views are the only right ones, also tend to weaken support for representative democracy. Expectations about what institutions ought to do vary and conflict according to race, gender, ethnicity, sexual preference, and attitudes toward the family, abortion, drugs, and immigration. Consensus is difficult to build on such polarized blocs. Political theorist Jean Bethke Elshtain explains that to the extent that citizens retribalize into ethnic or other "fixed identity" groups, differences become more exclusionist. When it becomes impossible to negotiate differences, democracy is strained.

The Fallout of Watergate and the Vietnam War

Throughout the history of the republic, Americans have been critical of their government. Skepticism, with dollops of cynicism and distrust added, is a constant in American politics. And most would view some degree of skepticism as healthy for a political system. It may be that, as some scholars maintain, the recent period of low public trust is not an aberration; rather, it is the relatively trusting era of the 1940s and 1950s that is unusual in the annals of American politics. According to such reasoning, distrust and cynicism are nothing new and thus should not concern us. Yet, the American discontent since the traumatic events of Watergate and Vietnam is of a nature that is quite different from what went on earlier. The distinction between the skepticism of the past and the cynicism of the present is important: what might be perceived as a difference in degree is actually a difference in kind.

In the case of Watergate, President Richard M. Nixon authorized criminal acts during a political campaign that would have led to his impeachment if he had not resigned. The Vietnam War was a government failure—it was unpopular, unsuccessful, and cost many lives. If these two events are responsible for nothing else, they undoubtedly contributed to the way in which the media deal with government and politics. In the period before these events in the late 1960s and 1970s, the media conceived of its role as not only reporting the news but also choosing what not to report because the consequences might be harmful. Journalists shared with members of Congress and state legislators a community of interests. This is no longer true. Now the relationship is adversarial. Public officials are fair game, indeed big game, and investigative reporting (of the Watergate type) commands great respect in the journalism trade.

The Negative Role of the Media

How Americans orient themselves toward their political institutions depends in large part on what impressions they get from the media. The media are the principal storytellers about government, politics, and political institutions. No single story in print or on television shapes people's orientation, but the cumulation of coverage has effects. And for the media, the very definition of news is a negative one. When legislatures are working well, they are not particularly newsworthy. When there is controversy, conflict, or deadlock, they are newsworthy. In the words of Thomas E. Patterson, an expert in this area, "The media's bad news tendency has heightened Americans' disillusionment with their political . . . institutions."

It used to be that cynicism was the province of political cartoonists, whose avowed role was to lampoon politicians and politics, sometimes savagely. Now the media in general play that role, not just a small coterie of political cartoonists.

David Schribman, a journalist himself, attributes the change in the news media as a factor contributing to the diminishment of public trust in Congress. He explains that twenty years ago reporters for the major national newspapers and the three major television networks covered Congress by chronicling the events on the floor, in committee, and in subcommittee. They wrote "straight" news accounts. By the 1980s, however, congressional reporters were writing with an emphasis on drama and disagreement and heightened attention to criticism from outsiders.

National news coverage about Congress and most state legislatures also has become progressively more negative in recent decades. According to Joseph Cooper, a scholar of Congress, the message framed by the media is far from neutral in its effects: "Politics and politicians are covered in ways that highlight conflict and controversy, on the one hand, and personal ambition and ethical lapses, on the other. . . . The defining impression created is of Congress as a bunch of politicians squabbling over the distribution of benefits to special interests and jockeying for personal power while the needs of the country are ignored." The media are in an economic maelstrom, competing furiously with each other for advertisers and audience—ultimately for survival. Whether covering Congress in Washington, D.C., or legislatures in Tallahassee, Olympia, or St. Paul, journalists often go for the jugular, seeking out the most sensational stories of scandal and corruption. One of the media's favorite subjects is campaign finance, which they consistently cast in the most negative light. Most reports make it appear that campaign contributions explain virtually all legislative behaviors, with incumbents doing whatever their big contributors want.

Beyond the news media, the entertainment media also project a negative image of politics and politicians. A study by the Center for Media and Public Affairs, done for the Council for Excellence in Government, examined the depiction of public officials and political institutions on prime time television service from 1955 through 1998. The conclusion was that prime time entertainment gave public service "little notice and less respect," portraying politicians and bureaucrats as serving their own interests or special interests rather than the public interest. In the 1990s three out of four comedy or drama episodes on TV pictured the political system as corrupt. A 2001 update of this study found that the situation had improved considerably. Today three out of five episodes portray positive images of government, perhaps a ripple effect from the success of the NBC series *The West Wing*. In fact the study attributes a substantial increase in the ranking of elected officials among all occupational categories to *The West Wing*.

Increasing Partisan Competition

Americans value competition, in politics as in sports. The political system today is almost as competitive as it can be, largely because of the resurgence of the Republican Party in congressional and state legislative elections, especially in the South, in the 1990s. In the 2000 elections, both parties had a chance to win the presidency and gain control of the House of Representatives and the Senate. The national balance after the elections remains close. The presidency itself was decided by a few votes in one state. The U.S. Senate was evenly divided, with 50 Republicans and 50 Democrats (until Sen. James M. Jeffords of Vermont left the Republican Party to become an Independent), and the division of the two major parties in the U.S. House was close, with 222 Republicans and 211 Democrats (2 independents made up the total of 435 representatives).

Competition is just as vigorous at the state level. Currently about two-thirds of the ninety-nine state senates and houses can be won by either party; the other one-third are dominated by one or the other of the major parties. During legislative sessions in 2002 Democrats had control of seventeen legislatures and Republicans seventeen, and the senate and house were split between the two parties in fifteen states. Three chambers were tied.

Competition is more appealing to Americans in theory than in practice. Campaigns are hard fought because the stakes are high and either side has a chance to win. Campaigns often stress the negative. Candidates highlight what is right with themselves and, in stronger terms, what is wrong with their opponents. An opponent's positions, record, supporters, character, and ethics are all challenged. Campaign consultants insist that the negatives are what voters attend to and remember. Because negatives are considered to be effective, candidates use them heavily in advertising. One candidate wins the election, but neither candidate nor the political system comes out of the contest unscathed. Some research suggests that those citizens exposed to negative advertisements are significantly less likely than those exposed to positive advertisements to express confidence in the political process.

The widespread use of government or the legislature as a target in political campaigns has further undermined public trust. Even congressional and state legislative incumbents run against the political institutions in which they serve. Years ago, congressional scholar Richard F. Fenno, in his book *Home Style*, described how members of Congress, in order to bind themselves to their constituents, disassociate themselves from "the government" and "the politicians" who run it. They run for Congress by running against it. This strategy, according to Fenno, is "ubiquitous, addictive, cost-free and foolproof," but hard on Congress and its members. "It's the system that's at fault," candidates charge. "Elect me and I will change it." If voters hear from challengers and incumbents alike that the legislature itself is at fault, why shouldn't they believe it? After all, both sides are saying it.

In the view of the public, the worst thing about campaigns is the money raised and the money spent. It is hardly surprising, in view of the competition and the stakes involved, that the two parties do their utmost to raise funds for the necessities of contemporary campaigns in targeted races: television, radio, direct mail, polls, and professional consultants. No one knows how much is enough and each side fears that the other side might get an edge by outspending it. Both the media and campaign finance reformers relentlessly assert that political contributions buy access, influence, and even votes, corrupting the entire system and virtually everyone in it. The public, for the most part, buys these unsubstantiated charges.

Two-party competition has also affected the internal processes of Congress and state legislatures, and in ways that the public finds unsavory. The heightened level of partisanship in Congress—interrupted at least for a while after the terrorist attacks—and many state legislatures, and the campaign-related activities of the legislative parties, turn many voters off. They refer derogatorily to what goes on in the nation's legislatures as "just politics." They don't realize that keeping an eye on the electorate is a major way in which representatives and representative assemblies try to be responsive to and win support from their publics.

The Polarizing Effect of Interest Groups

Interest groups are not new on the American scene; Madison in *Federalist* No. 10 pointed to the potential mischief of "factions." In the past forty years, however, the interest group system has undergone major changes. The number of organized groups that make demands on Congress and state legislatures has mushroomed, giving rise to what has been called an "advocacy explosion."

Not only are more groups represented by more lobbyists, but "single-issue groups"—focused, ideological, and noncompromising—play a significant role in contemporary politics. Groups whose issues are race, gender, sexual orientation, abortion, guns, or capital punishment do not serve as moderating influences in politics, as traditional interest groups once did. They believe firmly in their cause and would rather fight it out than compromise. Even business groups, which in earlier times were represented by broad-based associations, nowadays are more focused and organized in single industries or simply by single firms, all of whom lobby legislatures.

A group's membership is more involved in the articulation of interests than in previous years. The success of the environmental, consumer, and civil rights movements demonstrated the efficacy of grassroots lobbying. Other groups learned the lesson that the "outside game," which relies on persuading group members or the public generally to put pressure on legislators, can be as important as the "inside game," in which lobbyists work directly on legislators. Today any organization with substantial numbers of members or employees will try to develop grassroots capacity so that it can mobilize people to contact their representative when an issue of concern arises. To mobilize the rank and file, the organization must emphasize its stakes in the issue. This requires dramatic and militant rhetoric and more extreme claims. If a grassroots campaign does not win, or accomplishes less than promised, many people are sorely disappointed, even aggrieved.

Given the high levels of expectation by various interest groups and their members, dissatisfaction with the political system is the likely consequence. As Joseph Cooper writes: "Yet, even when action does occur, it does not necessarily relieve alienation in any quick or automatic fashion. Rather, positive action normally produces negative feelings for both advocates and opponents. The compromises inevitably involved in passing major legislation lead advocates to see the action as impaired or flawed, whereas opponents are distressed that the legislation passed." If one side wins big, the other side will be enormously unhappy and blame the system. If neither side wins or loses big, neither will be completely satisfied and both will blame the system. The system rarely comes out ahead.

Legislators as "Outsiders"

Members of legislatures attack their own institutions and present themselves to their constituents as outsiders. They seldom rise to their own collective defense, and they too blame the legislature for not producing the correct results.

Not until members have leadership responsibilities—chairing a committee or serving in a majority party leadership position—does their orientation change from advocacy to consensus building. Newly elected legislators come to the capitol with agendas that represent their beliefs, the needs and views of their constituencies, and commitments made during their campaigns. The legislator's principal objective (in addition to being reelected) is to enact his or her agenda, just as an interest group's objective is to enact its agenda.

Legislators feel frustrated and even disaffected when the session is over and they have achieved too little of what they set out to do. They simply have not been able to get a majority of their colleagues to agree to each of the items on their list. One can imagine the avalanche of new laws and programs, if every legislator's agenda won acceptance.

It varies by legislator and by state, but relatively few of the "good" proposals that new members bring with them are endorsed by the legislature. In Congress hardly anything gets enacted in the form in which it was introduced. Even fewer of the proposals of members in the minority are likely to become law. Rarely do legislators blame themselves for what they fail to achieve. They appreciate that not everyone can get everything, but they still blame the leadership, the committee chair, the other body, or even their own house. When they succeed, they claim credit; when they fail, it is the fault of the "system."

Given the many and diverse agendas, failures have to abound. It takes a while for members to adapt to a system in which they may have to work for years to get something into law. In most legislatures substantial numbers of new members experience frustration and dissatisfaction. As long as the principal responsibility of members is the advancement of their own agendas, they are unlikely to see things from an institutional point of view. Leadership roles force legislators to broaden their perspectives and take responsibility for advancing common agendas. Those in leadership are more likely to see the merits of a system in which conflict usually gets resolved, issues get worked out, and the public appears to benefit.

Generalizing from the Worst Cases

Among the 535 members of Congress and 7,424 members of the fifty state legislatures, each of whom engages in thousands of transactions every year, there are bound to be cases of unethical or corrupt behavior. A few legislators probably are corrupt, some are oblivious to ethical considerations, and others are simply stupid. All of the above have been sent to the capitol by the voters. But the overwhelming majority is neither corrupt, unethical, nor stupid. Unfortunately, citizens base their assessment of the whole on the extremely small parts that they see, hear about, and recall, aided by the news media that focus on the small parts and portray them as bad. "To the extent that bad deeds receive more attention than good ones," write social psychologists Diane C. Mutz and Gregory N. Flemming, "this coverage is likely to be negative." And even if the media covered the good deeds of Congress and state legislatures as much as their scandals, most people would more likely remember the negative examples.

People often generalize from the worst cases, not the best. Still, if they generalized from their own representative to Congress as a whole, the results would be very different. Approval rates for individual members of Congress, as surveyed by the American National Election Studies since 1980, have ranged from 80 to 90 percent. Similarly, the ratings of individual state legislators are high. But the approval ratings of Congress and state legislatures are much lower. The differences in public assessments of their legislator and their legislature stem partly from a more positive view of the personal and close and a more negative view of the impersonal and distant. The same principle applies to public assessments of schools. Only about one-fifth of those polled give the nation's schools, which are remote, an A or B grade. One-half give schools in their own community, which are nearer, an A or B. But about two-thirds of those polled give the schools attended by their own children, which are closest, A or B grades. It's easier to be negative toward something that is abstract than something that is part of one's experience.

The Legislative Process Is Incomprehensible and Distasteful

The American political system was not designed for people to understand. The framers sought to check and balance power, between the branches on the one hand and the federal and state governments on the other. It is unlikely that many Americans, even in the formative years of the republic in the 1780s, had a solid sense of how the system worked.

Americans today have even less of an idea of how representative democracy works. Ordinarily, they do not learn from the media, except in extraordinary circumstances such as the determination of Florida's popular and electoral votes in the presidential election of 2000. Otherwise, even if they observe the legislative process first hand, as on C-SPAN, they will probably find it mystifying. As David M. Shribman writes, "[c]loture motions, quo-

rum calls, votes on rules, sessions in the Committee of the Whole are difficult concepts to grasp (or even to explain). For that reason, unannotated
coverage of a legislative session often has an unintended effect: It brings the
action into a viewer's living room, but at the same time it makes the action
seem farther away, not closer."

Watching the senate or house of a state legislature from the visitors'
gallery can also be a disillusioning experience. While bills come up for a vote
on the floor, members scurry from desk to desk chatting with one another
instead of listening to perfunctory debate on the bills. Although spectators
are appalled by what they consider to be legislative negligence, the fact is that
legislators are really doing their job. They are negotiating with one another
on issues that still have to be settled. Those measures that come to the floor
for a vote nearly always have been worked out earlier—in committee or in
caucus—and members know how they will vote. Although the legislature
functions as it should, it does not operate as the public would expect.

The legislature is incomprehensible to people largely because the process
is not orderly. Rather, it is messy, even chaotic. As scholars Kenneth Newton
and Pippa Norris write in an examination of confidence in public institutions, "Other things being equal, most of us are liable to distrust that which
we understand least, and since the 1960s the American political system has
almost certainly spun well beyond the comprehension of all but a tiny minority of American citizens."

To the distrust that stems from lack of comprehension add the distaste
people have for the process itself. Although Americans express a devotion
to democracy in the abstract, they have little appreciation for what democracy entails in practice. They do not wish to see uncertainty, competing interests, confusion, bargaining, compromise, conflict, or any of the other
features that are central to a legislative body in a representative democracy.
Americans, as political scientists John R. Hibbing and Elizabeth Theiss-
Morse have shown, simply do not like the normal practices of democratic
politics and political institutions.

Civic Education Hasn't Been Up to the Job

Political scientists Mary A. Hepburn and Charles S. Bullock III offer a dis-
tressing account of contemporary civic education in high schools, whose

focus is on other subjects. It is rather rare, in fact, to find an American government course required in secondary schools. The subject of citizenship is taken up in the interstices of social studies curriculums. Students, in any case, are indifferent to learning about politics and government. Part of their lack of interest stems from the negative messages they hear outside of school, but it also relates to how textbooks and teachers present government and politics. At a time when entertainment is ubiquitous, the teaching of civics often lacks spark.

Texts invariably focus on formal processes to the exclusion of the real-life political maneuvers, which are much less definitive. Take the familiar diagrams of "how a bill becomes a law," a feature of just about every textbook treatment. According to congressional scholar Roger Davidson, these presentations "are about as accurate a guide to the legislative landscape as the Renaissance explorers' map of the New World." The major land masses are identified and labeled, but the contours, distances, and routes of travel are ignored or distorted. Although students reading a text may acquire information, they will not get a realistic feel for the untidy nature of the legislative process and representative democracy.

Many social studies teachers, moreover, share the cynicism toward political institutions and politicians that permeates the contemporary environment. Although they often focus on real-life political maneuvers, they are likely to suggest that such stratagems are quite unsavory and not up to democracy's standards. In their contrast of the rough and ready reality of politics to democracy's shining ideal image, the reality comes out as severely wanting. Teachers reject the actual processes with righteous disdain, dismissing what goes on in legislative bodies as "politics as usual." They, like most of their fellow citizens, according to Hibbing and Theiss-Morse, do not appreciate that "politics as usual" is democracy in action.

In Sum

It is hardly a wonder that people think what they do about the institutions and practitioners of representative democracy. There is much to criticize, and criticism is encouraged in a democracy like ours. But the negative, critical, and accusatory are about all people normally see and hear. Competing messages are extraordinarily rare. Only faith or firsthand experience could have made Americans view representative democracy much differently. Those who do see the merits of the system are likely to have participated themselves or be close to people who have taken part. These positive souls are the unusual ones; it is the normal majority whose cynical orientations dominate the American scene today. It is to that normal majority that discussions in the following chapters are specifically addressed.

Sources and Suggested Reading

The data in the section "What People Think" draw largely on the American National Election Studies of the University of Michigan, which have surveyed Americans on a regular basis for about thirty-five years. These data are reported in Joseph Cooper, ed., *Congress and the Decline of Public Trust* (Boulder: Westview Press, 1999). In this book, Cooper's chapters "The Puzzle of Distrust" and "Performance and Expectations in American Politics: The Problem of Distrust in Congress" are especially insightful. Cooper's volume also contains a worthy contribution from David M. Shribman, "Insiders with a Crisis from Outside." The introduction, by Robert D. Putnam, Susan J. Pharr, and Russell J. Dalton, in Pharr and Putnam's *Disaffected Democracies: What's Troubling the Trilateral Countries?* (Princeton: Princeton University Press, 2000) puts the American case in a larger context. Also relevant in this volume is the chapter "Confidence in Public Institutions: Faith, Culture, or Performance?" by Kenneth Newton and Pippa Norris. Another valuable study, edited by Norris, is *Critical Citizens: Global Support for Democratic Government* (New York: Oxford University Press, 1999). Additional useful data are provided by Everett Carll Ladd and Karlyn H. Bowman, *What's Wrong? A Survey of American Satisfaction and Complaint* (Washington, D.C.: American Enterprise Institute Press, 1998). The data on the views of fifteen-to-twenty-five-year-olds toward politics are from the Youth Civic Engagement Survey, funded by a grant from the Pew Charitable Trusts to Cliff Zukin, Scott Keeter, and Molly Andolina. The survey was administered January 29–February 25, 2002 to 1,166 Knowledge Networks panel members.

The discussion in the section "Why People Think the Way They Do" draws on some of the same works mentioned above: the introduction to Pharr and Putnam's *Disaffected Democracies;* Newton and Norris's "Confidence in Public Institutions"; and Shribman's "Insiders with a Crisis." George F. Will's *Restoration* (New York: Free Press, 1992) should also be read for a sharp critique of legislative performance. The "excess of democracy" is discussed by Samuel P. Huntington, "The Democratic Distemper," *Public Interest* 41(fall 1975): 9–38, and is also treated in Russell J. Dalton, "Political Support in Advanced Industrial Democracies," in Norris, *Critical Citizens,* and "Value Change and Democracy," in Pharr and Putnam, *Disaffected Democracies.* Morris P. Fiorina's "Extreme Voices: A Dark Side of Civic Engagement," in *Civic Engagement in American Democracy,* ed. Theda Skocpol and Fiorina (Washington, D.C.: Brookings Institution Press, 1999), presents an interesting view, as does Jean Bethke Elshtain's *Democracy on Trial* (New York: Basic Books, 1995). Michael Schudson's *The Good Citizen* (New York: Free Press, 1998) should also be read. Most important on what people believe is John R. Hibbing and Elizabeth Theiss-Morse, *Stealth Democracy: Americans' Beliefs about How Government Should Work* (Cambridge: Cambridge University Press, 2002).

Also useful are Joseph Cooper, "Performance and Expectations in American Politics"; David M. Shribman, "Insiders with a Crisis from Outside"; Diana C. Mutz and Gregory N. Flemming, "How Good People Make Bad Collectives: A Social Psychological Perspective on Public Attitudes Toward Congress"; Roger Davidson's "Congress and Public Trust: Is Congress Its Own Worst Enemy"; and John R. Hibbing, "Appreciating Congress," all in Cooper, *Congress and the Decline of Public Trust.* A study of how the public regards Congress is provided by John R. Hibbing and Elizabeth Theiss-Morse, *Congress as Public Enemy* (Cambridge: Cambridge University Press, 1995). On the media, in particular, see Thomas E. Patterson, *Out of Order* (New York: Vintage Books, 1994), and Joseph N. Cappella and Kathleen Hall Jamieson, *Spiral of Cynicism: The Press and the Public Good* (New York: Oxford University Press, 1997). The Council for Excellence in Government's study of the attitudes toward government of popular television shows can be found at http://www.trustingov.org/research/govtv. Our discussion of civic education draws on Mary A. Hepburn and Charles S. Bullock III, "Congress, Public Trust, and Education," in Cooper, *Congress and the Decline of Public Trust.*

2

What Did the Framers Have in Mind?

AS THE NEW YORK CONVEN-
tion, meeting in 1787,
considered ratifying the
U.S. Constitution, Alexander
Hamilton, perhaps the
strongest advocate of a
powerful executive branch,
was called upon to defend
the most populist element of
the constitutional framework,
the House of Representatives.
Hamilton responded with the
definitive statement, "Here,
sir, the people govern. Here
they act by their immediate
representatives." Regardless of
his personal preferences,
Hamilton knew that the
House was the cornerstone of
representative democracy.

Every two years the voters could assess the quality of their representation,
thus holding their legislators on a short leash. The framers placed great
power in the hands of members of Congress, but they also made sure that
the lawmakers would be responsive to their constituents. That arrangement still defines the nature of American representative government,
whether on Capitol Hill or in fifty state capitols.

The Constitution forged in 1787 continues to define the conduct of
American politics in the twenty-first century. The Supreme Court places

limits on legislative actions, much as Congress reshapes the president's initiatives to fall in line with its collective preferences. And through the veto power, the president can reject the judgment of congressional majorities. In our separation-of-powers system, change rarely comes easily; the framers of the Constitution took the idea of representation seriously and worried a good deal about the potential excesses of placing ultimate power in the hands of the people.

In this chapter we examine the historical context of American representative democracy, especially as it came to life in the hands of the reformist elite who crafted the Constitution. Because of the infrequency of successfully amending the Constitution, the United States continues to operate under the framework laid out in Philadelphia in the summer of 1787. In fact, the only constitutional change to the original structure of the national legislature came in the Sixteenth Amendment (1916), which mandated the popular election of U.S. senators. After placing the framing in historical context, we will turn to the goals of the framers and how they crafted a legislature to meet their goals. Their vision of human nature, coupled with their intellectual strength and their experiences throughout the Revolutionary era, produced a new vision of representative democracy that still affects our day-to-day politics, well over two hundred years later. In fact, examining what the framers had in mind will provide an important starting point for our assessment of representative democracy.

Framing the Constitution in Historical Context

The idea of representative democracy stands at the center of both the American Revolution and the subsequent establishment of a constitutional regime. Colonists rallied around the cry, "No taxation without representation." At first, their target was the British Parliament, and most thought that this legislative body would respond to their pleas. After all, as British citizens they assumed that they could petition Parliament to redress their grievances. At the same time, they had no formal representation in the House of Commons, so there were no direct linkages between members of Parliament and the colonial constituencies.

In the decade that followed the passage of the widely despised Stamp Act of 1765, colonists discovered, to their consternation, that Parliament was less responsive than they ever imagined. Even though the hated Stamp Act was repealed, Parliament instituted a series of import duties to generate the revenues that paid the salaries of royal governors. This source of funding freed the governors from the power of the purse exercised by colonial legislatures, which were well established from Massachusetts to Georgia. Indeed, the very existence of legislatures, some dating from the seventeenth century, provided the colonists with examples of effective representative democracy and with places where their discontent could form the basis for deliberation and action—up to and including the establishment of the First Continental Congress in 1774. It was this body that passed various declarations and resolutions, with each colony casting one vote, that amounted to a declaration of war against England. And the colonial legislatures responded by endorsing these declarations and sending representatives to the Second Continental Congress, which, after attempting to petition the king for redress of colonial grievances, adopted the Declaration of Independence in 1776.

Although we revere the individuals who made the American Revolution, our democracy was truly born in legislative bodies that represented the colonists' diverse interests, deliberated the crucial issues of the day, and articulated the collective complaints of both the established colonies and this new entity that would become the United States. Even before there was a country, the continental congresses established their legitimacy through the representation of the colonies, and indirectly, their citizens. Remarkably, the nascent United States conducted its war of revolution without a chief executive. As political historian James Sterling Young observed, the country was "born with a legislative body and no head."

When the framers of the Constitution met in Philadelphia, they drew extensively on their rich and varied personal experiences within the Continental Congress and their respective colonial legislatures. In fact, by 1787 representative democracy already had a storied history in the Western Hemisphere. By 1690, of the twenty-one British North American colonies all but Newfoundland had created a legislative assembly, led by Jamestown in 1619. The British House of Commons served as the model for the lower house of most colonial assemblies, but these bodies were more democratic and more responsive to the electorate than was the House of Commons, at least at first. And colonial legislators kept in touch with their constituents, either through the petitions that they received from interested parties or by circulating proposed pieces of legislation in their home districts.

As they began the work of creating a new governing document, the fifty-five framers—forty-six of whom had served in colonial assemblies—were part of a society that had nourished strong legislative bodies for more than a century. Not only were they grounded in the theory of representative democracy, they had been active participants in colonial legislatures, most with long histories of successful governance.

They had faith in representative democracy, to be sure, but they also understood, first hand, the problems of forging majorities and governing. Constructing a legislature that was both powerful and limited would be no easy task, but no group of men had ever been better equipped for such political engineering.

Constructing the Legislative Branch

The weaknesses of Congress under the Articles of Confederation were profoundly debilitating in that the national legislature could not require states to fund the military, even as the young country fought the Revolutionary War. Rather, Congress had to request the states to contribute to the war effort. Moreover, Congress represented the states, not their citizens, and required approval of all states to enact meaningful legislation. In short, fears of a powerful, centralized government had rendered the authors of the Articles of Confederation excessively cautious in devising any concentration of authority, which made governing difficult during the war and nearly impossible in its aftermath.

Fully understanding the problems of too much centralized power, as in the British monarchy, and of too little centralization, as in the Articles of Confederation, the framers sought to construct a new kind of representative democracy with a strong, but not unchecked, national legislature. During their constitutional deliberations in Philadelphia, the fifty-five representatives of the states devoted far more time and energy to discussing the nature and powers of the legislature than to any other topic. The framers justified such attention in that, given the representational strength of the legislature and its powers to spend and tax, this branch of government might well abuse its considerable power. Moreover, with their substantial experience as colonial legislators, they were familiar with the institution that they were creating.

In addition, the framers were a highly political bunch, acutely aware that they were trying to create something new while at the same time acting as a "reform caucus" whose job it was to forge workable institutions for political decision making. In a real sense, the framers operated much like a body of compromising legislators within the context of the Philadelphia convention. They devised various ways in which the legislature itself could be:

1. A powerful national assembly that could make authoritative policy decisions
2. A representative body, broadly responsive to its citizens
3. A body capable of effective deliberation
4. An institution subject to both internal and external checks on its authority

Achieving any of these goals would have been a victory; achieving them all was truly a triumph. Let's look in detail at how each of the goals was achieved.

A Powerful National Assembly

When the Philadelphia convention opened, the delegates held few core beliefs in common. They were suspicious of human nature, to be sure, and "they wanted to get rid of democratic 'excess' and 'follies.' " Still, as James Madison put it, they sought to "eliminate or lessen 'the inconvenience of democracy,' but only in a manner 'consistent with the democratic form of Government.' " What brought together the members of both the so-called Federalist and Anti-Federalist factions was their mutual understanding that the Articles of Confederation had failed miserably in concentrating national power. Before designing a legislative body that would create effective modes of representation and generate productive deliberation, the framers had to agree to forge an institution that could wield power when clear majorities favored a certain course of action. Once this general point of agreement was reached, the delegates could turn their attention to other, more contentious issues. The convention initially granted broad authority to the new Congress, but later the delegates decided to define eighteen specific powers that empowered the legislative branch while simultaneously limiting its authority.

One of the flaws of the Congress as a representative and deliberative body under the Articles of Confederation was its inability to tax and spend in coherent, predictable ways. The framers understood that legislative power came from control of the government's purse strings, so they gave Congress great control over taxing and spending. Although chief executives have since grown more powerful through their ability to propose budgets and administer expenditures, this legislative "power of the purse" has been a hallmark of legislative authority at both federal and state levels of government.

In addition, the framers invested Congress with two other major grants of authority: the power to impeach the president and the power to declare war. Impeachment has rarely been employed, and the chief executive has undermined the power to declare war in a variety of military actions, such as Korea and Vietnam. Still, these powers remain important sources of preeminent authority for the legislative branch of government. Such grants of power derived directly from Congress's status as the branch of government tied most closely to the public. If legislators abused their power, the people could "throw the rascals out."

Representation

During the 1780s, several states broadened the number of people who were eligible to vote. To be sure, women and slaves were not among them, and some property restrictions continued to apply, but overall participation increased substantially. Equally important, as Alvin Josephy notes, "Annual elections, open sessions of legislatures, roll-call votes, and the publication of bills and journals became an established part of government." Although the state legislatures provided the framers no single model, these bodies offered real-life experiences and alternative methods for linking constituents and representatives.

For the framers, the legitimacy of the government came from the consent of the governed, and they constructed a House of Representatives with strong, direct connections to the growing electorate. Each House member would represent approximately 30,000 individuals—a smaller number than in 2001 was represented by lower-chamber members in thirty *state* legislatures. With two-year terms of office and modest constituencies, representatives would constitute a body described by Virginia's convention delegate George Mason as "the grand depository of the democratic principle of government." At the same time, most framers had little desire to give "the people's branch" free rein. An unfettered House might well prove dangerous, especially as seen through the eyes of the aristocratic participants of the Philadelphia gathering. If House members were to reflect the views of relatively small numbers of constituents, senators would represent states, not individuals. As James Madison concluded in *Federalist* No. 45, the Senate's composition would be "at once a constitutional recognition of the portion of sovereignty remaining in the individual States and an instrument for preserving that . . . sovereignty."

As a result of twentieth-century court decisions and legislation, the U.S. House of Representatives and all state legislative bodies must follow the standard of "one person, one vote." But the Senate, far more today than when it was constructed, stands as a striking exception to the proposition that all citizens should be represented equally. For example, in California, each U.S. senator represents almost 34 million state residents, whereas in Wyoming the figure is 494,000 persons per senator.

The framers expressed their further reliance on the states, as well as their profound fears of the public at large, by mandating that U.S. senators be selected by state legislatures, a practice that continued for more than 125 years. The Philadelphia convention thus communicated its clear intent that senators would engage in a representational relationship with their constituents that was distinct from how House members addressed theirs. Political scientist Elaine Swift argues that the framers modeled the Senate on the British House of Lords and that the framers saw the House of Lords as "the fulcrum of that country's remarkable equilibrium, playing a crucial role in maintaining the kind of conservative social, economic, and governmental orders that they wished to see reign in the United States." More than two hundred years after the Constitutional Convention, the Senate stands as the only American legislative body that does not apportion its membership on the basis of population, a fact that offers systematic, if modest, advantages to smaller states.

In the end, the framers found an acceptable balance of representation. The House might well respond to the emotions of the moment, whereas the Senate, with its staggered six-year terms and indirect elections, could reflect the interests of the states and their aristocracies, even if it did not ultimately become an American House of Lords.

Although the framers enjoyed considerable experience in state legislatures and within the Continental Congress and were thoroughly familiar with the British Parliament, their views about representative democracy were far from uniform. In fact, like other democratic theorists, they battled over the nature of representation. Alexander Hamilton defended the Constitution's design for a Congress closely linked to the electorate. Members of the House of Representatives would need to be responsive to the wishes of their constituents, in part because each legislator would be "one of us" as a prominent member of the district's electorate and in part because the two-year term and the relatively small constituency would guarantee close scrutiny. The Anti-Federalists, who saw a real danger that citizens would lose control over their government, vigorously opposed Hamilton's Federalist, pro-Constitution position. As one opponent put it, "If we make the proper distinction between the few men of wealth and abilities, and consider them . . . as the natural aristocracy of the country, and the great body of the people, the middle and lower classes, as the democracy, this federal representative branch will have but very little democracy in it."

These differing views of representation have come to be labeled "delegate" and "trustee," respectively. That is, legislators are seen as either exactly reflecting the views of their constituents as delegates or exercising independent judgment as trustees. Of course, as we will explore in detail in Chapter 5, most lawmakers act as both delegates and trustees at different times.

A Deliberative Assembly

Discussing the nature of deliberation in the American legislative context, Joseph Bessette concludes, "Those who created the American constitutional system believed that on most issues, most of the time, deliberative majorities would not exist outside government, but rather would be formed through the operation of the governmental institutions, as the representatives of the people reasoned about public policy for their constituents." The framers sought to encourage men of talent to consider important issues through a reasoned, deliberative process that would, in the end, lead public opinion. To do this, they had to address several issues including controlling the effects of majority faction; limiting the power of the legislature; electing strong, public-spirited political leaders; designing a legislative institution that would encourage deliberation; and promoting a consideration of the national interest, as opposed to those of a region or narrow factions.

Majority Faction. Of all the legislative problems facing the framers, none was more serious or potentially destructive than the possibility that a majority faction could work its will to the extent that it would injure minority factions that would be powerless against such a strong and coherent coalition. The framers did have an immediate, practical example to draw on. In 1785–1786, the Rhode Island legislature faced a currency crisis by passing legislation that the state's supreme court subsequently declared unconstitutional. The state legislators retaliated by aggressively attacking the court's legitimate action. The Rhode Island legislature acted precipitously and with little debate to challenge a court ruling; in other words, a "majority faction" had acted to deny individuals and a minority their rights. With this concrete example in mind, Madison emphasized conditions that would foster deliberation among a variety of interests, represented within the national legislature. In particular, he viewed the very size of the American Republic as a great benefit. Representing large numbers of diverse interests, the legislature would discourage majority factions and, if they formed, make it difficult for them to control the government.

Limiting the Power of the Legislature. Aside from the explicit limitations incorporated into Article I of the Constitution, the framers both strengthened the hand of the executive and separated the executive from the legislative branch. This separation-of-powers structure, in concert with a strong, independently elected president, meant that the legislative branch could not dominate the executive and that it would have to be able to defend its policy decisions. Debate and deliberation are the methods that Congress and for that matter state legislatures use to defend their decisions. Effective deliberation can also enhance legislative power without threatening the executive's authority, because it demonstrates that the legislature's enactments are based upon reasoned debate, not legislators' whims.

Electing Strong Leaders. Through their extensive experience in state legislatures, the framers understood, first, that the most qualified citizens did not always find their way into elected assemblies, and second, that the quality of legislative discourse derived directly from the quality, broadly defined, of those chosen as representatives. A key reason why the framers chose to have state legislatures elect senators indirectly was to maximize the chances that senators would have substantial experience and a broad view of the national interest.

Encouraging Deliberation. In the 1780s the Massachusetts General Court (legislature) had more than three hundred members, and other states also had large bodies, especially considering their populations. Although not all the framers agreed, Madison and others contended that smaller bodies would enhance the chances for meaningful deliberation; in fact, large numbers of legislators would make them susceptible to manipulation by a demagogue. As Madison put it, "In all very numerous assemblies, of whatever characters composed, passion never fails to wrest the scepter from reason." So, no matter how qualified the legislators, large bodies tended to discourage effective deliberation. Anti-Federalists railed at the small size of the original House (sixty-five) and Senate (twenty-six), but the majority of the framers came down on the side of enhancing discourse at the expense of reducing the representation of parochial interests.

If size was their first structural condition, the framers' second consideration was the length of legislative terms: the longer the better. Again, the Senate was the centerpiece for this goal, in that its members were to serve six-year terms, longer than any elected officials at either the state or national level. And Senate terms would be staggered, so that at any point only one-third of the senators would be newly elected. Even the two-year House

term doubled the single year of service that was standard for most state leg
islatures in those days.

In concert with the small size of both House and Senate, relatively long
terms for their members would encourage extended discussions of difficult
issues, especially in the Senate. Indeed, the so-called upper chamber
emerges as an extraordinary legislative institution—one that is protected
from the passions of the public at large and rooted in the sovereignty of the
individual states. Much of the Constitution was new, but the construction
of the U.S. Senate, seen as a kind of American House of Lords, was especially imaginative.

The Public Interest. Although Madison designed an array of checks
and balances to thwart self-interested factions, he also foresaw in *Federalist*
No. 51 that "a coalition of a majority of the whole society could seldom take
place on any other principles than those of justice and the general good."
This suggests that he had high hopes that reasoned debate within the legislature by those who represented a variety of interests would produce policies that would reflect a broad public interest.

Constraining the Legislative Branch

However much the framers wanted to create a powerful branch of government to fulfill their goals of a representative democracy, they understood
from the outset that legislative power must be constrained, especially given
the potential abuses by majority factions. Although they did have confidence that a large, diverse republic would control many possible excesses,
they ultimately agreed on building government structures that would limit
legislative power both *within* the institution and *outside* it.

Bicameralism: Internal Constraint. When the framers met in 1787
both their own experience and the dominant political theories of the day
led them to assume that they would create a bicameral legislature (two
chambers), which could balance the interests of the many and the few. In
fact, no debate was required before the delegates approved Madison's initial
formulation that the "legislature ought to consist of two branches." And the
reasoning was straightforward: the Senate, as a smaller, more elite, even
aristocratic, body, could check the excesses of the more democratic lower

chamber. As Madison put it, the Senate would bring "coolness" to the heat generated by the passions of the directly elected House of Representatives.

If the existence of two chambers was a foregone conclusion, the composition of the Senate was anything but. The framers fought energetically over how best to provide the Senate with some semblance of representativeness while retaining its capacity to limit the House's potential excesses. In the end, the decision to give all states the same number of senators was forged in power politics that pitted the more populous states against the smaller states. This was so even though, as political scientists Frances Lee and Bruce I. Oppenheimer note, "no political issues united large states against the small states." It was the *potential* for abuse that united the small states, whose delegates feared that the Senate would not be able to play its balancing role if the large states dominated.

At the same time, the equal representation issue was *not* central to how the framers viewed the Senate, which was to be a "small, elite body, relatively independent of popular majorities." With the requirement that both houses pass legislation, the Constitution institutionalized a serious internal check on the actions of the legislative branch.

The Separation of Powers: Constraint within the Constitutional System. In *The Democratic Republic* Martin Diamond, Winston Mills Fisk, and Herbert Garfinkel point out, "The constitutional design . . . depends on an executive and judiciary capable of *combating* the legislature." Although bicameralism imposes major limitations on the legislative institution, it pales before the most profound brake on the Congress—the separation of powers. That is not to say, however, that the separation is absolute. It is not, nor can it be. But with separate bases of power, the legislative, executive, and judicial branches must share and compete over the exercise of power. At the same time, each branch must husband its own authority. In the Philadelphia convention Madison became especially concerned that, given the impeachment power, Congress might well control the executive. In a famous passage of *The Federalist Papers,* he makes the core argument for a separation-of-powers structure: "The great security . . . consists in giving to those who administer each department the necessary constitutional means and personal motives to resist encroachment of the others. . . . Ambition must be made to counteract ambition. The interest of the man must be connected to the constitutional rights of the place." This means that the self-interest of those in the executive and judicial branches must be supported so that they can resist the powerful pull of legislative majorities that purport to reflect the public will.

Formally, the presidential veto and the Supreme Court's ability to declare a law unconstitutional provide the most profound institutional support for separated powers. The Congress must continually consider whether a proposed law will trigger a presidential veto, which can be overridden only with two-thirds' majorities in each house; likewise, it must frame legislation that will pass the Court's constitutional muster. Although the framers clearly outlined the veto power, their treatment of the judiciary can only be described as cursory. Still, they put in place a system that allowed Chief Justice John Marshall in *Marbury v. Madison* (1803) to construe the Constitution as granting the Court the authority to decide whether a law is constitutional or not.

As they drew up a document that would create a powerful representative democracy, the framers remained aware of the need to limit the legislature's powers. From the vantage point of more than two hundred years later, one can scarcely argue that they did not do their job with great skill. Passing legislation in the American system has rarely been a simple task.

The visions of the framers have affected how Congress and the fifty state legislatures have conducted their business from the 1790s to the present. The bicameral, separation of powers framework has held up remarkably well, whether in Washington, D.C., or Olympia, Washington. At the same time, as the Philadelphia delegates pursued their political goals and careers over the subsequent decades, they invented democratic institutions, such as political parties, that were designed explicitly to overcome the limitations they had placed on the legislative process. In the end, the difficulty of passing legislation has been one of the central themes of American politics. And this difficulty flows from the constitutional system that emerged from the Philadelphia convention. If Americans experience difficulty in understanding the workings of representative democracy, they might look first to the decisions made by the architects of the Constitution.

In Sum

In *The Democratic Republic* Diamond, Fisk, and Garfinkel argue,

> A major problem in the American Republic . . . is the democratic choice of . . . wisdom and virtue—democratic choice because the whole system rests upon choice by majority rule; wise and virtuous representatives because of the republican belief that government of and for the people more competently solves problems and protects liberties when it is conducted by such representatives than by the people themselves.

For the framers, representative democracy was a necessary, if not sufficient, condition for the new enterprise of the American Republic to succeed. In particular, they made incisive observations about the quality of elected officials, the people's connections to their legislators and the role of public opinion, the influence of factions, the nature of the legislative process, and the ultimate accountability of elected representatives. Their thinking shaped American representative democracy in the Constitution and continues to affect how contemporary legislatures renew the promise of effective representative government.

With their characteristic mix of hope and trepidation, the framers placed confidence in the willingness of local leaders to serve in Congress and, by inference, as state legislators. Part of one's obligation as a community leader was to serve, and legislators with varied backgrounds would put themselves forward. If the people did occasionally elect ill-suited representatives to the House, senators would cool their passions. As Madison observed in *Federalist* No. 62, the Senate would be composed of those with substantial experience, trust, and knowledge, who could be expected, in their maturity, to place local interests aside. We will consider this subject in more detail in Chapter 4.

For all the Constitution's constraints on the use of power, the framers did ultimately place their trust in "the people" to govern through their representatives. Madison expected majorities to arise not from single broad consensual interest but from a series of coalitions, which would bring together legislators from various states and constituencies. Public opinion—in an era long before survey research was invented—would find its way into the legislative chambers through a diverse set of lawmakers who would assess their constituents' preferences and interests. Legislators would both interpret and feel bound by public opinion, as they came together in Congress across the country. Indeed, at a time of no mass communication, conversations among legislators might well reflect the most up-to-date manifestation of national pubic opinion. In Chapters 3 and 5, the role of public opinion in the legislative process will be examined further.

Directly related to the idea of public opinion is the crucial concept of factions. Here Madison turned the classical political theorists on their heads, so to speak, by asserting that the very breadth of interests ("factions" in his terms) contained within a very large republic would constitute an absolute benefit. Like any good politician, Madison may have been making lemonade out of the lemons that he possessed, but his argument has become a foundation of representative democracy. In *Federalist* No. 51 he states, "In the extended republic of the United States, and among the great variety of interests, parties, and sects which it embraces, a coalition of a majority of the whole society could seldom take place on any other principles than those of justice and the general good." Such a conclusion may seem too rosy in the light of more than two hundred years of conflict among competing interests, but contemporary pluralist scholars would argue that Madison's optimism was, in the end, well justified. We will take a closer look at this issue in Chapter 6.

For many observers of legislative life over the course of the American experience, the process of governing has been seen as too fractious, too messy, and too difficult to understand. The framers, as practical politicians and veteran legislators, saw the lawmaking process as central to bringing together diverse interests. Although selfish points of view are articulated, the process of building majorities requires that virtually all legislators, regardless of the factions they represent, make concessions. Thus, compromise, usually through deliberation, is the method by which legislatures get things done. Chapter 7 continues our exploration of how representative democracy resolves conflicts among a host of interests.

One final worry of the framers and of all democratic theorists is how to make certain that their constituents will hold legislators accountable. Madison argued that only frequent elections can provide the legislature with the proper "dependence on, and . . . intimate sympathy with, the people." Just as they designed the House for immediate accountability, they structured the Senate for greater reflection. Still, each biennial election can change the Senate profoundly, even though only one-third of its seats are open in any given year. Thus, accountability is blended with reflection. Accountability remains an important issue facing all legislatures, and Chapter 8 will offer a detailed consideration of how legislators are held accountable for their actions.

In short, the framers thought long and hard about the nature of representative democracy. And they were optimistic, although not foolishly so, over its prospects. That remains our position, too, more than two centuries later.

Sources and Suggested Reading

Above all other sources, *The Federalist Papers* (New York: Bantam, 1989, among various editions) provides a direct connection to the framers and their campaign for ratification of the Constitution. There are any number of accounts of the Constitutional Convention, including Catherine Drinker Bowen, *Miracle at Philadelphia* (Boston: Little, Brown, 1986); Clinton Rossiter, *1787: The Grand Convention* (New York: Norton, 1987); and, especially on the politics of the convention, Calvin C. Jillson, *Constitution Making: Conflict and Consensus in the Federal Constitution of 1787* (New York: Agathon, 1987). See also Leonard Levy, *Essays on the Making of the Constitution,* 2d ed. (New York: Oxford University Press, 1987).

For a traditional political science approach to the founding as it plays out across American politics, see *The Democratic Republic,* by Martin Diamond, Winston Mills Fink, and Herbert Garfinkel (Chicago: Rand McNally, 1966). This text is especially good on the separation of powers. For more on this topic, see several of Louis Fisher's books on presidential-congressional relations, including *The Constitution between Friends* (New York: St. Martin's, 1978).

On the role of the Senate, see Elaine K. Swift, *The Making of an American Senate* (Ann Arbor: University of Michigan Press, 1996), and Frances Lee and Bruce I. Oppenheimer, *Sizing Up the Senate* (Chicago: University of Chicago Press, 1999). For an excellent discussion of legislative deliberation, see Joseph M. Bessette, *The Mild Voice of Reason: Deliberative Democracy and American National Government* (Chicago: University of Chicago Press, 1994). See also James Sterling Young, *The Washington Community, 1800–1828* (New York: Harcourt Brace Jovanovich, 1966) and Alvin M. Josephy Jr., *On the Hill: A History of the American Congress* (New York: Touchstone, 1979).

3

Where Do People Stand on Issues?

WHAT IF ALL PEOPLE IN A certain society, both the rulers and the ruled, were in perfect agreement on every political issue? Would there be any need in such a society for people to be careful in selecting and monitoring those who were to make political decisions? No. The actions of the rulers would be consistent with the preferences of the ruled. With such remarkable consensus, the identity of the rulers probably wouldn't matter. Selection by lot would be a

perfectly reasonable way of choosing rulers. It is only when people admit that a completely consensual society is unrealistic that the vital details of representative arrangements assert themselves as central components of the governing process. When important differences exist among the people of a society, the canons of democracy dictate that these differences should be reflected either by giving everyone in the society a voice or by ensuring that everyone in society is represented when key decisions are made. Since ordinary people have little stomach for personally engaging in constant political disagreements with their neighbors, disagreement makes representative democracy necessary.

The level of political agreement in society is, in other words, a key test of the need for representative democracy. The more agreement there is perceived to be, the less necessary the institutions of representative democracy become. And a startling number of people harbor the belief that the political views of most ordinary Americans do not contain important differences. Indeed, much of the puzzling fondness of modern Americans for proposals to weaken representative structures can be traced back to beliefs about the absence of political diversity. Are Americans correct in their beliefs that society is highly consensual? Answering this question is the primary focus of this chapter and a key factor in determining the need for representative democracy.

What the Public Believes

What is the evidence that Americans persist in believing that substantial consensus exists in the country on political issues? One source is focus groups. Focus groups bring eight to twelve ordinary people together in a casual setting to visit with each other. They are a good technique for determining people's perceptions and concerns. The comments of participants in a series of focus groups conducted in late 1997 by John R. Hibbing and Elizabeth Theiss-Morse nicely illustrate the tendency of many people to see consensus. Eight of these sessions were held across the country and with a wide mixture of participants. In one session, for instance, Mike (full names are withheld to protect anonymity) stated that "80 percent of the people [in the United States] think one way. . . ." In another, Lisa said that "in the end, a majority will want the same thing, the same end." And in a third, JoAnn observed that "there is more consensus [in the country] than we think." Given the amount of apparent acrimony in the political system (except after highly unusual major crises such as the 2001 attacks on the World Trade Center and the Pentagon), this perception of consensus seems surprising. How can so many people be convinced that consensus on political matters is the norm and not the exception in the modern United States? To answer, we need to look more carefully at the perceptions and convictions of people.

Perhaps people believe that even though a consensus does not exist on specific issues it does exist on underlying values and goals. Although Americans may fight like cats and dogs about whether to spend more or less on the military, on schools, and on housing for the poor, they could be united on broader goals such as freedom, equality, a strong America, a good economy, and humane treatment of all people. After all, the focus group participants quoted above made no claims that Americans agree on specific policy issues; only that they "think the same way" and "want the same thing."

No doubt some people who see consensus believe that it stops with these basic, largely inarguable, goals and value beliefs. But a closer look reveals that many others see consensus as more pervasive and specific than that. In the late spring of 1998, as part of the same study, Hibbing and Theiss-Morse also commissioned a random national survey of nearly 1,300 American adults. Among many other things, respondents were asked the extent to which "the American people agreed on the most important problem facing the country." Notice that this item asks respondents about consensus only on the identity of a problem, not on the solution to that problem. Thus, although it does not address basic values, the item does address perceived consensus on the general issue of the problems that society should treat as priorities. Consistent with the focus group comments, people tended to see substantial agreement as to the most important problem. Of the three permitted responses, just one out of five respondents said "very few" Americans agreed, whereas one out of three stated that "most" Americans agreed on the most important problem. The rest took the middle option of "some" agreement on the key problem. The perception is that there is substantial agreement on the most important problem facing the country.

A second survey item shifted the respondents' attention to the matter of consensus on the best way to *solve* whatever problem was identified as the "most important." Naturally, people admitted that there is somewhat more disagreement on solutions than on identification of the problem, but even then nearly two out of three said either "some" or "most" people agree on the solution. Perhaps of even more concern were the answers to a different survey item. This one asked respondents to agree or disagree with the following statement: "The American people disagree with each other so much that politicians need to compromise." Survey respondents have a bias toward giving "yes" answers, so in this case the level of perceived disagreement in society is probably being overestimated. Moreover, the bar has been set very low. The statement addresses only whether there is enough disagreement to necessitate any compromise at all on the part of politicians. It seems likely that everyone would recognize there is enough disagreement to require at least some compromise in order to reach a solution. But nearly one-half of all respondents disagreed, thereby suggesting the startling idea that the level of consensus among ordinary Americans is so high that politicians do not need to compromise.

The responses to these survey items indicate that the common claim for consensus probably goes beyond agreement on values to agreement on more pointed matters such as particular problems and specific solutions to those problems. Besides, a consensus only on broad matters such as freedom, equality, and the desire for a prosperous economy is not much of a consensus at all, since these goals are universally desired by people everywhere. When the people claim to see political consensus in America, they are not just thinking of consensus on broad goals. What else, then, could explain their stubborn belief in consensus?

A likely explanation is this. People recognize that political agreement is not pervasive in the country. After all, they hear the disputes and see the election returns. But they may believe that if it were possible to strip away the rhetoric and emotion engulfing the political arena, people would find that down deep they all see the political realm in similar terms. Many people attribute observed disagreements not to the real feelings of ordinary people but to unnecessarily divisive political parties, greedy politicians, combative media, and demanding special interest groups. The American people are of a piece, the logic goes, but these other entities make it appear as though disagreement abounds. The people seem to be saying, "Sure there is political disagreement, but it is traceable to ignoble forces rather than to ordinary Americans."

A focus group participant named Ben spoke for many when he said that "politicians are always fighting even though they are supposed to be working for the common good." In Ben's view and that of many other citizens, the common good is not up for debate. In fact, if there is a dispute over the common good, then someone, or maybe everyone, involved in the dispute must actually be interested in an uncommon good—probably their own self-interest. For many people, disagreement almost becomes the way they divine politicians' intent. If elected officials are in a dispute with other politicians, then they are not serving the interests of real Americans.

People are turned off by any part of the political system that doesn't pretend to speak for all people. Political parties and special interests are seen as selfish and as the source of the allegedly faulty impression that people disagree with each other. As April puts it, "political parties cause much diversity not only in our government but also in the American public as a whole." Notice the contention that parties cause, not just reflect, societal diversity. Special interests are viewed with even more disfavor, since, by definition, they are speaking for the interests of only one group of Americans. Anthony believes special interests have created a "tyranny of the minority. . . . Some people will defend [groups] and say that without them the politicians wouldn't know what the people wanted . . . but this doesn't make sense to me. The groups aren't representative of people as a whole so how could they say what the people as a whole would want?"

As was the case with Ben, Anthony seems to believe it is impossible to represent the views of part of the people; only the people "as a whole." According to most people's view of the political world, anything that pits people against people is a sign that the system is misfiring because if people's honest feelings—not those trumpeted by the parties and special interests—were revealed, those feelings would be amazingly monolithic.

The general tenor of people's focus group comments suggests they are upset because it seems to them that politicians, parties, and special interests spend too much time dealing with trivial, "fine print" issues when they should be tackling the larger concerns that really matter. The people don't necessarily see an aptitude for the details of public policies as a beneficial quality for a politician to possess, since it may be a sign that the elected official is not in tune with the real interests of the people. In fact, the people may even be thinking that the more a politician knows about the specifics of policy, the less he or she knows about what ordinary people want and need. The polls taken during the 2000 election campaign, as well as those conducted on election day itself, demonstrated that many of the people who planned to vote, and then voted, for George W. Bush believed Al Gore would be more competent to handle policy problems. This pattern of behavior is not anomalous because policy competence is not something on which the people place a great deal of value. Consider the following comments that were offered by a focus group participant named Linda: "I think part of the problem is that [those who run for office] . . . believe so strongly in one thing. . . . They have to have something that drives them to make them even run for office these days. And so sometimes I think you get the wrong kind of people in government that way. . . . He's got his own agenda. . . . He's not doing it for service to the people."

Linda doesn't want her politicians offering specific proposals because, if they do, then maybe not everyone would agree with the proposal. If this were the case, then the politician would not be serving the people but would instead be pursuing "his own agenda." In doing so, the politician would not be representing the interests of all people and, as we have seen, this is not what the people want. Even though "the devil is in the details," policy specifics make it more difficult for the people to continue in their belief that there is a consensus, and as such they don't like to consider the details of specific proposals.

The public's belief that there is general consensus within the American population on the issues that are important and deserve to be addressed is particularly dangerous to representative government. The result of this belief is that people are unable to understand why the government is addressing issues other than those that are important to them. Rather than realizing that different issues are important to different people and that the government's agenda itself is a compromise among popular interests, people draw the conclusion that the government must be dealing with a certain issue only because of the undue influence of special interest extremists. When legislatures seem to be spending almost all their time on issues that are unimportant to a given citizen, that citizen may still approve of the legislature if he or she thinks the issues are important to other real Americans. But if that given citizen believes all Americans care about the same issue, when the government is dealing with other issues he or she will conclude that the agenda is being set by atypical special interests. The belief that ordinary people agree on the appropriate government agenda leads many people to lose respect for legislatures and other institutions of representative democracy.

In sum, the public view is that although not everyone agrees on every issue, there is general agreement on the important, core matters. A society that appears divided is probably just one in which parties and special interests have pushed the people out of their relatively unified view of the political world and into counterproductive, artificial, warring camps—or else it is a society in which politicians have become seduced by the intricacies of policy details. If these artificial disputes and this fascination with unimportant policy minutia could be set aside, the people are convinced that it would then become apparent that down deep where it matters—in other words, on policies that are nontrivial—typical Americans usually agree with other typical Americans.

Why People Are Eager to Perceive Consensus

This perception of a popular consensus that has been unnecessarily distorted by apparent but false divisiveness is a comforting one. It allows people to perceive themselves and their fellow citizens as innately sensible, agreeable, and other-regarding. All distasteful traits are projected to vague and impersonal entities such as political parties, special interests, and self-serving legislators. In subscribing to this view, people are likely falling victim to the well-known psychological tendency known as "false consensus." This is the proclivity of people to overestimate the extent to which others agree with them. Experiments have found, for example, that those people whose favorite color is blue tend to over-predict the percentage of the population whose favorite color is blue. It is not surprising, then, that those people who favor a certain issue position—say, increasing spending on the military—tend to believe that more people agree with them on that position than is actually the case.

The reasons for this tendency are obvious and deeply rooted in human nature. First of all, we tend to associate with people who are similar to us in certain respects. And if they are similar to us in certain respects, this increases the odds they will be similar to us in others. People who live in the same neighborhood, work at similar jobs, have children who attend the same schools, or enjoy the same leisure pursuits are more likely to agree with the political views of their fellow travelers than they are to share the views of those with whom they do not come into contact. Therefore, when politics is discussed in the real world, more often than not, most of the people with whom people interact agree with them.

Moreover, well-known patterns of personal interaction exacerbate the appearance of compliance. Specifically, a process of "group-think" frequently pervades discussions. Group-think is when a view stated by one discussant discourages those with contrary views from offering up their own views for group consideration. Those who agree with the initially stated opinion may say so, but those who don't come around to the new position or remain silent, thus giving the appearance of more consensus than really exists. People are social creatures and we prefer to have a sense of belonging, of sharing with our colleagues, and of being a part of something bigger than we are. Part of this belonging often includes agreement on political issues of the day, so citizens have a psychological stake in believing that other reasonable people share their views. This stake may lead people to use what are sometimes called "perceptual screens" to ignore information that provides evidence of dissension and to take in any evidence of a consensus among all members of society—or at least all those who are of good heart. We all know those who delight in being contrarian, but for most people believing that others agree is an important vindication of their own beliefs.

When people are presented with direct evidence that their own views are not universally shared, they have an amazing capacity to denigrate the legitimacy of opposing views, thereby preserving their sense of consensus. A good example of this is provided by the following focus group exchange.

> *Bob:* When the President says I think we need to do this for the country blah blah and all that, they [members of Congress] ought to see if they can do it rather than work hard not to do it and kill it, right?
>
> *Delores:* But that started a long time ago when they allowed the protestors and the demonstrations to come in front of the White House or wherever. They pitch their little thing and confuse the whole issue. And then everybody gets all excited and this has to be acted on.

Bob: The government has to listen to the 10 people who feel this way but that's only 10 out of millions.

Linda: Those 10 people that get up there and protest are the ones that are listened to because they are protesting.

Bob: We are the silent majority.

These focus group participants have convinced themselves that disagreement, in this case at least and probably many others too, is attributable to the noisy protests of "10 people." The truth of the matter, however, is that whatever cause they have in mind is certainly important to far more than ten people. Rather than treating dissenting voices as expressions of legitimate real-person concern, they have been portrayed as the bleating of a handful of undeserving and demanding malcontents. Bob, Delores, and Linda are not bad people. Indeed, there is no reason to believe they are anything other than fairly ordinary, well-intentioned individuals, and this is why their inclination to dismiss views different from their own is instructive and important.

The pattern of thinking evident in this focus group is actually quite typical. As we have seen, when people do acknowledge the existence of disagreement, they often make it out to be caused by people who are unusual or selfish. A widespread belief is that a "silent majority" is in fundamental agreement on important issues. Disagreement becomes a sign that whoever is disagreeing must not be in sync with most Americans and the cause of not being in sync, as we have seen, is usually traced to special interests and, relatedly, to the self-serving interests of the political decision makers themselves.

The people's view on this matter draws some support from academics. For example, political scientist Morris P. Fiorina contends that the primary source of people's dissatisfaction with government is that so many elements of government are not in the policy middle—where the people are. Thus, when the people see one party arguing from the right and the other party arguing from the left, they are disillusioned and wonder why there has to be disagreement at all. Why are politicians unable to see that the people are in the middle? Why do they try to pull people toward one extreme or the other? Fiorina even makes a persuasive case that people's tendency to vote for a divided government, with one party controlling the executive branch and the other controlling the legislative branch, is their way of trying to get public policies that are "in the middle." As such, Fiorina's view of a consensual public frustrated by a nonconsensual set of political actors is perfectly consistent with the view of many ordinary Americans.

People's basic vision, then, is that, because they are composed of atypical, noisy activists, and because they command an inordinate supply of resources, special interests and party extremists usually get much more than is deserved, thanks largely to the willingness of officeholders to provide assistance. Americans do not like to think of any interests as special; they like to think of all interests as the same, as being a part of the general interests of the majority. The contempt for special interests and extremist party insiders is perfectly consistent with the people's common interpretation that quiet majority interests are legitimate, but noisy special interests are not.

The Actual Level of Consensus

So far, we have seen that most Americans believe there is substantial consensus on political matters among ordinary people, and we have offered some arguments and findings from psychological research that explain why people would harbor such a belief. Now it is time to address directly the matter of whether or not Americans are correct in their perceptions of political agreement.

In truth, the level of consensus people attribute to Americans as a group is grossly inflated. Despite many Americans' belief to the contrary, it turns out that the American people don't agree on much of anything in the political arena. The 2000 elections, if nothing else, would seem to have demonstrated conclusively that Americans are politically divided. They are divided at the national level and in many of the states. After the 2000 elections, control of the legislature was divided in about one-third of the states, one house with a Democratic majority and the other with a Republican majority. In more than half the states governors had to work with a legislature that had at least one legislative chamber controlled by the opposing party.

But for all the extraordinarily competitive outcomes at the legislative level, the clearest indication of the country's political division was of course provided by the 2000 presidential race. In that contest, Americans divided their votes for president more evenly between the top two candidates than at any time in the history of the republic. The vote totals were so close that weeks after the election we still did not know the outcome in three states and, therefore, did not know the identity of the forty-third president of the United States. Recounts became the order of the day, and every fine point of the voting and tabulating process was scrutinized because, with a margin so minuscule, any change had the potential to produce a different winner. The Florida recount, upon which the election hinged, continued to be in dispute, and the U.S. Supreme Court finally decided the issue, in favor of George W. Bush. Out of approximately 103 million votes cast, Al Gore received a little over half a million more votes than Bush, a difference of just half of 1 percent. Are Americans in agreement on political issues? Recent voting behavior suggests the answer is so clearly no that the question itself is preposterous.

If the focus is moved away from elections and toward opinion on various policy issues, disagreement is also readily apparent. It would seem, in fact, that Americans do not even agree on the identification of the most important problem facing society, let alone on the best way of solving that problem. In the 1998 Hibbing and Theiss-Morse survey described earlier, when people were asked to identify the most important problem, the problem receiving the most mentions was "crime," which just edged out "a decline in values and morals." But each of these issues was mentioned by only 7 percent of the respondents (less than 100 of 1,263 total). Nineteen separate "problems" (see Table 3-1) were identified as the most important by twenty or more people—an amazing absence of agreement on just the identification of society's most important problem. Contrast this *actual* dearth of consensus with the *perceived* prevalence of consensus described in earlier parts of this chapter. The conclusion has to be that, contrary to what Americans tend to believe as a society, we do not come close to a situation in which people agree on the most important problem.

To be sure, this survey of public opinion on the most important problem facing America was conducted before the terrorist attacks on New York's World Trade Center and on the Pentagon in September 2001. In the wake of traumatic national events like that, there may well be more consensus on

Table 3-1 The Most Important Problems in America

1. Crime	8. Unemployment	14. Too much government spending
2. Moral values	9. Poverty	15. Social Security
3. Drugs	10. Welfare system	16. Government too powerful
4. Corruption in government	11. Economics	17. Lack of religion
5. Education System	12. Taxes too high	18. Healthcare system
6. President Clinton	13. Racism	19. Homelessness
7. Budget deficits		

Source: 1998 Gallup Survey on Political Processes, conducted for John R. Hibbing and Elizabeth Theiss-Morse with support from the National Science Foundation (SRB-97-09934) and reported in their *Stealth Democracy: Americans' Beliefs about How Government Should Work* (Cambridge: Cambridge University Press, 2002). The problems listed are those mentioned by at least twenty survey respondents, in order.

the most important problems, but such catalyzing events are rare and their effects on public consensus are likely to be temporary. Even so, by May 2002, when Harris Interactive asked people to name the top two issues that the federal government should address, only 30 percent chose terrorism, while the rest divided their choices among other issues.

When attention is shifted to the appropriate strategies for addressing important problems, divisions multiply. For example, when all respondents were asked whether crime should be tackled by "addressing the conditions that cause crime" or by "getting tough with criminals," 47 percent leaned toward the "conditions, not criminals, cause crime" approach, but 34 percent adopted the "lock 'em up and throw away the key" approach. Another 19 percent could not pick between the two and wanted to follow both strategies. Among the eighty-two respondents (6.5 percent of the sample) who saw crime as the most important problem, the tough-on-criminals strategy, not surprisingly, was slightly more popular than it was among the entire population. But the interesting point is that divisions of opinion on the best strategy for dealing with crime persist even among those who see crime as the most important problem. Of the eighty-two people saying crime was America's biggest problem, thirty-five favored addressing the conditions that cause crime in the first place and thirty-four supported getting tough on criminals. The remaining thirteen wanted to do both at the same time. Opinion could not be any more divided than that. Even those few who agree that crime is the most important problem tend to disagree on the proper solution. And, of course, even more variation is introduced if people are allowed to register the intensity of their feelings on various matters.

The evidence just presented with regard to crime could be duplicated for virtually every other policy area. People disagree on whether or not a particular issue is the most important problem facing the country, they disagree on what to do about it, and they have varying intensities of feelings about the benefits of various strategies. Regardless of what the people believe (or want to believe), the level of policy disagreement among members of the American public is astounding.

This same conclusion is evident in many other soundings of the American public. A nearly identical pattern of results was found, for example, in a survey conducted by Peter Raducha in the summer of 2000 that focused exclusively on youth (sixteen-to-twenty-five-year-olds). When asked to identify the single most important issue facing our country today, youth mentioned homelessness/poverty most often, compared with the "crime" response that was top on the list of the sample of adults mentioned earlier. But the key point is that, just like the older respondents, the younger ones were badly split on the identity of the most important problem. Homelessness/poverty was selected by just 8 percent of all respondents. The youth were then asked what advice they would give the president on how to solve the sixteen most frequently mentioned problems; on only one of the sixteen issues did a majority of respondents agree on what to tell the president about the problem. And even this single exception, dealing with environmental problems, hardly indicates real consensus: 66 percent proposed telling the president that leadership on environmental issues needed to be stronger. This option is so broad as to be meaningless and still leaves open the possibility that dissension would exist if the policy choices were more specific. In any event, no other solution to any of the sixteen "most important problems" was supported by at least 50 percent of the young people.

Disagreement doesn't stop with beliefs about which issues the government should first address. In 1998, as in other election years, the American National Election Studies survey at the University of Michigan administered a detailed questionnaire to a large random sample of Americans. Several issue-oriented questions were included, and the results generated drive home the extent to which disagreement is rampant. One question in that survey asked if people thought "we had gone too far in pushing equal rights in this country." Forty-five percent agreed, but an almost equal 42 percent disagreed and thought "we had not gone far enough." The remaining 13 percent could not decide. Another question asked if "organized religious groups should stay out of politics or is it important for them to stand up for their beliefs in politics." Forty-seven percent said organized religious groups should stay out of politics, and 51 percent said they should stand up for their beliefs, with the remainder saying they did not know.

More specific policy proposals raised in the items posed to respondents by the American National Election Studies survey in both 1998 and 2000 and reported in Table 3-2 display about as much division as is humanly possible. On school vouchers just over 46 percent favored vouchers and just fewer than 48 percent opposed them. The rather complicated question about placing limits on foreign imports in order to protect American jobs resulted in a large percentage of respondents (over 39 percent) confessing they had not thought much about this issue. But the telling point is that of those who did venture an opinion, 52.5 percent favored new limits on imports and 47.5 percent opposed such limits.

Of those responding to a question about health insurance, 53 percent believed there should be a government insurance plan and 47 percent believed there should not be such a plan. Forty-eight percent of the respondents said companies that had a history of racial discrimination should be forced to have an affirmative action plan, leaving 52 percent saying that such a requirement should not be in place. And divisions are not confined to obscure economic issues. On hot-button social issues such as homosexual rights, integration of schools, and abortion, deep splits were in evidence in the results of the 2000 American National Election Studies survey. To cite just one example, 45 percent thought that gay or lesbian couples should be legally permitted to adopt children and 55 percent thought they should not be.

Results from policy-related questions on surveys other than those conducted by American National Election Studies show the same contour. Regarding gun contrl, 53 percent wanted to enforce current laws more stringently and 45 percent wanted new gun laws to be passed (September 2000). Military intervention? In June 1999, 47 percent expressed the belief

Table 3-2 Americans Disagree on the Issues (in percent)

Question	Yes or first option	No or second option
1. Do you favor or oppose school voucher programs?	46%	48%
2. Some people have suggested placing limits on foreign imports in order to protect American jobs. Others say that such limits would raise consumer prices and hurt American imports. Do you favor or oppose placing new limits on imports?	53	48
3. Should there be a government insurance plan or should individuals pay medical expenses through private insurance?	53	47
4. Should companies that have discriminated against blacks have to have an affirmative action program or should companies not have to have an affirmative action program?	48	52
5. Should gay or lesbian couples be legally permitted to adopt children?	45	55
6. Should current gun control laws be more stringently enforced or do we need new gun laws?	53	45
7. Do you believe that the situation in Kosovo is worth going to war over?	47	47
8. On abortion, would you say that you are more pro-choice or pro-life?	48	43
9. Which of the following do you think is the bigger risk to the Social Security Trust Fund: continuing the current method of funding Social Security or allowing stock market investment of Social Security funds?	51	42

Source: National Election Studies, 1998 and 2000.

Note: Responses were to public opinion questions in the NES surveys of 1998 or 2000. Percentages given are rounded and include those who expressed an opinion, excluding those who had no opinion.

that the situation in Kosovo was "worth going to war over," and 47 percent believed it was not. Averaging three polls taken in 2000, 48 percent considered themselves to be pro-choice on abortion and 43 percent viewed themselves as pro-life. And in June 2000, 51 percent of respondents believed continuing the current method of funding Social Security was a bigger risk than allowing funds to be invested in the stock market, whereas 42 percent believed the opposite. On issue after issue, the American public is deeply divided over the proper course of action.

Particularly in recent years, another method of measuring the public's policy preferences is to take note of ballot measure results. In twenty-four states it is possible for the people to vote directly on policy matters that have been placed on the ballot through the initiative or referendum process. The advantage of this approach is that it is an indicator of people's behavior as opposed to their hurried responses to pollsters. The method of tapping public views may be different, but the message of a nonconsensual American people is the same. Some ballot measures produce lopsided results. In the wake of the disaster at Columbine High School, for example, Colorado passed ballot language mandating background checks at gun shows by a 70-30 vote, and in California a widely publicized proposal to create school vouchers was defeated by better than a 2-1 vote. But many other results confirm that people within given states are not in sync. We focus specifically on the referenda that occurred in conjunction with the 2000 election. Again in Colorado, a proposal to legalize medical usage of marijuana passed but only by 54-46 percent. In Maine, a proposal to permit doctor-assisted suicide failed by just 18,000 votes out of 650,000 cast. South Dakota and South Carolina each abolished certain types of lotteries by close 54-46 percent margins. Finally, the state of Washington voted down a controversial charter school proposal by 52-48 percent.

In Sum

Although it may be natural to want to believe that people all operate from a singular and definitive viewpoint, people need to recognize that no consensus exists either on the appropriate agenda for the government or on solutions to important, specific, political issues in the United States. Make no mistake, Americans *do* share many basic goals and aspirations. This was apparent after the terrorist attacks in September 2001, when the country was virtually united in its support of the president, in its desire to bring to justice those responsible, and in its passionate efforts to help to rebuild. Even in noncrisis times, Americans agree on goals such as economic prosperity, good schools, safe streets, justice, and freedom. In this sense, the focus group respondents who claimed that Americans tended to "want the same thing" are correct.

Nevertheless, we must point out that agreement on matters such as these is not very meaningful. Where in the world has there ever been a people who longed for economic ruin, incompetent schools, and rampant crime? And terms such as justice and freedom are so broad and nebulous that agreement on them is vacuous. Two people could both claim to want justice and freedom and could still disagree on every political issue of significance. Americans do agree on goals, but only when those goals are couched in language so broad as to render disagreement all but impossible.

The implication of Americans' contention that ordinary people pretty much all agree is that politicians would all agree too, if they were really in touch with the people. But a public that is united in its desire for peace, prosperity, justice, and freedom is not necessarily a public united in the conditions, if any, under which abortions should be legal; in its desire for new gun control laws; on whether or not to recognize same sex unions and marriages; and on whether taxes should be levied on sales or income. People don't agree on values and, as indicated by the data presented earlier in this chapter, they certainly do not agree on priorities. People have vastly different ideas about the most important problem facing the country and they have vastly different ideas about how government should prioritize its spending. Some may think the most urgent need is to help the handicapped; others, to foster education for young people. Some may want to provide health care for those who cannot afford it; others, to enhance military capability. And even within these broad categories there is more disagreement. Among those who wish to enhance the country's defenses, some want to build a missile defense system, some want to spend more on traditional weapons systems, and some want to shift spending into antiterrorist approaches to defense. Some want to close unneeded military bases, and some want to leave them open. Does knowing that the public wants peace help a representative to understand the people's preferences on any of these matters? It does not.

Americans do not agree on political specifics. Perhaps because of this, they tend to pass off policy specifics as inconsequential. Whether the government devotes scarce resources to a missile defense system or to enhancing intelligence and antiterrorist capabilities matters greatly, and over the years the signals coming from the public on this matter have been cloudy at best. The devil is in the details. Saying there is agreement on the goal of defending the country is not the same as saying we agree on the best way to defend the country. Allegedly trivial matters quite often are the decisive element in whether or not we will be successful at achieving widely shared goals—and, as we have seen, we do not come close to agreement on the best way to achieve our goals.

Finally, disagreement in the political arena cannot be dismissed as merely the product of a few wild and misguided protestors. The number of "protestors" is usually greater than imagined and, even if this were not the case, views held by a small number of people are not necessarily misguided. People need to recognize that views can be legitimate even when many others in the population do not share those opinions. Democracy is about allowing input by everyone, not just by those who are convinced that their views are identical to those held by the majority. People should recognize that by pretending that their own views are those of all real Americans and by demeaning views that are different from their own they are behaving in a very human but dangerous fashion. Disagreement on central political issues exists among the real people of America, and it exists to a degree that is grossly underestimated by most of those same people.

Regarding the people's alleged policy centrism, sadly, much of it is illusory. Individuals who do not have strong beliefs on particular matters tend to select middling responses. Take the case of survey respondents who are asked to place themselves on a scale from 1 to 7, with 1 representing strong opposition to affirmative action, 7 representing strong support for affirmative action, and 4 representing something in between. Those respondents without strong feelings on the matter will be attracted to a response of 4. Americans certainly are moderates in many regards, but on numerous specific policy issues uncertainty or indifference magnifies their apparent centrism. A middle response is the safest way of getting the questioner to go on to the next question. In truth, the more people know about a topic the less likely they are to answer "4." The difference between centrists and others is not the difference between real people and special interests; rather it is often the difference between those who do not know or care and those who do know and care.

Political parties and special interests may on occasion exacerbate conflict, but it is unreasonable to claim they are the source of it. To take just two examples, have parties and special interests manufactured the opinion split on education vouchers? Isn't it possible that the people on their own could come to different conclusions on the complex issue of providing taxpayer dollars to church-supported schools? Would the people be in agreement on this difficult issue if parties, special interests, and self-serving politicians did not exist? No. What about efforts to promote equal rights for all? Is it any wonder that, in light of all the different experiences and exposures people have had, some will be more supportive of additional policies to pursue equal rights while others will conclude that the country may already have gone far enough? Parties and special interests are not necessary to account for popular division in this policy area. The people are perfectly capable of disagreeing with each other—and they do.

Believing that all other sensible people in society agree with you is easy and comforting. It is also misleading because it can encourage the erroneous conclusion that any time government is working on an issue that is not of interest to us, it is working on an issue that is not of interest to the American people generally. In a democracy, diversity should be welcomed, not defined away. Disagreement is a vital part of life in a modern, highly populous, differentiated, technologically complex, ethnically diverse, mobile society such as ours. False consensus does not help people understand representative democracy.

James Madison made an excellent case that democracies actually have a better chance of surviving in large, diverse societies than in small, homogeneous ones. Madison recognized that the best way to keep disagreement from turning society into a "spectacle of turbulence" was to ensure that many, many interests were present. Constantly changing issues and coalitions, Madison recognized, would diffuse the dangers of conflict. By contrast, if a group convinced itself that it was a majority, then no protection would be afforded "the weaker party." As a result, the health of society would be imperiled. If democracy is even conceivable in the context of political consensus, it would paradoxically be threatened by that consensus. Rather than pretending the people are consensual we should actually hope they are not. And, fortunately, the empirical data demonstrate conclusively that diversity of political views in the United States exists in abundance.

Sources and Suggested Reading

Data on public sentiments toward a variety of policy issues are available many different places thanks to the proliferation of polling agencies asking issue-oriented questions. Students can easily access the pollsters' Web sites and see for themselves that the American people do not agree with each other. Good sites include:

> http://www.gallup.com
> http://www.cnn.com
> http://www.washingtonpost.com
> http://www.icpsr.umich.edu/NES
> http://www.nytimes.com
> http://www.icpsr.umich.edu/gss

The icpsr.umich.edu/NES site was the source for many of the results presented here. Results from the election of 2000, including ballot measure results, can be found at http://www.cnn.com.

Perhaps the most inclusive scholarly analysis of public opinion on policy issues over the course of the last fifty years is contained in Benjamin Page and Robert Shapiro, *The Rational Public* (Chicago: University of Chicago Press, 1992). Also relevant is Michael X. Delli Carpini and Scott Keeter, *What Americans Know about Politics and Why It Matters* (New Haven: Yale University Press, 1996). For an expanded discussion of some of the points made and data sources used in this chapter, see John R. Hibbing and Elizabeth Theiss-Morse, *Stealth Democracy: Americans' Beliefs about How Government Should Work* (Cambridge: Cambridge University Press, 2002). Elisabeth Noelle-Noeman, in *The Spiral of Silence: Public Opinion—Our Social Skin* (Chicago: University of Chicago Press, 1984), provides the best treatment of the tendency of groups to project more agreement than is actually present. Morris Fiorina's stimulating arguments on the causes of divided government and the moderation of the American people can be found in Morris P. Fiorina, *Divided Government*, 2d ed. (Boston: Allyn and Bacon, 1996). See also Fiorina's essay entitled "Extreme Voices: A Dark Side of Civic Engagement," in *Civic Engagement in American Democracy*, ed. Theda Skocpol and Morris P. Fiorina (Washington, D.C.: Brookings Institution Press, 1999). As the title indicates,

Fiorina believes that anything other than middle-of-the-road beliefs are potentially a "dark side" of American politics. We, on the other hand, worry that what often passes for middle-of-the-road beliefs is really just a dearth of policy knowledge and conviction. When people move out of the center, therefore, they have not necessarily moved toward the dark side. Finally, for more details on the survey of youth referenced in the chapter, see Peter Raducha, "Preliminary Results of a Nationwide Survey of Youth, July 2000" (Program for Governmental Research and Education, Oregon State University).

4

What Makes Legislators Tick?

FOR REPRESENTATIVE DEMOCracy to work, our elected officials should be driven by public-regarding motives, not by personal financial gain. They should seek to improve the quality of life for their constituents, their community, their state, or the entire country. The pressure to raise funds to support their political campaigns should not unduly affect legislators' public policy decisions. Legislators should behave ethically and when faced with conflicts of interest should disclose them and should not participate in an issue when they have a direct financial interest in its outcome.

To evaluate legislators according to these criteria we need to explore why they run for office in the first place, what the job is like, why they do or don't derive satisfaction from it, how they run campaigns, and what influences their decisions. In short we will explore in this chapter whether or not the widespread public view described in Chapter 1 that legislators are corrupt is correct.

Who Runs for the Legislature and Why

What motivates people to run for elected office? Many of them like politics and the idea of public service. Some come from political families. A parent or uncle or aunt serves or has served in office. There are political families like the Kennedys, Bushes, and Gores at the national level. Many states have their own political families that have sent numerous men and women into politics. Others are drawn to politics as a result of their experiences as volunteers in political campaigns or as interns in legislatures. Still others decide to run for public office after working in state or local civic and advocacy groups, such as the League of Women Voters, a parent-teacher organization, or a statewide taxpayers' association.

A survey of nonincumbent candidates for state legislatures in 1998 reported that the most common types of candidates were white (less than 7 percent were not), male (22 percent were women), in their forties or fifties (only 5 percent were under thirty), had attended college (only 22 percent had no college at all, of whom only 6 percent had less than a high school degree), had incomes of more than $50,000 (12 percent earned less than $30,000 and 15 percent more than $120,000), and characterized themselves as moderate or conservative (only 12 percent said they were very liberal or very conservative). Three-quarters of them had lived in their community for more than ten years. This candidate profile is a picture of middle- to upper-middle-class America.

The most frequent occupational background of these candidates was business employee or owner (30 percent), followed by retired (15 percent) and attorney (10 percent). Most of the remaining 45 percent had been employed in education, government, real estate and insurance, health care, or farming or ranching.

Legislative office is not the first public office for many people in states such as California, Massachusetts, Michigan, New Jersey, and Ohio, which have strong traditions of starting politicians in local office before they move to the state level. Such politicians have been mayors or council members in their towns, commissioners of their counties, or members of school boards in their districts. Their careers in public office were already under way. This is even truer for members of the U.S. House of Representatives, approximately half of whom previously served in state legislatures.

The 1998 state legislative candidate survey found that one-third of the candidates were self-starters—it was entirely their idea to run for the legislature. Approximately half of them said that they had thought about the idea of running, but someone else had also encouraged them to run. About one-fifth said that they had not seriously thought about running until someone else suggested it to them. People and organizations that may actively recruit people to run for the legislature include legislative leaders, state and local party organizations, and interest groups.

Most people run for the legislature because they have a commitment to public service. They want to do good. For them, good is service to their constituencies, their states, and the public interest as each of them sees it. Public service exercises strong appeal for legislators. A former speaker of the Michigan House of Representatives puts it this way: "Most people run [for the legislature] with some level of idealism—to leave the state and the community better for their children than they found it. Why do people teach or go into the ministry? I think it's very much the same thing . . . it's the same call to public service."

Some people who run are driven by public policy concerns—to improve education, change the health care system, or revise tax policy. They have agendas to propose and goals to accomplish. Candidates bring with them or develop a variety of dispositions regarding public policy issues. These dispositions shape both their campaigns and their votes if they reach the legislature. Their outlook on public policy is fashioned from their families, the communities they live in, their work experience, and their political party. It is not surprising that a male farmer from a rural area has attitudes toward the environment different from those of an urban woman whose political experience is as a social activist. People who run small businesses are likely to see business regulation differently from the way a labor union member from a large city would see it. Democrats are more likely than Republicans to favor government intervention and to be less resistant to higher taxes or government spending.

Other candidates care more about taking care of constituents back home than about particular issue areas. They want to help their constituents by providing service, developing new community projects, and connecting them to their government. Most see government as an instrument to accomplish goals; some see government as an obstacle that prohibits citizens from accomplishing their state or local goals or agendas. Almost all of them say that they want to run for the legislature because they want to make a difference.

Undoubtedly, there are also candidates for whom the potential power and prestige of political office are an attraction. Most legislators are comfortable with power, although it may not be their prime motivation. A few probably think that getting elected to the legislature will help their private businesses by making them more visible in the community. Many are politically ambitious, and a few see the legislature as a path to a higher-paying job.

In reality, a mix of motivational factors—personal background and political history, public service, policy issues, constituent service, power, prestige, ambition—plays into the decision of most candidates to run for office.

What the Job Is Like

Newly elected legislators find that the job varies greatly because the institutional settings in Congress and among different state legislatures vary so much. To understand legislative life we need to have a sense of these different settings. A fundamental difference that we will first introduce and then explore in more detail is the distinction between "citizen" and "professional" legislatures.

Dating back to the founding of the nation there has been a strong ethos in American politics that we should have "citizen legislators"—men and women who leave their work and communities to take up the public's business for a brief period of time and then return to their communities. They are expected to be like Cincinnatus, the Roman general who left his plow to lead the troops in battle but returned to till his fields when the war ended. The idea of citizen legislators is attractive because of the image of our elected officials maintaining their roots in their communities and occupations while taking time off to serve the public good. Americans also like citizen legislators because it appeals to a strong cultural value that favors limited government.

Congress gave up the idea that it was possible to be a part-time legislature and still be a coequal branch of government more than fifty years ago. The California Legislature moved to nearly full-time status in the late 1960s, and most of the other more populous states (with the notable exception of Texas) followed suit in the 1970s. As these legislatures demanded more time of their members, they usually, although not always, increased their compensation and provided them with more staff resources. Together these greater resources of time, compensation, and staff define the more "professional" legislatures. The argument for the professional legislator is that large, diverse, complex states (or the nation as a whole) require greater time and expertise from legislators to maintain an independent legislature that is able to balance the power of the chief executive.

A key variable in understanding citizen as opposed to professional legislatures is the amount of time required to serve in the legislature. The length of legislative sessions varies from less than two months in a biennium in Kentucky and Wyoming to virtually year-round in Congress, California, and Massachusetts. It is not enough, though, to look only at the number of days in session to measure the time demands of the job, because session length does not include the days legislators spend at the capitol during interim periods for committee meetings. Nor does it include the hours and hours legislators spend dealing with constituents in their districts throughout the year and the all-consuming demands of election season every two, four, or six years.

Taking into account session time, interim work, constituent service, and political work, Figure 4-1 shows estimated time commitments for legislators in Congress and in the fifty states. It is definitely a full-time job in Congress and, as mentioned before, at least a three-quarter, if not full-time, commitment in the professional legislatures of ten of the largest population states. In ten states with citizen legislators, service usually requires one-third of their time or less. The remaining thirty states are somewhere between the two extremes in a range of one-third to three-quarters time required of a legislator. Legislators in these in-between, hybrid states often face a dilemma between a public that wants them to be citizen legislators and increasing complexities of public business that pressure them to spend more time on the job. Over the last thirty years the time demands on legislators have increased within the categories of citizen, professional, and hybrid legislatures.

In both hybrid and citizen legislatures there are always some legislators who spend much more time on the job than others do while the legislature is out of session. This may be because they love the work and have the time

Figure 4-1 Time Demands of Legislative Work

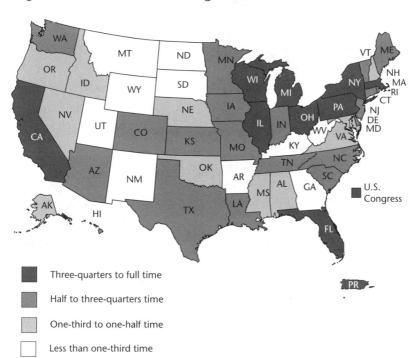

Three-quarters to full time

Half to three-quarters time

One-third to one-half time

Less than one-third time

Note: Estimated proportion of a full-time job spent on legislative work includes legislative sessions, interim committee work, constituent service, and election campaigns.

to commit to it or because they are legislative leaders. Leaders who have responsibility for the management of the institution, agenda setting, and public representation of the body find that they must commit much more of their time to legislative business than average legislators. On the other side, there are a few legislators who spend as little time at the capitol or with their constituents as possible. This may be because they are lazy, not motivated, or prefer to devote their time and attention to their private business.

During session, all legislators face a crowded calendar. Committee meetings are likely to begin early in the morning, and floor sessions may extend into the night, especially at the end of legislative sessions. In between there are constituents and lobbyists to see and bills to prepare and study. Congress and the more full-time legislatures tend to hold sessions Tuesday through Thursday each week, reserving the Friday through Monday period for legislators to return to their districts to meet with constituents or carry out their personal business. Most of the citizen legislatures with strict constitutional limits on their sessions, though, work intensively every weekday until the end of the session.

Figure 4-2 shows a busy day in the life of a California state senator. This day includes a caucus meeting, two committee hearings, a floor session, six meetings with constituents and lobbyists, an interview with a reporter, a briefing for schoolchildren, and four receptions. Fourteen major issues are on the agenda for the day, beginning with the state budget in the morning and ending with the regulation of predatory lending by financial institutions in the afternoon. For some people this schedule would be daunting and exhausting; for others—and this includes most people attracted to legislative service—it is exciting.

How do the time commitments that different legislatures demand relate to the amount they are compensated? Except for Congress and a few of the more professionalized states—such as California, Michigan, New York, and Pennsylvania—legislative compensation tends to be low, as shown in Figure 4-3. In a few legislatures, such as Montana, New Hampshire, New Mexico, South Dakota, and Utah, pay is so low that serving in the legislature more closely resembles volunteer work. New Hampshire is an extreme case. The salary for New Hampshire legislators is only $100 per year, but the legislature meets for nearly six months out of the year. About the only people who can serve in that legislature are ones that have a spouse who is the primary wage earner or some other source of independent income.

In Congress and in the state legislatures that provide salaries that are sufficient for legislators to make a living, the capital is distant from the population centers; most members thus have to maintain homes in both the capital and their districts, severely limiting any potential financial gain from legislative service. Although these legislatures provide reimbursement for some of the costs associated with travel to and from the capital, it is rarely enough to cover the added financial burden. Simply put, legislators are not getting rich through service in Congress or state legislatures.

Figure 4-2 A Day in the Life of a California Legislator

Sen. C.'s Calendar	May 23, 2001

Wednesday, May 23

8 am			
9 00	Democratic Caucus meeting re state budget and confirmation of governor's appointment of director of environmental protection		
10 00	Senate Revenue & Taxation Committee hearing—land use and water resources bill		
	Bee reporter re land use/water resources bill		
11 00	Senate in Session—State budget, child care, cell phones & driving	Sen. Chuck G., Rep. Mike M., Mark T. (PG&E) re blackout notification	
12 pm			
1 00		Maple School—21 8th grade students—Your Ideas Count! pamphlet	
	Senate Revenue & Taxation Committee—SB 1123, manufacturing investment credit, 5 bills on agenda, yours is last		
2 00	District constituents w/ CA Restaurant Assn. re energy crisis, workers' comp, food safety		
	Ruben L. w/ CA City Attorneys Assn. constituent from district re SB 71, workers' comp.		
3 00	Phil E., Maureen O. re SB 476, summary judgment, burden of proof		
	Eleanor P. w/AARP in district re prescription drugs		
4 00	Mike E. w/client Roland A., owner of mortgage company, re predatory lending		
5 00	Public Employees' District Council Reception		
	Ca. Restaurant Assn. Reception	League of CA Cities Reception	
6 00– 8 00			Antonio V. for Mayor Reception

Figure 4-3 Estimated Annual Compensation of Rank-and-File Legislators

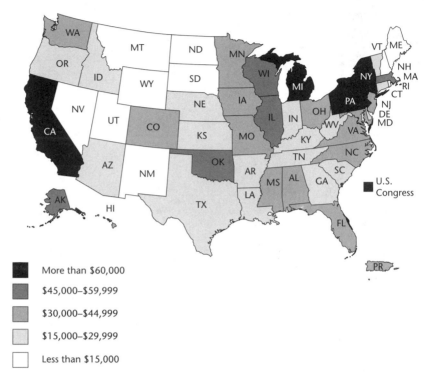

More than $60,000

$45,000–$59,999

$30,000–$44,999

$15,000–$29,999

Less than $15,000

Note: U.S. Congress annual compensation is $135,000.

Most legislators sacrifice income by serving in the legislature. In fact, a fair number could be working as lawyers, developing their own businesses, or running big companies—jobs that would compensate them much more. For most lawmakers, serving in the legislature is a part-time job. They have to take time off from work to serve. Teachers may have to go on unpaid leave from their school district for several months, lawyers can handle fewer cases, farmers must hire help or rely on family members to handle their chores, and insurance salesmen can't sell as much insurance. The compensation that legislators receive from the state seldom makes up for what they lose in outside income. Although a few attorneys and other professionals may gain business because of their public visibility, service in the legislature hurts lawmakers' private careers more often than it helps.

The bottom line is that few—if any—legislators stay in the legislature because of financial rewards. In so many other careers, financial income plays an important role in the choices that individuals make. That is not the case for those who enter the ranks of Congress or state legislatures. Fundamentally, they are in it for the satisfaction the job brings.

In addition to the pressure of time and the low compensation, there are two other reasons why the job of a legislator is not an easy one. First, legislators must make thousands of difficult choices. They have to decide not only what bills they want to introduce but also whether to vote aye or nay on countless bills in committee and on the floor. Table 4-1 shows the number of introductions and enactments in each legislature. The range of bill introductions includes less than 900 in Alaska, North Dakota, and Wyoming; nearly 8,000 in Congress; 15,000 in Massachusetts (where every citizen has the right to introduce a bill); and more than 30,000 in New York. There is no simple explanation for the variation among the states as to the number of bills introduced or the proportion enacted. Idiosyncratic local traditions, constitutions, and rules more often than not explain the differences. Each of the bills is likely to be considered and voted on at three or four different stages in the same legislative chamber. At many of these stages amendments may be offered, so the number of decisions legislators must make multiplies rapidly. It is a large workload. The fact that these decisions affect people's lives makes the task even more difficult.

Second, legislators' activities are all in the public domain. Every decision a legislator makes is on public record and subject to challenge and criticism. Media coverage of legislators' work can be heady stuff; it can also be disheartening and embarrassing. Especially during election campaigns, any personal or family flaws or peccadilloes are likely to be aired in the newspapers. Legislators are often placed in the position of defending their record in public.

With all the difficulties of the job, what are the rewards? Why do people continue to serve? For those who enjoy challenges, the legislative process is about as challenging as anything one can tackle. The politics and the excitement of making critical decisions affecting the future of the state and

Table 4-1 Legislative Bills Introduced and Enacted, 1998 and 1999, Regular Sessions

State	Introductions	Enactments	Percent
Alabama	3,625	824	23
Alaska	837	259	31
Arizona	2,117	680	32
Arkansas	2,041	1,362	67
California	5,391	2,125	39
Colorado	1,213	682	56
Connecticut	4,522	650	14
Delaware	1,166	529	45
Florida	5,052	853	17
Georgia	2,490	969	39
Hawaii	7,351	698	9
Idaho	1,469	837	57
Illinois	6,522	812	12
Indiana	2,392	213	9
Iowa	2,271	437	19
Kansas	1,846	464	25
Kentucky	1,333	357	27
Louisiana	4,400	1,532	35
Maine	2,201	947	43
Maryland	4,644	1,451	31
Massachusetts	15,020	912	6
Michigan	3,402	742	22
Minnesota	6,656	422	6
Mississippi	7,039	1,082	15
Missouri	2,498	350	14
Montana	1,013	522	54
Nebraska	1,394	489	35
Nevada	1,167	691	59
New Hampshire	1,894	653	34
New Jersey	5,814	427	7
New Mexico	4,203	516	12
New York	32,263	1,566	5
North Carolina	3,115	739	24
North Dakota	881	554	63
Ohio	1,235	280	23
Oklahoma	3,601	784	22
Oregon	3,091	871	28
Pennsylvania	4,764	340	7

Table 4-1 (continued)

State	Introductions	Enactments	Percent
Rhode Island	7,273	1,404	19
South Carolina	2,731	571	21
South Dakota	1,208	606	50
Tennessee	3,431	1,286	37
Texas	5,561	1,487	27
Utah	1,465	742	51
Vermont	1,147	212	18
Virginia	4,113	1,999	49
Washington	3,948	781	20
West Virginia	2,724	636	23
Wisconsin	2,715	494	18
Wyoming	745	328	44
Puerto Rico	2,729	450	16
State totals	201,723	39,656	20
U.S. Congress	7,732	394	5

Source: The Book of the States, 2000–01 (Lexington, Ky.: Council of State Governments, 2000).

nation are stimulating. "It's great to sit around over dinner, talking policy or strategizing. It's an intoxicating environment," says a California senator. A Nebraska senator comments, "I live for the last three or four weeks of the session—when everything comes together, we're going a mile a minute and things are getting done. It's barely controlled chaos, but somehow it works. It's exciting." Life in the legislature is rarely dull, and in the final weeks or days of a session the pace may even be frenetic.

For those who feel the call to public service, being able to influence public policy, help their community, and play in an exciting political game are satisfactions enough. The power that legislators wield is also an incentive. Power is necessary to get things done and provides its own sense of reward, but the power of individual legislators is limited by other players such as their colleagues in the chamber, the leaders of their legislature, members of the other chamber, and the president or governor.

A few of those who are elected to the legislature don't like the experience and leave after a term or two. Some have to leave because they cannot afford to stay financially. Their children may be approaching college age or a law practice may require more of their attention. Some don't leave until their health gives out. Others retire because they are afraid that they can't win re-election.

Still others leave to run for higher office—members of the U.S. House for governor or a U.S. Senate seat and state legislators for Congress or a statewide position. A survey of state legislators who left legislative service in 1987–1988 found that 6 percent of them ran for governor or other statewide office, 5 percent for Congress, and 4 percent for judicial or local government office.

This raises a question as to whether lawmakers who have ambitions for higher office such as congressional representative, U.S. senator, governor, or even president have different motivations from those of other legislators. Do their ambitions influence their behavior while they are in office? Probably they do. Ambitious legislators tend to pursue legislative strategies that make their work more newsworthy. They are also likely to espouse policies that have a broad appeal to the larger constituencies they wish to serve rather than just their own districts.

These different motivations for aspiring public officials are a problem for representative democracy only if they distract from public-regarding motivations that make the system work. Achieving ambition for higher office is a form of personal gain, but it is not likely to be a significant financial gain because, as already noted, legislative office does not usually lead to financial reward. The wider ambitions of some legislators actually have a beneficial effect for the system by making elected officials more responsive to broader constituencies. Their greater visibility may make them more effective legislators. Besides, the system of representative democracy as a whole profits by having legislators gain experience and knowledge at one level of government and applying them at another.

In addition to dealing with ambition for higher elected office we must also consider instances in which serving in the legislature may lead to a better-paying nonelected job. Former legislators make effective lobbyists because they know the people and the system, so some are able to make a good living as legislative advocates after leaving the legislature. Other former legislators obtain executive branch appointments that pay well and lead to careers in administration. Although the instances of former legislators becoming lobbyists or executive agency officials are fairly visible, they are relatively small in number. For the most part a better-paying job related to the public sector is a by-product of legislative service rather than a principal aim.

So far, the reasons that we have discussed as to why people leave the legislature deal with voluntary retirement. Taking all the reasons for voluntary retirement together, only about one in ten members of Congress or state legislatures chooses to leave legislative service at the end of each biennium. A second set of reasons for leaving falls in the category of involuntary retirement. Besides death and disability (statistically small factors) there are two causes of involuntary retirement: term limits and election defeat. We will save discussion of these factors for Chapter 8.

At this point, we will merely point out that term limits are an increasingly important cause of membership turnover in seventeen states but that election defeat causes very few legislators to leave. Once elected, most members choose to remain in the legislature and are able to get reelected. Although their jobs vary greatly by level of government and from state to state, they like and derive satisfaction from their service. To continue our examination of what makes legislators tick, we need to consider the role that elections play in the life of legislators with particular attention to the subject of campaign finance and its influence on legislative decision making.

How They Campaign

If they find legislative life fulfilling, legislators have to concern themselves with the next campaign for reelection. They can continue in public service only by winning more votes than their opponent wins in the next election. So they worry about what their constituents think about them and about the issues. In the larger states—and just about everywhere in competitive districts—the impending campaign is never far from legislators' minds.

Fund-raising is often an ongoing activity. Is it any wonder that officeholders who like their jobs don't want to lose?

Even incumbents from relatively safe districts take little for granted. They are always looking over their shoulders for a primary election opponent. They have seen colleagues whose districts were even safer than their own struck by electoral lightning and do not want it to strike them. So they campaign hard. In populous, competitive districts, election campaigns are likely to be exhausting marathons that last several months. Many legislators represent small enough districts that they can campaign door-to-door evenings and weekends. All of them appear at candidate forums and debates. If they can afford it, they buy radio and television advertisements. Most make use of direct mail. Campaigns require not only the time and effort of candidates, they also require financial resources.

The range in the cost of legislative election campaigns is great. In 1998 the average winner of a race for the U.S. House of Representatives spent $675,000, whereas U.S. Senate winners spent an average of nearly $5 million. In large, competitive states like California, Illinois, or Ohio, candidates for the legislature sometimes spend $1 million or more, although expenditures of a few hundred thousand dollars are more common. In smaller states with citizen legislatures like South Dakota, Vermont, or Wyoming, in contrast, it is unusual for candidates to spend more than $10,000 on a state legislative election campaign. In small rural districts dominated by one party in Arkansas, Maine, or North Dakota, candidates for the legislature may spend only a few hundred dollars for filing fees, printing, and postage. There is a strong relationship between the population of legislative districts and the amounts of money candidates spend on elections. Generally, the bigger the district, the more money is spent.

Legislators who do not need to raise a lot of money can support their campaigns with contributions from family and friends and groups in their district that support them because they already are allies. In U.S. Senate races, high-stakes congressional elections, or highly contested legislative races in the big states, candidates must reach beyond their families, friends, and district-based political supporters to raise the money necessary to win elections. Their sources of campaign funds include individual contributions, candidates' personal funds, legislative party leaders, political party organizations, and the political action committees (PACs) of interest groups. In congressional races in 1998 on average slightly more than one-half of all campaign funds came from individual contributors, about one-third from PACs, and less than 10 percent from candidates' own funds and political parties combined. High-cost state legislative races follow a similar pattern, with a somewhat more significant portion coming from PACs and legislative party leaders. In spite of all the attention given to the role of PACs in campaign fund-raising, most campaign funds come from individual contributions.

In the more expensive races campaign fund-raising requires substantial time and effort from the candidates over an extended period. How many of the 8,000 members of Congress and state legislatures are subject to these kinds of pressures? Probably a much smaller number than most people think. Although it is impossible to say for sure how many legislators are potentially subject to campaign finance pressures, it is reasonable to guess that about 2,000 (25 percent) fit into this group. This includes only a very small portion of legislators in the smallest states (less than 10 percent, mostly legislative leaders who raise money for their colleagues), a quarter of those in medium population states, about one-third of the members in the larger states and the U.S. House of Representatives, and virtually all U.S. senators. Another way of guessing at this number is that there are approximately 2,400 legislative districts in the country with populations of more than 100,000 people. These districts are large enough that candidates are likely to have to use more expensive retail (mass mailings, media) than the low-cost wholesale (door to door, one-on-one) marketing techniques. Using these two methods, we estimate that only 25–30 percent of all state and federal legislators have substantial campaign fund-raising needs.

How They Make Decisions

The good news is that almost three-quarters of all legislators don't raise enough money that we need to be concerned about their integrity in relation to campaign funds. The bad news is that about one-quarter of them have to raise so much money that we need to consider whether or not campaign funds have a corrupting influence on their behavior. Our political culture today is so suspicious of the role that political money plays in influencing legislators' actions that we must examine the extent to which fundraising pressures distort legislators' priorities by coloring how they spend their time, whom they choose to see, or how they vote on issues. A second question of integrity that we must also address is the problem of conflict of interest—whether or not legislators benefit personally from their public decisions.

To understand these issues of integrity better let us introduce a hypothetical lawmaker. Senator Strong is a Republican state legislator from a competitive, suburban district in a large state. He owns a successful small business, is an avid outdoorsman, has served in the legislature for ten years, and chairs the commerce and industry committee. In his last election to the state senate against a strong opponent, he spent $150,000 and was narrowly reelected. Some of his largest contributors came from the tobacco industry and the National Rifle Association (NRA).

During the legislative session Senator Strong faces decisions on two particularly controversial issues. The first one is a bill requiring restaurants to offer segregated seating for smokers and nonsmokers and to ventilate the smoking area. The bill is introduced by the chair of the health committee, is referred to her committee, and easily receives a "do pass" recommendation to the full senate. But because the bill deals with business regulation the senate president also refers the bill to Senator Strong's commerce and industry committee for a recommendation. At the urging of Senator Strong, his committee recommends that the bill "do not pass," and with his leadership on the floor of the senate it is defeated. A major newspaper in the state that supports the restaurant smoking measure editorializes that Senator Strong is "in the pocket of big tobacco." The second issue is a gun control measure that requires background checks of gun purchasers at gun shows. Despite aggressive lobbying by the NRA, Senator Strong casts the deciding vote in the senate in favor of this bill. In the following discussion of how legislators make decisions we will elaborate on Senator Strong's decisions on these two bills.

The subject of campaign finance and its influence on legislators' behavior pervades political discourse in America. The media harp on it. Candidates for elected office—from president to county assessor—accuse their opponents of being "tools of the special interests." Government reform organizations trumpet alleged correlations between campaign contributions and legislators' roll call votes. An example of the inflamed rhetoric of the reformers can be found in the headline on a May 2001 statement by the president of Common Cause on Vice President Dick Cheney's energy task force report: "Big time donors get major league payback, non-donors get higher energy bills and a dirtier environment." The implication is that politicians' votes follow the money.

Let's examine the issue in detail. As we will discuss in Chapter 6, a great many organized interests have a stake in the outcome of legislative decisions. Many of these groups have political action committees that give campaign contributions, usually to legislators who are predisposed to support their positions. The contributions are designed to help reelect friends and allies. In the case of Senator Strong, he had long worked for the rights of gun owners before being elected to the legislature with the help of the NRA. Similarly, his votes in favor of smokers on tobacco issues had been consistent over time, so the tobacco industry regarded him as an ally and wanted to help him stay in the legislature. In other words, the campaign contributions that he received followed his votes, rather than the votes following the money as insinuated by the newspaper editorial.

Before looking at the influence of these campaign contributions on legislators' actions, we need to understand a whole range of other complex dynamics that affect lawmakers' choices:

1. *Constituents.* Legislators pay close attention to their constituents' views because they are products of their communities and think in similar ways, they want to do good for their districts, and most want to be reelected to office. Senator Strong voted for the gun show background check bill because of strong, united opinion in his district in favor of tighter control on the sale of guns, engendered by an incident of school violence in a neighboring community involving guns purchased at a gun show. On matters that are important to their districts and on which most of their constituents agree, nothing except perhaps their own values is likely to sway legislators from voting the predominant opinions found in their districts.

2. *Legislators' core principles and beliefs and their public records.* Many legislators come into public service with strong dispositions toward public policy issues that grow out of their work and family experiences and their socioeconomic background. Their professional or occupational backgrounds are likely to be particularly influential in forming these beliefs. It is understandable that teachers support bills benefiting education, that doctors favor bills advancing health care, or for that matter, that a president and vice president, having spent much of their careers in the energy industry, would favor greater energy production. One reason Senator Strong opposed the bill concerning smoking in restaurants was that as a small business owner he was not sympathetic to more state regulations for restaurant owners. His vote on the gun control bill was more surprising for going against his core beliefs and values as an outdoorsman and Second Amendment advocate than it was for opposing the position of a major campaign contributor. As lawmakers gain experience in the legislature these views and beliefs grow stronger, and they build a public record on issues. This record is subject to attack from their opponents in election campaigns, especially if the record shows frequent changes in positions or other inconsistencies. Beyond the natural tendency for people to behave in ways that match their personal beliefs, there is pressure to maintain consistent views.

3. *Legislative leaders and political parties.* Political parties tend to have strong influences on legislators' behavior. People who run for public office choose one party or another, usually on the basis of their core principles and beliefs. All but a few legislators in the country are elected under the banner of one of the two major parties. In order to get ahead and achieve positions of influence that allow them to achieve their policy goals, legislators must respond to their party's leaders, who usually are trying to advance a party policy agenda. Party caucus meetings reinforce the admonitions of party leaders and in some states bind party members to vote for the party position. Senator Strong's party caucus had not taken a formal position on the matter of smoking in restaurants, but in keeping with Republican principles in favor of limited government, most of his fellow Republicans voted the same way as he did.

4. *The merits of the issue.* There are few issues in American life on which everyone agrees. Usually there are merits on both sides, just as there are organized interests on both sides. On the restaurant smoking issue Senator Strong had to balance the merits of improving public health and the comfort of nonsmokers against the merits of supporting limited government and protecting the property rights of business owners. In the end he judged that this was not a good issue for the state to enact a "one size fits all" policy and voted instead to allow local communities to make their own decisions. The contentious legislative process on this issue, as on most issues, ensured that the merits on both sides were thoroughly argued.

5. *The executive branch.* Because of presidents' or governors' abilities to dominate media attention, their positions as party leaders, and the powers of their office, chief executives wield influence over legislators' decisions. They are lightning rods that can cause legislators to go one way or another, depending on whether the governor or president is of their political party. Executive agency officials also can have a significant effect because of their specialized knowledge, larger resources, and greater expertise.

6. *Legislative committees or trusted colleagues.* Legislators cannot be experts on all the hundreds of issues that come before them. On matters on which they don't know a lot or don't have strong positions, they rely on the recommendations of the legislative committees that have studied the issue in more detail or on colleagues they know are knowledgeable in the area.

7. *Family and personal friends.* Legislators' personal connections help to define their core values and beliefs in the first place. On some issues they may feel more accountable to friends and family than to almost anyone else. A former Colorado legislator says, "I found it more difficult to say 'no' to my friends than to the people who contributed to my campaign."

These influences on legislators' actions are complex, highly interrelated, and almost impossible to isolate on any given issue. With this broader context of factors influencing legislators' decisions in mind, we are now in a position to focus on the potential effects of large contributions on their actions. We will look at three areas of potential influence: time, access, and votes.

1. *Time.* There are three dimensions to the effects of campaign funds on legislators' time. First, legislators (and their challengers in elections) may have to spend inordinate amounts of time raising money, time that they could more productively spend on something else. To the extent that this may be true, it is likely to be a significant problem only in the months immediately before an election. Second, the desire of legislators to satisfy their major contributors with whom they are in agreement may lead them to make commitments early in the deliberation process, thereby reducing the lawmakers' flexibility to change their minds or compromise at later stages of consideration. For example, Senator Strong might have committed himself at the outset of the session to voting against the antismoking proposal before hearing all the arguments, both because of his strong personal beliefs and his desire to please campaign contributors. Third, legislators may be induced by campaign contributions to devote more time to the causes that they and their supporters agree on than they might otherwise devote to issues that don't have wealthy or powerful advocates. Contributions from the tobacco industry might have encouraged Senator Strong to take more of a leadership role on the smoking-in-restaurants issue than he might otherwise have done.

2. *Access.* The main thing that large campaign contributors expect to obtain is access—the ability to make sure their message is heard. The time demands of most legislators are so great that they cannot see everyone who wants to bend their ear. They have to make choices. Many legislators say that contributors get more of their attention than noncontributors do. All else being equal, this may be so. But even if there were no need to raise campaign funds, many of these major contributors would get more attention from legislators because they are major employers or large institutions in their districts or states, they represent large numbers of people, or they are particularly well informed on important issues. In the words of former U.S. senator Dan Coates, "A contribution is by no means necessary to obtain a meeting, and a meeting is no guarantee of results." In the case

of the smoking in restaurants bill, the tobacco industry probably would have been able to talk to Senator Strong even without contributing to his campaign. On the gun control issue, the NRA got Senator Strong's ear but not his vote. We will elaborate on the subject of access in Chapter 6.

3. *Votes.* Except in unusual cases of corrupt or venal legislators, contributions rarely affect outcomes on the major issues of public policy. On the big issues the other factors that we have enumerated, especially constituency position, party agenda, and the legislators' own beliefs, play a greater role. In some cases, contributions may influence a legislator's voting decisions on the margins if the issue is of low importance to his or her constituency or if the member has no position on the issue. Or it might cause a legislator to pay more attention to the group's policy justification for its position, so without being aware of the influence of the contribution, a legislator might decide to vote for the group's position. In this way, contributions may soften potential opposition or activate potential support. They are more likely to influence how active and vocal a legislator is on an issue than they are a legislator's basic position or vote.

After reviewing the academic literature on campaign finance, Bradley Smith, a law professor and member of the Federal Election Commission, concludes: "The assertion that lawmakers vote to please financial contributors is simply not supported by the bulk of systematic evidence. Serious studies of legislative behavior have overwhelmingly concluded that campaign contributions play little role in floor voting. . . . Empirical studies show that the influence of contributions is dwarfed by party agenda, personal ideology and constituent desires."

Thus, we conclude that the overwhelming majority of legislators can and do maintain their integrity even though they are constantly raising money for political campaigns; only a few can't and don't. What do these contributors get for their money that they wouldn't get otherwise? Not much. They get what any political supporters or local influential people would get—courtesy, an ear, and consideration. Perhaps they get it somewhat more readily than noncontributors might. Despite public and media suspicion, there is no evidence that campaign contributions significantly influence legislators' decisions.

Besides the influence of campaign funds, a second major element of public concern about legislators' motivations relates to conflicts of interest. The news media and public watchdog organizations often criticize legislators for serving on committees that have jurisdiction over their personal occupations or for voting on matters that affect their own industry. For example, in press reports about a report entitled "Our Private Legislatures—Public Service, Personal Gain," the director of the Center for Public Integrity was quoted as saying, "You'd better watch these people very closely. Not all of them are working for the public interest. Some of them are feathering their own nests." The report goes on to castigate state legislators because "more than one in five sat on a committee that regulated their professional or business interests" and some worked for organizations that lobby state government or received income from a government agency.

Remember that most states have citizen legislators who supplement their legislative incomes with income from private employment. There is always the potential for conflicts in which the public good can lose to the individual legislator's personal gain. James Madison's argument that our country has multiple, competing interests in the policymaking process is especially applicable to our citizen legislatures. His point was that the number and diversity both of our citizenry and our elected officials prevent any one interest from prevailing over the others.

Legislatures have enacted statutes and rules to disclose and guard against conflicts, and legislators are expected to abstain from participating on an issue when they have a direct financial interest in that issue. Ethics experts generally agree—and most ethics laws specify—that it is acceptable for legislators to vote on matters affecting themselves and everyone else in a class or industry but not on issues that help them or their spouses specifically.

But to the public, following the letter of the law may not look right, and these days an appearance of conflict can be almost as damning as a conflict itself. The accusation about legislators serving on committees that regulate their industry falls in the category of an appearance of a conflict. The whole idea of a citizen legislature is that our system benefits from the knowledge that teacher-legislators bring to education policy, doctors and nurses contribute to health care issues, or, in our example, Senator Strong adds to the subject of business regulation. Doesn't it make sense for legislators to ask to serve on committees in which they have knowledge, interest, and expertise?

The problem is that the reformers worry not just about actual conflicts in which elected officials benefit personally from their public actions (the equivalent of a smoking gun) but also about the appearance of a conflict (possession of a gun regardless of whether it is used in the commission of a crime). This creates a dilemma both for legislators and the voters who elect them.

Prohibiting outside employment and getting rid of the citizen legislator is the only way to resolve the problem. Congress, by far our most professionalized legislature, has chosen this route, but it is the only legislative body in the United States whose members are banned from earning any outside income. Few states have been willing to raise legislative salaries to a level high enough to justify preventing legislators from earning outside income. Most people in most states prefer the idea of a citizen legislature. As long as we want to continue citizen legislatures we have to accept the potential for some conflicts of interest.

Finally, campaign contributions or the prospect of enriching one's own business or profession may significantly influence the few lawmakers who can be swayed by financial considerations. There have been scandals involving bribery, campaign funds, and personal enrichment schemes throughout American history. In the 1980s the FBI conducted sting operations to catch suspected legislators in the act of accepting money in exchange for votes. Abscam, the FBI's congressional operation, resulted in the conviction of six house members and one senator. Similar stings caught state legislators in Arizona, California, Kentucky, and South Carolina.

Often the penalty for such transgressions is conviction of a crime and fines or imprisonment. In other cases public reprimands, other slaps on the wrist, or bad publicity embarrass legislators or lead them to step aside in the wake of scandals. In 1989 U.S. House Speaker Jim Wright resigned after accusations that he had profited from shady financial dealings. More recently the House Ethics Committee issued a reprimand to Rep. Bud Schuster of Pennsylvania, the chair of the House Transportation Committee, because of his relationship to a former staff member who lobbied his committee. He also received extensive bad publicity for his close ties to the transportation industry. Eventually he resigned his seat in Congress.

Despite the wide publicity that these cases of malfeasance receive, they are relatively infrequent occurrences. Although a few legislators may be corrupt and a few more may be ethically challenged, the overwhelming majority of American legislators are honest men and women who are trying to meet high standards that have become even higher in recent years. Lee Hamilton, a highly respected member who served in Congress for thirty-four years, says, "People like to dwell on misbehavior. In my experience in Congress probity is the rule, not the exception." Every institution, including every legislative chamber, has a few bad apples. But that is no reason to assume that the entire barrel is spoiled.

In Sum

In our examination of what makes legislators tick we have found that the overwhelming majority of them are inspired by their wish to serve the public. Although not all of them embody the Madisonian virtues of experience, trust, and knowledge, in general they are a dedicated group who want to help their constituents, strengthen their communities, and improve public policy at the state or national level. Depending on the type of legislature in which they serve, the pressures on them may vary substantially, but most of them like their work and pursue strategies that allow them to continue in it. One of the things that varies the most from Congress to state legislatures and from state to state is the need to raise funds to finance their campaigns. For those who have to raise large amounts of money campaign finance is one added pressure on top of many that influence their decisions. Simple efforts to correlate political money and roll call votes are gross oversimplifications of the complex motivations of legislators. A more sophisticated understanding of the multiple factors that affect legislators' choices is required to make sense of representative democracy. Conflicts of interest are an inevitable result of having citizen legislatures. Because Americans value their part-time legislatures and believe that the public benefits from legislators' ties to their communities that result, the public must rely on ethical practices by legislators to avoid any potentially negative effects of conflicts of interest. All but a few bad actors in the legislatures meet our standards for effective representative democracy.

Sources and Suggested Reading

A highly readable personal account of legislative life that touches on all the themes in this chapter is *The Art of Legislative Politics* (Washington, D.C.: CQ Press, 1994), an account by Tom Loftus of his career in the Wisconsin Assembly. The most useful study of who runs for legislatures and why is Gary Moncrief, Peverill Squire, and Malcolm Jewell's *Who Runs for the Legislature?* (Upper Saddle River, N.J.: Prentice-Hall, 2001) from which the data on candidates for state legislatures in this chapter are taken. Gary Moncrief and Joel Thompson include many valuable articles on legislative careers in their *Changing Patterns in State Legislative Careers* (Ann Arbor: University of Michigan Press, 1992). Alan Ehrenhalt's *The United States of Ambition* (New York: Random House, 1991) is a provocative journalistic account of the motivations of candidates for elective office in several states. Excellent reviews of the academic literature on legislative careers include Gary Moncrief, "Recruitment and Retention in U.S. Legislatures," *Legislative Studies Quarterly* 24 (May 1999); John R. Hibbing, "Legislative Careers: Why and How We Should Study Them," *Legislative Studies Quarterly* 24 (May 1999); and Burdett Loomis, "The Motivations of Legislators," *American Legislative System*, vol. 1, ed. Joel H. Silbey (New York: Scribner's, 1994). The diversity of the settings in which legislatures operate is covered by Karl T. Kurtz in "Understanding the Diversity of American State Legislatures," *Extension of Remarks*, American Political Science Association Legislative Section Newsletter, June 1992.

As its title suggests, *Unfree Speech: The Folly of Campaign Finance Reform* (Princeton: Princeton University Press, 2001), by Bradley Smith, has a strong bias but contains a useful summary of the amount of campaign spending, the arguments for and against the corrupting influence of campaign finance, and the potential consequences of reform. Studies and reports that favor campaign finance reform can be found on the Web sites of Common Cause (www.common-cause.org) and the Center for Responsive Politics (www.opensecrets.org). Although now somewhat dated, Frank J. Sorauf's *Inside Campaign Finance: Myths and Realities* (New Haven: Yale University Press, 1992) is a valuable resource. The only full-length treatments of state campaign finance are *Campaign Finance in State Legislative Elections*, ed. Joel A. Thompson, Gary F. Moncrief, and Herbert E. Alexander (Washington, D.C.: CQ Press, 1998), and *The Day after Reform*, by Michael J. Malbin and Thomas L. Gais (Albany: Rockefeller Institute Press, 1998). *Legislative Labyrinth*, by Diana Dwyre and Victoria Farrar-Myers (Washington,

D.C.: CQ Press, 2000), provides a case study of campaign finance reform legislation in Congress.

The best treatment of the subject of conflict of interest is Alan Rosenthal's *Drawing the Line: Legislative Ethics in the States* (Lincoln: University of Nebraska Press, 1996). See also the Center for Public Integrity's Web site (http://www.publicintegrity.org) for a critical report on state financial disclosure laws.

5

How Are Legislators
Linked to Their Constituencies?

FOR REPRESENTATIVE DEMOC-
racy to work, a connection must
exist between representatives
and the constituents in their districts. Constituents must have
access to their representatives to
express their views or ask for
help. Representatives must service their constituents and connect them with government.
They must also take their views
and interests into account in
performing their function as
lawmakers.

How the Public Sees
Representation

As we noted in Chapter 1, the public is schizophrenic on the subject of representation. On the one hand, people think their own representative does a
pretty good job in "representing" them. Public opinion polls offer supporting evidence, as do election results that show incumbents winning 80–90
percent of the time in both Congress and state legislatures. Part of this success rate comes from the built-in advantages of incumbency, but part is attributable to their constituents' belief that they are doing a good job.

One piece of evidence is furnished by a study of evaluations of how
members of Congress responded to communications initiated by

constituents. Responses to communications expressing opinions satisfied 49 percent of constituents (20 percent were not satisfied). Responses to communications seeking information satisfied 64 percent (8 percent were not satisfied). And responses to communications seeking help satisfied 61 percent (16 percent were not satisfied).

Although people appear to feel that their own representative cares about them, they do not feel that way about legislators in general. If only legislators would listen to ordinary people. If only they would stay in touch. If only they were not professional politicians. If only they were like plain people—having to go to regular jobs, having to live on modest salaries, and having to balance a budget. The problem, according to many Americans, is that legislators don't listen to regular folks and aren't like them. In this chapter we will explore how accurate this public view is and assess the effectiveness of the links between legislators and their constituents.

How Legislators Feel about Their Constituencies

Contrary to what the public believes about representatives in general, legislators care more about their constituencies than anything else in their political lives. They care for three major reasons.

First, legislators naturally identify with their constituents—as one of them and not simply as their agent. Most have lived in their districts for years. But whether they have grown up in their districts or have lived there for only a relatively brief time, the attachment is strong. Their constituents are friends, neighbors, people they have met. Many legislators not only live in their districts but work there as well. Although members of Congress may not, by law, earn income to supplement their government salaries, legislators in the fifty states can and do practice law, sell insurance, and continue other occupations, albeit on a restricted basis. Thus, they have occupational, familial, and friendship ties in the districts they represent. Legislators, with few exceptions, feel at one with the people where they live. Wanting to represent them comes naturally to them.

Second, legislators believe that representing their constituents is a significant part of their role in a representative democracy. They take the business of representation seriously, because they want to do a good job. This does not necessarily mean that they think of themselves as "delegates," acting in response to the demands or wishes of constituents, rather than as "trustees," acting according to their own judgments on behalf of constituents. However they conceive of their representational role, their constituencies are foremost in their minds.

Third, legislators are motivated to care about their constituencies, if they want to be reelected (or elected to higher office), as nearly all of them do. Indeed, as Richard Fenno points out, "there is no way that the act of representing can be separated from the act of getting elected." If members of Congress or of state legislatures cannot win, they can't represent anyone. No one wants to be rejected by the voters at the polls, even if he or she is thinking of retiring from political life anyway. The scars one suffers with defeat last a long time, and legislators are loath to bear them. So they pay attention to what their constituents say, what they want, and what they need.

How Legislators Relate to Their Constituencies

How legislators relate to their constituencies depends on many things. District size is one of the most important. At the federal level, U.S. senators represent states that range in size from California with 33,871,648 people to Wyoming with 493,782. Representing states like California, Florida, New York, and Texas is a lot different from representing states like North Dakota, South Dakota, Vermont, and Wyoming. Each congressional district has 609,000 constituents. Members of virtually every state legislature have substantially fewer constituents. Their districts vary enormously from state to state, as shown in Table 5-1.

Only in California are some districts larger in population than U.S. House districts. Each of California's 40 state senators represents about 846,791 people. At the other extreme, the least populous states have comparatively small populations in each of the legislative districts. In New Hampshire, for example, each of the 400 house members in a single-member district has 3,089 constituents (although some multimember districts have larger populations).

Table 5-1 Legislative Districts

State	Senates		Houses	
	Seats	Dist. pop.	Seats	Dist. pop.
Alabama	35	127,060	105	42,353
Alaska	20	31,347	40	15,673
Arizona	30	171,021	60	171,021[a]
Arkansas	35	76,383	100	26,734
California	40	846,791	80	423,396
Colorado	35	122,893	65	66,173
Connecticut	36	94,599	151	22,553
Delaware	21	37,314	41	19,112
Florida	40	399,559	120	133,186
Georgia	56	146,187	180	45,480
Hawaii	25	48,461	51	23,756
Idaho	35	36,970	70	36,970[a]
Illinois	59	210,496	118	105,248
Indiana	50	121,610	100	60,805
Iowa	50	58,526	100	29,263
Kansas	40	67,210	125	21,507
Kentucky	38	106,362	100	40,418
Louisiana	39	114,589	105	42,562
Maine	35	36,426	151	8,443
Maryland	47	112,691	141	37,564
Massachusetts	40	158,727	160	39,682
Michigan	38	261,538	110	90,349
Minnesota	67	73,425	134	36,713
Mississippi	52	54,705	122	23,317
Missouri	34	164,565	163	34,326
Montana	50	18,044	100	9,022
Nebraska	49	34,924	NA[b]	
Nevada	21	95,155	42	47,578
New Hampshire	24	51,491	400	3,089
New Jersey	40	210,359	80	210,359[a]
New Mexico	42	43,311	70	25,986
New York	61	311,089	150	126,510
North Carolina	50	160,986	120	67,078
North Dakota	49	13,106	98	13,106[a]
Ohio	33	344,035	99	114,678
Oklahoma	48	71,889	101	34,165
Oregon	30	114,047	60	57,023

Table 5-1 (continued)

State	Senates		Houses	
	Seats	Dist. pop.	Seats	Dist. pop.
Pennsylvania	50	245,621	203	60,498
Rhode Island	50	20,966	100	10,483
South Carolina	46	87,218	124	32,355
South Dakota	35	21,567	70	21,567[a]
Tennessee	33	172,403	99	57,468
Texas	31	672,639	150	139,012
Utah	29	77,006	75	29,776
Vermont	30	20,294	150	4,059
Virginia	40	176,963	100	70,785
Washington	49	120,288	98	112,917[a]
West Virginia	34	53,187	100	18,083
Wisconsin	33	162,536	99	54,179
Wyoming	30	16,459	60	8,230
Puerto Rico	29	133,107	52	74,233
U.S. Congress	100	NA	435	645,632

Source: National Conference of State Legislatures.

Note: District size is calculated by dividing the number of seats into the total 2000 population. District sizes are for single-member districts in states with mixed district types.

[a] Two-member districts.
[b] Unicameral legislature.

Representation probably is easier in smaller than in larger districts. Smaller districts are likely to be more homogeneous, with fewer organized interests and fewer competing ones. In districts with fewer than 50,000 or so people, representatives can have personal contact with a sizeable proportion of constituents. Geographical size and shape also affect the nature of representation. Urban districts are more concentrated, whereas rural districts are more dispersed. In California, state legislative districts range from 18 to 28,991 square miles. New York's range from 1 square mile to 4,731 square miles. Colorado's districts range from those in Denver, which are roughly 6 square miles each, to a district of 12,916 square miles that covers the entire northwest corner of the state.

Whether the district is large or small and whether the legislator is a member of Congress or a citizen legislature, representatives find it important to establish a connection with constituents and a presence in their constituencies. This is done in several different ways. Members of Congress spend as much time as they can in their districts. Many manage to get back home every weekend. Many, and especially those with school-age children, don't even bring their families with them to Washington. Those with greater seniority and more electoral safety travel back and forth less often. They can pay relatively more attention to the legislative part of their job than to the constituency part.

Because Congress is in session practically the entire year, except for scheduled "constituency work periods" and vacations, the physical presence of members in their districts has to be limited. But professional staffs in their states and districts extend their presence on a full-time basis. U.S. senators allocate on average one-third of their personal staffs to offices in various parts of their state, whereas representatives keep about half their personal staffs in one or several district offices.

State legislators can spend more time in their districts than members of Congress. State legislative sessions are shorter than congressional ones, especially in the citizen legislatures described in Chapter 4. In small northeastern states like Connecticut, Delaware, Maryland, New Jersey, and Rhode Island, legislators can commute to the capital each session day, spending evenings back home. Even in larger states, where populations are concentrated in and near the capital, many legislators commute. In Massachusetts practically all do. In Nebraska, those from Lincoln and Omaha do. And in Minnesota, legislators from St. Paul and Minneapolis have no difficulty getting home every night. Long interim periods, closer proximity to the capital, and Tuesday-Thursday session schedules in some states mean that legislators spend more time at home.

When they can, legislators present themselves to constituents and constituency groups in their districts. They make the rounds. In suburban districts they visit with the Chamber of Commerce for breakfasts, the Rotary Club for lunch, and perhaps the Board of Realtors for dinner. The League of Women Voters may meet on a Sunday afternoon, and the sportsmen's club may have a get-together on Saturday night. In urban districts, the routine is different—churches and neighborhood associations get special attention, as do town hall meetings scheduled by the representatives themselves. In some districts legislators talk mainly about policy; in others they present themselves in more down-to-earth terms.

In the most populous states, legislators have district offices or allowances to pay for space as well as staff to support their efforts at home. California, Florida, and New Jersey are examples. Like members of Congress, legislators from these states also have budgets for newsletters to inform constituents of what they are doing on their behalf. And many have Web sites of their own to supplement those of their state legislatures.

Few legislators, from either more competitive or less competitive districts, take lightly their relationships with the folks back home. They invite requests from constituents; make time to respond to their phone calls, letters, or e-mail; and juggle busy schedules in order to be available for their visits to the capitol or sacrifice time at work or with their families in order to visit with constituents in their districts.

How Legislators Serve Their Constituencies

Legislators fulfill their representational function by rendering constituent service to individuals, which is commonly known as "casework." In the congressional offices, one major function of personal staff is to provide assistance to people who are having problems with federal departments and agencies. Representatives intercede with bureaucracies handling social security benefits, civil service pensions, immigration proceedings, veterans' benefits, and so forth. Casework is about the same at the state level, although cases tend to be fewer (particularly in wealthier districts, where constituents are less apt to request assistance). The problems relate mostly to unemployment compensation, welfare, health and hospitals, roads and highways, traffic, drivers' licenses, insurance, and occupational licenses.

Depending on the state, anywhere from one-third to two-thirds of legislators would cite constituency service as an important, or even the most important, part of the job of being a legislator. If they have personal staff in their districts or capitols, as they do in about one-third of the states, the casework burden is greater in general but easier on the legislators themselves (see Table 5-2).

But whether they have staff or budget to do the job, legislators everywhere will write the letters and make the phone calls necessary to intervene on behalf of a constituent. They will sometimes ask for action or a decision that complies with a constituent's request; they will more often ask that the case be expedited, so that constituents can be assured that they are getting fair and timely consideration. Constituents who receive such help from their legislators are inclined to be appreciative and feel better connected to their government system.

Not only do representatives service individual constituents through casework, they also service their districts as a whole with project work. The difference between these services is not only the number of people receiving benefits but the nature of the benefits themselves. Federal grants, building construction, and highways are major projects. Funds for supporting local arts programs, building a playing field for a high school softball team, and renovating a roller-blade park are minor projects. But all are important to at least some people in a legislative district.

Every district can justify its own special needs, and usually the district's justification has merit. Representatives strongly believe that part of their job is going to bat for groups that come to them for assistance. It is ironic, therefore, that legislators are accused of trying to get "pork" for their districts in one breath and of being unresponsive to their constituents in another. It may be that what people think their representatives get for their own districts are meritorious projects, but what other representatives get for other districts is pork.

Efforts by legislators to bring resources to their districts (and prevent resources from being taken away) extend further. Little is more important to legislators as representatives of their districts than federal or state aid channeled to local units of government—counties, municipalities, and particularly school districts. Legislators try to ensure that the funding formula enacted into law benefits their constituencies as much as possible. For example, state aid to public schools commands tremendous attention from

Table 5-2 States and Jurisdictions That Provide Year-Round Personal Staff to Members, 1998

State	Senate Capitol	Senate District	House Capitol	House District
Alabama	◆			
California	◆	◆	◆	◆
Connecticut	◆			
Florida	◆	◆	◆	◆
Hawaii	◆		◆	
Illinois	◆	◆	◆	◆
Louisiana		◆		◆
Maryland	◆	◆	◆	◆
Massachusetts	◆		◆	
Michigan	◆		◆	
Minnesota	◆			
Missouri	◆	◆	◆	
Nebraska	◆			
New Jersey	◆	◆	◆	◆
New York	◆	◆	◆	◆
Ohio	◆		◆	
Oklahoma	◆			
Oregon	◆		◆	◆
Pennsylvania	◆	◆	◆	◆
South Carolina	◆			
Tennessee	◆		◆	◆
Texas	◆	◆	◆	◆
Washington	◆	◆	◆	
Wisconsin	◆	◆	◆	◆
Puerto Rico	◆	◆	◆	
U.S. Congress	◆	◆	◆	◆

Source: The Book of the States, 2000–01 (Lexington, Ky.: Council of State Governments, 2000).

Note: Some other states provide members with shared or session only personal staff.

state legislators. How does the allocation of funds compare with that to other districts? How does it compare with previous allocations? When it comes to devising or revising an aid formula for education, public welfare, highways, or general support, legislators have one primary concern: that their constituency comes out ahead.

The work that legislators do for their districts is believed to pay off handsomely. It benefits individual constituents and the constituency overall, and it also benefits the members of Congress and state legislatures who perform such services. They see results back home, and they also see results in their efforts to win reelection. One reason why so many incumbents do well at staying in office is that they do well in providing casework, projects, and other goodies for their electorates.

How Legislators Express Constituency Policy Views and Interests

When it comes to expressing concern, helping constituents with their government-related problems, or getting state aid and projects for their constituencies, representatives have a relatively straightforward role. It is not difficult for representatives to know what to do in pursuit of their districts' interests. On symbolic matters on the one hand and material concerns on the other, the mandate is: heed and express constituency concerns, bring home the bacon, and help the folks back home who have run afoul of government. Acting as an agent for the constituency on policy matters is more difficult, however.

Just how legislators represent their constituencies on matters of public policy depends on four sets of factors. First is the representative's conception of the representational role. Second is the constituency and the nature of its interests and views on various issues. Third is the communication from constituency to representative on issues in question. Fourth are other forces that come into play in the legislative process.

The Legislator's Representational Perspective

In his speech to the electors of Bristol in 1774, the English member of Parliament Edmund Burke advanced the case for the representative in the role of trustee:

> [Constituents'] wishes ought to have great weight with him; their opinion high respect; their business unremitted attention. It is his duty to sac-

rifice his repose, his pleasures, his satisfactions, to theirs—and above all, ever, and in all cases, to prefer their interest to his own. But his unbiased opinion, his mature judgment, his enlightened conscience, he ought not to sacrifice to you. . . . Your representative owes you, not his industry only, but his judgment: and he betrays, instead of serving you, if he sacrifices it to your opinion.

Many political theorists support the Burkean position, agreeing that the representative as trustee must do what is best for constituents, using experience, judgment, and wisdom in making his or her decisions. Other political theorists disagree, maintaining that the representative's duty is, as a delegate, to reflect accurately the wishes and opinions of those who are being represented.

In her theoretical work on representation, Hannah F. Pitkin allows for a continuum, ranging from a "mandate" theory of representation, where legislators assume delegate roles, to an "independence" theory, where they assume trustee roles. At the mandate/delegate end, representation occurs only when the representative acts on explicit instructions from constituents. The representative is an agent of the constituency, a tool or instrument by which the constituency registers its will. Further along the continuum, the representative exercises some discretion but is required to consult on controversial issues and then do as the constituency wishes, or else resign from office. Toward the middle of the continuum, a representative acts as he or she thinks constituents would want, unless they give instructions to the contrary, which the representative must obey. Proceeding further toward the independence/trustee position, the representative acts as he or she thinks is in the interests of constituents, unless they give instructions to the contrary, which have to be obeyed. Near the independence/trustee position, the representative must do as he or she thinks best, except insofar as one is bound by campaign promises. At the very end of the continuum the representative, once elected, is entirely free to use his or her own judgment in making decisions.

The public, on its part, probably believes that legislators ought to be bound by the views of their constituents. For example, a poll on the impeachment of President Clinton asked whether members of Congress should reflect public opinion or do what they think best. Almost twice as many respondents thought senators and representatives should reflect public opinion as thought they should do what they think best.

How do legislators see themselves? If pressed to choose, most would identify more with the trustee than with the delegate role. Over the years, political scientists have given considerable attention to legislators' roles. In 1962 John C. Wahlke and his associates, in a classic study of the legislative system, analyzed representational role orientations of members of the California, New Jersey, Ohio, and Tennessee legislatures. The role that predominated in each of the four states was that of trustee. Studies since then have produced similar results.

Legislators choose the trustee role, not because they reject the views or interests of their constituents or because they think their own beliefs should necessarily take precedence. There are virtually no legislators who believe district views are inconsequential. On very few issues, however, do legislators' conscience and constituency come into conflict. There are even fewer where a legislator would choose conscience over constituency. Legislators choose the trustee role because they regard it as the only viable one given the greater knowledge they have as a result of their involvement in the legislative process on the one hand and the paucity of constituency attention to most issues on the other. Their constituents, even if attentive, are far removed. As one Florida legislator commented, while "the public sees a snapshot, legislators see full-motion video." While apologizing for sounding elitist, a former member of the Florida Legislature nonetheless had to admit, "You [that is, legislators] do know more."

The Constituencies and Their Interests

The nature of legislators' constituencies and constituency beliefs on many issues precludes the delegate role. A legislator has little real choice other than to decide on the constituents' behalf, in line with what the legislator believes are their interests or in response to factors that for the most part are not constituency related.

Whether the constituency is a congressional district of nearly 700,000 or a state legislative district of about 3,000 or 4,000, the constituency as such offers little guidance on how legislators should act on the overwhelming number of issues. If, for instance, representatives wanted to play a delegate role on issues, they would have to know which constituents in their districts they were responding to; what views, if any, their constituents held; how strongly their constituents felt; how they divided; and whether a constituency mandate existed.

Legally, a representative's constituency consists of all those people living within a specified district. Demographically, a constituency may be mainly urban, suburban, or rural. It may be largely white or predominantly black or Hispanic. It may be affluent or poor. The more heterogeneous the district, the more difficult it is to represent, given its diverse interests. Politically, a constituency is less than the entire population; politically, it consists of those people who vote or who are eligible to vote. Even the electorate as constituency can be subdivided—into "primary" and "reelection" constituencies, the former being a representative's strongest supporters and main source of campaign funds and endorsements, and the latter being those who voted for the representative at the last election. Generally, the representative has to keep all these constituencies in mind, although on different issues the representative keeps one or another constituency in the forefront while others are further back.

Each of these demographic and political constituencies is factored into a representative's thinking. Nobody is left out, as a Republican in the Florida house explained. In a district of about 108,000 people, he won 40 percent of the vote in the primary and 54 percent in the general election. A total of 14,000 people voted for him and sent him to Tallahassee. That, he figured, was about 20 percent of the electorate. The other 80 percent either did not vote for him or simply did not vote, but, according to his understanding as a representative somehow he had to accommodate the 80 percent as well as the 20 percent.

Whatever the predominant reference group, what are a constituency's views on policies? As Pitkin points out, a constituency does not have an opinion on every topic. A representative, therefore, cannot reflect what is not there to be reflected. The large majority of issues addressed at a congressional session and the overwhelming majority of issues addressed at a state legislative session engage only a small proportion of constituents in any one district. This does not mean that such issues are not important to at least some constituents.

Many of these are what might be called narrow "special interest" issues. They are of concern to automobile dealers, optometrists and ophthalmologists, attorneys, and so forth. They affect the well-being and the livelihoods of relatively small professional and occupational groups, industries, or businesses. They are not matters that command broad public interest or concern. One Florida legislator, for instance, pointed out that there was virtually no opinion in her district on 95 percent of the issues on which she had to vote. She recalled that one of her early votes affected the disposition of the Florida stamp on a beer can. No one back home really cared about beer-can labeling. "It is rare," she commented, "that I have a sense of really what my district feels on any issue, except the most major questions."

Despite the lack of constituency views on these kinds of issues, legislators hear a lot about such matters from organized interest groups, the so-called special interests. These groups represent the views and interests, not of geographical constituencies, but of professional, occupational, business, and labor constituencies, as well as those interested in social issues. Some of these groups, moreover, may have a significant membership or nonmember support within a representative's district. Still, the base is usually a tiny part of the overall population of the electorate.

On major issues, those of overall public concern, constituents do have opinions. But as we demonstrated in Chapter 3, their opinions may be so general that they offer representatives little guidance. Once complicating factors, such as trade-offs or specificity, are introduced, consensus breaks down. But the very stuff of legislative work in committees or on the floors of Congress and state legislatures is trade-offs, priorities, and specifics. Even if they so desired, they could hardly behave as delegates, instructed by their constituencies. On the overwhelming majority of issues, there are no instructions or, if there are instructions, they are mixed. Legislators have to decide on the basis of factors other than constituency views. Furthermore, on most legislative issues constituencies have little or no interest, and certainly little or no direct interest. One would have to stretch mightily to discern the effects on legislators' districts of the many bills that relate to the administration of government and the many that regulate competition among special interests. These bills have their effects, but not on legislators' constituents.

Communications between Legislators and Their Constituencies

Even if a legislator's constituents had views on an issue, and the legislator wanted to follow them, it would often be difficult to do so. Although many avenues of communication link representatives and constituents, the messages that are carried can be unclear and contradictory.

Legislators are constantly reaching out, inquiring into how their constituents feel and what they want. Legislators visit one-on-one with people in their districts, mail them newsletters inviting their comments, and send out questionnaires that solicit constituent opinions on a host of subjects. They write newspaper columns, hold town hall meetings, and invite constituents to district "capitol days." Increasing numbers of legislators have their own Web pages. Whether they reach out or not, legislators hear from their constituencies. They receive telephone calls, mail, faxes, and an increasing volume of e-mail.

Members of the U.S. Senate and the House of Representatives receive tabulations from their staffs that keep them abreast of communications reflecting the distribution of constituents' opinions on key issues before Congress. Such tabulations are likely to be done on a weekly basis, or even more frequently if the issue is especially controversial. These communications, whether spontaneously initiated by ordinary individuals or stimulated by organized interest groups, are not without effect on members. Indeed, some state legislators become concerned if they receive as few as half a dozen letters on a subject. Aware of the ability of special interests to manage the expression of opinion by constituents on a given issue, other legislators apply a discount rate to the messages they receive—unless they are handwritten. Most legislators, however, would rather not run the risk of ignoring any possible reflection of constituency views; they pay attention to whatever form a communication from a constituent takes.

Although voting participation in the United States may have decreased, the communication by citizens with their representatives has increased. And the sensitivity of representatives to local opinion has also risen. A Missouri legislator described changes in participation that have brought constituents closer to their legislators than they were twenty, thirty, or forty years ago. "When I came into the system as a senator, I got six letters, threw five in the wastebasket and said to the secretary, 'Tell the other S.O.B. he doesn't know what he's talking about.' That was about the relationship and attitude we all had." Not anymore, not by a long shot.

The question that legislators have to ask is whether those people they hear from are typical of average voters. An Ohio legislator doubts the representativeness of the constituents who speak out. "If you go to 100 meetings in my district . . . ," he commented, "you'll meet the same people 85 times." Over the past several decades public opinion polling has proliferated. Major newspapers, magazines, and the networks all conduct national polls periodically. We can find distributions of opinion on virtually any major issue and on many minor ones as well. These national polls, and what they reveal about the public's support or opposition to a measure, affect the struggle in Congress. Yet, the findings of national polls are too general to have much bearing on what is happening in the states. Statewide polls also are conducted on a regular basis by media outlets and universities in about one-third of the states. To some extent at least, lawmakers take them into account.

National and state polls most often work, not to change where lawmakers stand on an issue, but rather to buttress the already formulated position of one side or the other in the debate under way. In the legislative process, it is useful to be able to show a popular majority, or better still a large popular majority, in agreement with a particular proposal. Thus, the products of polls are among the grist for the deliberative process in the legislature.

But few legislators view public opinion polls as directive. For example, a 2001 New Jersey poll indicated that 59 percent of the respondents did not favor a sales tax cut if it would mean a reduction in state services. Members of the Republican majority in the legislature, however, had pledged a cut during the course of their campaigns. They were not going to renege because of a public opinion poll, and the chairman of the assembly appropriations committee pointed out how the poll results were inconsistent with the results of the election in which his party had pledged to reduce taxes. Another poll found that 70 percent of New Jerseyans favored an increase in tobacco and alcohol taxes to pay for charity care by the state's hospitals. Legislators were not about to raise taxes of any kind, no matter what a statewide poll indicated.

Probably the chief effect of polls is to restrain legislators, rather than to embolden them. Most would not rush ahead just because a poll showed a majority of people in the state or nation to favor something. They would need to know much more than any poll would be likely to tell them. But lawmakers take seriously the finding that a considerable proportion of people oppose something, especially if several surveys report similar results. A negative finding makes them think twice about the risks they may run in pushing a proposal.

The public opinion polls that matter most to legislators are those at the legislative district level. A representative is more interested in his or her own constituents' views than in the views of citizens of the entire state or nation. Rarely, however, is systematic polling done at the state legislative district level, so lawmakers lack reliable information on the distributions of opinion in the place that they represent and where they run. Occasionally, as part of intensive national or state grassroots and media campaigns, an interest group may commission polls in the districts of key or swing legislators. But such polls cannot be accepted at face value because the opinions may not be strongly held or persistent or because the sponsors, in trying to gain support for their own position, may pitch the question in ways that will elicit the answer they prefer.

Contemporary technology will probably enhance the effects of constituents' views. As long ago as 1981, political scientist Robert Dahl predicted that the new telecommunications technology would allow citizens to place questions of their own on the public agenda (and not only in states that authorize lawmaking by initiative and referendum). More recently, Lawrence Grossman offered the prospect of Americans sitting at home or at work, able to use telecomputer terminals, microprocessors, and computer-driven keypads, pushing buttons to tell their elected officials what they want done about important and less important matters. John Geer describes a scenario of constant referenda taking place via telephone, computer, or TV, allowing a member of the legislature to sample thousands of households on a particular bill before voting on it.

If (or when) legislators are confronted by electronic referenda of voters in their own districts, the pressure on them to respond positively to dominant views will increase further. People who participate in this system of "electronic democracy" may not be representative of the entire district. They are apt to be those who are attentive or concerned, those who vote. Accurate reflection of district opinion or not, a legislator will be hard-pressed to go counter to a significant majority of constituents who express themselves. The political cost could be high.

The channels of communication between legislators and constituents have increased in recent years. Legislators are in touch, as are constituents. Messages from the district get through, at times instantaneously. Yet, what the constituency wants on the many issues of public policy is seldom obvious, even to sensitive lawmakers with their ears to the ground.

In Sum

As part of the legislative orientation program of the Florida house in December 2000, several former members were asked to render advice to the sixty-three new members who had just been sworn in. Dale Patchett, who had served from 1976 to 1990, had this to say: "You each came here with your own personal philosophy, underlying beliefs and opinions. . . . Notwithstanding who you are or why you chose to run, you were elected by your peers to be their voice in Tallahassee. Never forget that they elected you to represent their views as well as your own." Richard Longley, who served in the house from 1972 to 1978 and in the senate from 1984 to 1986, put it this way: "When you seek office your platform should identify your beliefs on certain issues. When elected, you should continue to hold, and be guided by, those beliefs. . . . I voted my conscience and beliefs, and eventually a majority of my district disagreed with me. So be it."

There are all sorts of variations on such advice, but they probably all can fit into either the delegate or trustee model of representation. In practice the two models overlap; they are, in fact, compatible with one another and not contradictory. Lawmakers tend to be neither all-delegate nor all-trustee, but rather a mixture—delegates on some vital issues and trustees on most issues. On the one hand, they feel compelled to reflect the views of their constituencies when such views exist, are clear and overwhelming, and do not contradict the lawmakers' basic beliefs. This is what representatives believe they ought to do, and also what makes political sense for them to do. On the other hand, they feel obliged to look elsewhere for cues in the many instances in which the constituencies have no views as such or where they are sharply divided. This is what they believe they have to do, in part because they have no alternative.

On most issues representatives can be said to have leeway, as far as their constituencies are concerned. Not only do constituents have little interest or involvement, but also the effects of the issues on or in the constituencies are nearly impossible to discern. Such issues, however, may be of relevance to special interest groups. For example, a contract lobbyist in Texas categorized the legislation introduced at a typical session: about 100 bills had statewide implications and perhaps an additional 100 affected members' districts. "Another 4,800," he said, "don't appear on my radar screen at all." From a statewide or district perspective, these bills are inconsequential, whereas from the perspective of a group, a state agency, or a local government they may be quite important.

On some issues the constituency does have concerns, and the representative is presented with instructions. Usually, however, representatives receive more than a single set of instructions from more than a single group of constituents. Sometimes the only constituents who care are those who are members of interest groups organized both within and outside the constituency. Members of business organizations may be opposed to members of labor unions; doctors may be at odds with nurse practitioners; schoolteachers may be in conflict with school administrators. Instructions are in conflict and neither set expresses the views of most constituents.

At times, but not often, an issue may touch more people in a district than just the members of one interest group or another. A relatively large number of constituents may have views on questions such as abortion, capital punishment, or even mandatory sentencing. But unless one side is favored by a large (and possibly intense) majority, a representative still will have to choose between two sets of instructions—choice or life, death penalty or not, mandatory or discretionary sentencing. If opinion divides 75–25 percent, a constituency majority would appear to be clear. If the questions were correctly framed. If responses were correctly recorded. If views were strongly held. If they were stable. But what if the distribution was 60–40 percent or 55–45 percent? Is there consensus or dissensus, then? Which set of instructions should lawmakers follow if they want to represent their constituencies?

On a few issues there may appear to be a constituency mandate, and on even fewer a mandate might actually exist. In 2000 the Vermont legislature enacted civil union legislation, establishing the legal equivalent of marriage for gay couples. Vermonters were sharply divided, but in several districts in the northwestern part of the state, fervent majorities opposed legal recognition of any kind. Mandates opposing civil union probably existed in these places. In several districts Democratic legislators voted in favor of civil union and were defeated in their races for reelection, perhaps because of their stand on the issue. Their defeat, however, does not necessarily mean a mandate existed. The antis may have been better organized and more strongly motivated, and other factors may have contributed to the election results as well.

A representative may take to heart instances in which a majority favors one side and a minority the other. A recent and dramatic example occurred in Florida. After the 2000 election the Florida Legislature prepared to appoint its own slate of electors for George W. Bush when it appeared that the contest in the state might not otherwise be resolved before the electoral college deadline. A house committee reported a resolution to that effect, with Rep. Dwight Stansel, one of the Democratic members, voting with the Republicans on an issue that divided legislators sharply along partisan lines. Representative Stansel's northern Florida district, although heavily Democratic in registration, had voted overwhelmingly for Bush over Gore. Alluding to his constituents, Stansel indicated that he could not afford to vote with his party. "If you don't listen to them, you'll be home, and somebody else will be listening to them," he said.

Constituency mandates pertain when a substantial plurality of voters are in agreement and can be mobilized to express their views on an issue in political terms. Potential mandates rather than actual mandates motivate the representative, because it is impossible for a representative prospectively to know for certain if a mandate exists. In retrospect, it is easier to determine, because the best evidence is a representative's rejection at the polls for supposedly ignoring the will of the constituency. Of course, potential mandates differ in different constituencies. In agricultural districts support for farming is probably a mandate issue. Support for affirmative action, bilingual education, higher education, and government workers are examples of mandate issues in certain districts. In recent years, many voters have been in agreement on not raising taxes, and lawmakers have interpreted that as a mandate.

On issues like these, representatives risk their political future if they deviate from what appears to be a local mandate. Representatives seldom buck what appears to be a tide. Most often representatives are naturally aligned with their districts, so rarely do conscience and constituency clash. They and their constituents, at least most of them, are on the same side.

For legislators the bottom line is constituency. The first question they ask, explicitly or implicitly, before taking action is: "Will it hurt my constituency?" or "Will it hurt me in my constituency?" Whatever the issue, if district opinion is clear and vocal, the legislator will ordinarily follow suit. But since constituency mandates are few and far between, legislators ordinarily must rely on their own judgment. As we described in Chapter 4 they must weigh several factors, including the merits of an issue; their own beliefs; the arguments of various groups; and recommendations from legislative leaders, committees, colleagues, and the governor.

In a representative democracy legislators ought to act in the interests of their constituents and, insofar as possible, in accord with their wishes. This they certainly do. There may be a problem in the system of representation, but it is not that legislators are unresponsive to their constituents and constituencies. They not only manage to take care of their constituencies, but they also manage to work on behalf of their own convictions, their party's programs, and what they believe to be the interests of the state or nation.

Sources and Suggested Reading

This chapter draws heavily on Alan Rosenthal, *The Decline of Representative Democracy* (Washington, D.C.: CQ Press, 1998), 6–48. Data on the geographical size of districts are for the 1980s and are from Anthony Gierzynski, "Elections to the State Legislatures," in *Encyclopedia of the American Legislative System*, ed. Joel

H. Silbey (New York: Scribner's, 1994), 435–449. Data on communications between constituents and members of Congress are from Bruce Cain, John Ferejohn, and Morris Fiorina, *The Personal Vote: Constituency Service and Electoral Independence* (Cambridge: Harvard University Press, 1987). This book and *Home Style: House Members in Their Districts,* by Richard F. Fenno Jr. (Boston: Little, Brown, 1978), offer a close and careful look at representatives and constituencies. Another important work on representation is John C. Wahlke, Heinz Eulau, William Buchanan, and LeRoy C. Ferguson, *The Legislative System: Explorations in Role Behavior* (New York: Wiley, 1962). A brief but important treatment of the subject is by Linda L. Fowler, "Constituencies," in *Encyclopedia of the American Legislative System,* ed. Joel H. Silbey (New York: Scribner's, 1994), 399–418. For a thorough theoretical treatment, see Hanna F. Pitkin, *The Concept of Representation* (Berkeley and Los Angeles: University of California Press, 1967). On polling and electronic democracy, see John G. Geer, *From Tea Leaves to Opinion Polls* (New York: Columbia University Press, 1996), and Lawrence K. Grossman, *The Electronic Republic* (New York: Viking, 1995). The advice from former Florida legislators to new members is offered in a publication prepared by the James Madison Institute, *Points of Personal Privilege,* published in Tallahassee, November 2000.

6

How Special Are the Special Interests?

NARROW INTERESTS HAVE been suspect in American politics from the time of the founding. In *The Federalist Papers* James Madison expressed grave concerns about "factions"—his term for special interests. Madison wrote: "By a faction, I understand a number of citizens, whether amounting to a majority or a minority of the whole, who are united and activated by some common impulse or passion, or of interest, *adverse to the rights of other citizens, or to the permanent and aggregate interests of the community.*"

With no illusions, Madison saw factions as natural elements of society, "sown in the nature of man." That they were natural and omnipresent did not make them less dangerous. But, Madison argued, factions could not be eliminated without having an oppressive government. Nor was he willing to assume that "enlightened statesmen" would always be at the helm of the government. So, if factions could not be eliminated, they should be controlled. How? Madison assumed that numerical minorities (such as farmers, merchants, city dwellers) would be held in check by regular elections. His greatest concerns lay with majority factions, which might well deny minority interests their basic rights.

Still, let's be clear. Madison understood factions to be natural outgrowths of human tendencies. He viewed them as potentially dangerous and argued that their effects should be limited. In many ways, Madison's thoughts were not so far from contemporary public opinion with its great skepticism toward interest groups. But there's a crucial difference. From Madison's point of view, much of the vibrancy of a diverse country came from the expression of these distinct interests. The very fact that many different interests would be spread across a vast republic meant that it would be difficult for a single faction to dominate. Ever the realist, Madison concluded that to create a strong, vibrant new nation, the government should not seek to extinguish the many factions, but to control their effects.

Conditions for Representative Democracy: Interest Groups

Building on the arguments of the framers, we offer seven conditions for representative democracy and interest groups to work effectively together:

1. There should be no overarching "majority" faction that can dominate political life.
2. All major interests must be effectively represented. This does not imply equal representation, but the voices of bankers, bakers, and candlestick makers should be capable of being heard in legislative chambers.
3. A substantial number of groups should have large memberships to promote linkage between citizens and government.
4. Group members should belong to, or at least identify with, more than one group. Such crosscutting loyalties promote negotiation and compromise.
5. Groups' resources should be widely dispersed and varied.
6. There must be real competition among organized interests and no systematic losers.

7. As groups and legislators work together, there must be as much transparency as possible. That is, citizens need to have some sense of who is attempting to wield influence, which legislators are benefiting from lobbyists' largesse, and which interests are contributing how much to whose campaigns.

We will examine each of these conditions in detail. In the course of this analysis we will also consider the arguments of the critics of interest group politics in America. In the twenty-first century, the most common charge against legislatures is that they bow too much to moneyed interests like oil companies, large corporations, or agricultural groups. Reacting to the pluralist theorists of the 1950s, political scientist E. E. Schattschneider responded with his famous line that "the heavenly choir [of pluralism] sings with a distinctly upper-class bias." Many journalists, such as Elizabeth Drew, and some so-called public interest groups, such as Common Cause, have argued that permissive campaign finance laws have led to undue influence for corporations and other affluent interests.

More generally, the critics say that groups with concentrated interests—like the airlines in the wake of the September 2001 terrorist attacks—wield more power with legislators than do interests whose constituent base is broader and difficult to organize, such as airline passengers.

In addition, many critics argue that with so many groups organized on so many policy issues the legislature cannot act effectively on many pressing problems. And many organized interests are perfectly happy with the status quo, even if more general societal interests are often ignored.

As we saw in Chapter 1, these critics have had an effect on public opinion: an overwhelming number of Americans, young people especially, believe that a few big interests control the government. Our task in this chapter is to examine these charges and determine if the relationship between interest groups and legislatures is beneficial or detrimental to representative democracy.

Given the number and range of organized interests, and their extensive dealings with the Congress and the fifty state legislatures, we, like Madison, see the many bonds between groups and legislators as a positive element of representative democracy. Indeed, it would be difficult to imagine American representative democracy without a large and vigorous set of organized interests.

To go even further, we make the unambiguous argument that interest groups, as they have developed in American politics, are not just helpful to the functioning of representative democracy, but *essential*. Both legislators and organized interests represent substantial numbers of constituents. Likewise, they want the legislative process to produce certain kinds of results. And they both know that the people they represent are keeping an eye on them. Just as voters can remove legislators from office for poor performance, restive members can overthrow group leaders.

Those who label interest groups "special interests" or "pressure groups" usually intend to imply that they constitute a dangerous force within American politics because they want to use the legislative process for their selfish ends. If a few interests systematically dominate policymaking, such an interpretation would be justified. But this has not ordinarily been so. Ironically, under the right conditions, the very selfishness of groups can work to benefit society as a whole, because large numbers of groups will pursue their interests in a host of ways at both the state and national levels. The result will be that a rough approximation of a general interest will be served.

Why should the politicking of a large number of interest groups work in tandem with legislators to strengthen representative democracy? Let's first examine the conditions that allow this pairing to work productively and then turn to see how interests and legislators are linked together.

Examining the Conditions

The first condition that promotes an effective interrelationship of interest groups and representative government is Madison's vision of a plural society in which there is *no dominant majority*. Over time, despite tests like the Civil War and excesses like the internment camps for Japanese-Americans during World War II, this condition has been met. Farmers, merchants, laborers, veterans, environmentalists, gun enthusiasts, and hundreds of other groupings of citizens organized themselves into interest groups in the nineteenth and twentieth centuries. As national and state governments have grown in size and complexity, citizens have come to rely on groups to represent their interests. So too have corporations, trade associations, and other economic interests. The result has been a government system in which, with rare exceptions, no single group has been able to prevail for prolonged periods of time.

The second condition of the relationship between interest groups and legislatures is that *all major interests are represented.* Beyond the representation of important economic interests, this means that a reasonably effective organization exists to advocate for a group of like-minded individuals. In every state legislature, there is a wide range of lobbyists representing everyone from dental hygienists to canoeists to school voucher advocates. And in Washington the number of organized interests can only be guessed at—but one recent estimate put the total at 17,000 or so. The universe of groups not only represents a large number of interests but also changes continually. Thus, in the late 1980s few high-tech firms felt the need for serious representation in Washington. By the mid-1990s, when Congress was engaged in a complete overhaul of telecommunications policy, dozens of different high-tech interests came to Capitol Hill to plead their cases. Thus, in the 1980s these interests harbored "potential" groups. Subsequently, various groups of corporations or individuals recognized some common interest, and they mobilized to create a range of organizations to represent those interests.

Some groups are easier to represent than others. A handful of oil companies can form an effective organization; tens of millions of drivers, who habitually fill up their vehicles with gasoline, have a much more difficult time forging an organization, because their status as drivers doesn't define their lives. In general, consumers, whether of television, cars, or tobacco, have a more difficult time organizing than do producers, whose interests are strong and whose numbers are small. Still, organized groups do represent most important societal interests, and their major targets are usually Congress and the fifty state legislatures.

Third, a substantial number of groups should have *large memberships.* Such organizations are scarcely guaranteed great influence, but they do offer an important connection between citizens and the government. Although lots of organizations represent narrow interests, such as National Football League players or bow-and-arrow hunters, many groups in

American politics enjoy large, even very large, memberships. Most notable, perhaps, is the AARP (formerly the American Association of Retired Persons), which claims 34 million members; 16 million Americans belong to labor unions, a decline since the 1970s but still a substantial number. The Chamber of Commerce and the Sierra Club have hundreds of thousands of members, and the National Rifle Association (NRA) has more than 4 million. From the National Trust for Historic Preservation to the Christian Coalition, large numbers of like-minded individuals come together to take part in the political process.

Fourth, organized interests serve representative democracy if most *group members belong to, or at least identify with, more than one group.* Consider a Latina union member who belongs to her son's parent-teacher organization or the union member who strongly supports the NRA. Such overlapping memberships set the stage for a politics of compromise within American legislatures. With such multiple loyalties, individuals can see things from more than one perspective. Nearly eight in ten Americans belong to an organized group with a policy agenda—from Handgun Control to the Christian Coalition to People for the Ethical Treatment of Animals. About 40 percent of adults are members of two or more groups. Even without formally joining an organization, many individuals identify with that group (for example, spouses of union members or African Americans who don't pay dues to the NAACP).

Fifth, *group resources are widely dispersed and varied.* For example, the AARP does not have a political action committee (PAC) to distribute campaign contributions, nor does it advertise heavily to get its message across. Indeed, the AARP is quite restrained, in that it represents a broad cross-section of the public. But its immense numbers mean that it can whisper on Capitol Hill and still be heard. Conversely, Microsoft—a single company—is an interest that has no membership but has enormous financial resources and economic clout. An interest group like the American Civil Liberties Union (ACLU) possesses a relatively small (150,000) but strongly committed and resourceful membership. Overall, many groups benefit from any number of resources.

Sixth, for representative democracy to flourish in the American context there must be *real competition* among organized interests and no systematic losers. Some scholars have contended that business interests have a "privileged" position in American society, especially in light of their considerable financial resources. But other students of interest groups, like Jeffrey M. Berry, argue that since the 1960s citizens' groups have succeeded in reducing the advantages of the business community. Certainly in some states one or two interests historically dominated state politics. Copper-mining firms got their way in Montana, as did DuPont in Delaware, and the oil industry in Louisiana. But even in these states, countervailing interests have arisen to challenge the strongest corporate groups.

Finally, as groups and legislators work together, there needs to be as much *transparency* as possible. As we discuss in detail in the discussion of legislative ethics in Chapter 4 and the media's role in ensuring accountability in Chapter 8, the legislative process in America today is extraordinarily open. Citizens cannot know everything, but they—through the legislative press corps—have the information needed to understand what is happening in the capitol. Unhappy citizens can lobby key legislators or support those organizations that do. Or they can start an interest group, as victims of breast cancer have done in many states.

Although not all of these seven conditions are met all of the time in American politics, they provide an introductory outline of how groups function within and contribute to the legislative process, and they allow us to elaborate on how things actually work in this interrelationship.

Groups and Legislators: A Series of Exchanges

Since the first years of the republic, interests have sought to influence Congress; in turn, members of Congress have both relied upon and attempted to shape the attitudes of organized interests. Especially in the complex society of the twenty-first century United States, one cannot imagine Congress and state legislatures functioning without interest groups. How, then, can we analyze the varied relationships between groups and the legislature? At a general level, both groups and Congress are in the business of representing people and interests. But how? We suggest three overlapping lines of analysis: (1) the politics of *access,* the often-articulated goal of many interests;

(2) the role of *information* in affecting policy outcomes; and (3) the importance of *elections* in establishing the legislative context for decision making.

Before proceeding to lay out the elements of access, information, and elections, we should make two points. First, relationships between organized interests and lawmakers are reciprocal; that is, as much as interests seek to influence legislators, lawmakers also make demands of interests and seek to shape the thinking of their leaders and members. For example, as chair of the House Transportation Committee, former representative Bud Schuster, R-Pa., continually shaped the expectations and strategies of groups within the highway lobby. Second, many of the relationships between interests and legislators relate to money. Often the issues at stake for the interest groups involve substantial amounts of money. As we saw in Chapter 4, campaign contributions are involved and should be discussed, even if political scientists have found few solid links between such contributions and legislative action.

Access

In his thoughtful analysis of how members of Congress grant access and how organized interests gain it, political scientist John Mark Hansen focuses on the reduction of uncertainty by both legislators and groups. Interest groups and lawmakers work together so that each partner in the arrangement reduces the tremendous uncertainties of the legislative process. For legislators, uncertainty arises over winning reelection and rising to higher office. For interests, it relates to the effect of future policies and programs, especially those seen as potentially injurious.

In sum, access is a two-way street, with each side hoping to obtain higher levels of certainty at the lowest level of cost. Thus, in real-world settings, a long-time legislative supporter of the National Rifle Association may find it impossible to swallow that organization's opposition to waiting periods on gun purchases. But voting against such a provision might produce too much potential electoral backlash. Hansen sees access as evolving from the mutual assistance relationship that allows groups to gain influence in exchange for technical information. In establishing these ties, lawmakers choose among alternative groups that offer advice and information. But

groups have discretion as well, as they see⌐
make their case within the legislature.

The notion of access is also important in
groups' ties to Congress and state legislatures. T⌐
terest group leaders contend that campaign contri⌐
not buy influence but may help them obtain acces⌐
lawmakers. Although campaign reform advocates ma⌐
distinction without a difference, current laws prohibit⌐
commonplace in the first 150 years of the republic, when⌐
were paid by interests to produce desired legislation. Camp⌐
tions today usually follow access, rather than lead to it, as we⌐
ously argued. In the end, both legislators and groups value acces⌐
as falling short of guaranteeing influence. But for many lobbyists⌐
central to their ability to provide the information that they see as cru⌐
making their case.

Information

The exchange of information between organized interests and legislators
composes the core of their connections. In particular, scarce and reliable information is highly valuable, especially in the uncertain environment in
which much legislating takes place. Although policy-based information is
important, other intelligence can be equally, if not more, important. Inter-
actions between interest groups and Congress foster needs for three kinds
of information: policy, political (reelection), and procedural (internal to
the legislative process). Lobbyists and legislators continually attempt to reduce uncertainties by soliciting and exchanging various kinds of information, often within the context of extended, trusting relationships. This
makes sense, because both major interests have long-term goals to benefit
the various constituencies that rely on the same industry. For example, both
the automobile industry and a key legislative figure like veteran representative John Dingell, D-Mich., share concern for a healthy auto-manufactur-
ing sector.

The distribution of power in legislatures determines where groups will
seek to build strong bonds. Circa 1900, for example, the major congres-

figures were the top party leaders, who could control the process. In mid-1970s, in contrast, as both committee and party leaders struggled provide policymaking direction, organized interests needed to establish to dozens and dozens, if not hundreds, of members of Congress, many whom operated as independent entrepreneurs in a highly decentralized body. This fragmentation has been reduced since the mid-1980s, but lobbyists still find it important to court the rank-and-file of a closely divided Congress. In many state legislatures party leaders are key to the process, but in others committee chairs or influential individual lawmakers may require groups' attention. If nothing else, lobbyists must be flexible as they address the needs of all kinds of legislators.

One of the shibboleths of lobbying is that lobbyists should never be caught misrepresenting their clients, nor can they lie to legislators. According to the conventional wisdom, being caught in a lie means that the bonds of trust will be irreparably frayed. Yet, the stock-in-trade for most lobbyists is to present information that favors their position. Both lobbyists and lawmakers will color the truth through their reliance on policy narratives in the course of developing legislative alternatives. Regardless of the legislative body, lobbyists and lawmakers forge careers of crafting explanations for policies past, present, and future. One way to look at lobbying is to think of it as offering up various policy explanations to legislators, who can then select and adapt the ones they want to convey back to their constituents.

In the past, the exchange of policy information has been a relatively private undertaking, with lobbyists making their arguments in personal conversations. All contemporary surveys of interest group activity note the continuing importance of such communications. At the same time, framing explanations in public—through expensive scientific studies or large-scale public relations/advertising campaigns—has become more commonplace. So-called message politics has grown in importance, as lawmakers have come to understand that major policy decisions are often largely determined by how they are framed on the government agenda.

Elections and Majorities

For individual legislators, interest groups are almost always important elements of winning reelection, as they provide both pools of voters and cam-

paign contributions. But the broader electoral relationships between interests and legislators vary according to chamber, partisan margin, the balance of power between parties and committees, the safety of incumbents, and the costs of campaigning. Thus, in the 1920s, an era of few effective campaign regulations and a dominant Republican Party in Congress, well-heeled interests could "invest" in a national party and its incumbents, confident in the knowledge that these partisans would control the legislative process for at least the next two years. In the 1980s the Democrats' chief congressional campaign fund-raiser, Rep. Tony Coelho, D-Calif., made it clear to business interests that they would have to deal with a Democratic Congress for some time to come, and corporate contributions shifted sharply away from Republicans over the next few years. Likewise, in the states, organized interests must often confront an established majority party with which they disagree on many issues. For example, in Utah or Kansas, the state branches of the Democratic-leaning National Education Association must deal with Republican legislators who dominate both legislative chambers. By the same token, business interests in Hawaii or Massachusetts must forge relationships with the predominant Democratic majority.

Where there is a rough partisan balance, as in more than half the states and in the post-1995 Congress, organized interests operate within an environment that is both tempting and dangerous. They can make strategic decisions to back one party or the other, in the hope that their favored partisans will win control of the legislature. But if their party loses, they face the possibility of being shut out of the policy process—at least in terms of the majority party leadership. Given partisan parity, interest group "investments"—even very large ones—may have modest payoffs, in that narrow margins ordinarily increase the level of uncertainty over legislative outcomes.

In the end, organized interests contribute to the legislative process by competing among themselves, by subsidizing legislators through their provision of information, and by serving as checks on the claims of opposing groups. The linkages between groups and legislators are not always benign, but if they are reasonably well regulated and made as transparent as possible through various reporting requirements, they are beneficial to representative democracy, even when group motivations are narrow and self-serving. Indeed, converting self-interested motivations into actions that benefit the public at large is one of the unsung virtues of representative democracy.

Lobbying the Legislature

One secret of American lawmaking is that legislators and legislatures need lobbyists. Even in the U.S. Congress and a few highly professionalized state legislatures, where legislators enjoy great staff resources, interest group representatives provide a continuous flow of useful, even critical, information. In less professional bodies, the process of lawmaking could easily grind to a halt without the information provided by lobbyists. If legislators want to know something about agriculture, they can call the Farm Bureau and a dozen other, smaller groups such as beekeepers or organic farmers or farm implement dealers. If they want to know what raising the minimum wage will mean, they can talk to the National Federation of Independent Business, the Chamber of Commerce, and the American Federation of Labor–Congress of Industrial Organizations (AFL-CIO), as well as representatives from various think tanks. Lawmakers will get a range of responses, but they'll almost always come out better informed. Moreover, legislators know that by seeking information from several sources, especially when they are genuinely undecided, they will increase their chances of taking an appropriate position on a given issue. In addition, over time lawmakers come to know whose information they consider most useful and reliable.

What legislators want most—and what lobbyists can provide—is solid information, delivered in a timely, efficient manner. For lobbyists, this requires access, which allows them to deliver a message at the right time. One lobbyist, a former state senator, noted that if he wanted to talk to a key lawmaker, he would get to the capitol by 7 A.M. and catch the legislator before he got too far into the hurly-burly of the day. "I can get my business done in two or three minutes, once I can talk to him. Otherwise, it's hard to find an opportunity to have his undivided attention."

Lobbyists and their interest groups seek to influence legislative outcomes in numerous ways. First, they can try to persuade legislators that their positions should be adopted, both in terms of substance (a worthy program) and politics (a smart vote). Second, lobbyists can try to mobilize their grassroots supporters to pressure their representatives to support a particular policy. Third, they can seek to redefine issues, so that a given program, like prescription drug benefits, becomes something else, like a tax increase. Fourth, they can direct campaign funds to benefit legislators who agree with them. And fifth, they can seek to oust legislators who oppose them. It's worth noting that the first three of these techniques are the most direct and rely on information more than money to further the goals of their respective interest groups.

This is not to say that money is not important, either at the state or national level. Top-flight lobbyists command high salaries and large fees. Equally important in contemporary politics are grassroots campaigns that seek to pressure legislators by mobilizing their constituents. In the past, such grassroots techniques were used predominantly by large membership groups like labor unions or environmentalists that could prompt their loyalists to call or write their legislators. In recent years, however, some lobbying firms, such as Jack Bonner's in Washington, D.C., have created a specialty in pumping up grassroots support for legislative action. Often labeled "astroturf lobbying," such efforts can be expensive, and legislators often sniff out these campaign tactics. Indeed, one perennial problem for lawmakers is to separate useful information from noise. Again, if lobbyists and their groups can gain the confidence of legislators, they have a much better chance of getting them to listen—and this exchange usually works to benefit both lobbyists and lawmakers.

In fact, what lobbyists value most is the opportunity to make their case to key lawmakers and at an opportune moment. To take advantage of such access, lobbyists must establish trusting relationships with legislators. These relationships can come about in any number of ways. They have traditionally been fostered in social settings, ranging from a hunting trip to a golf outing or a convivial dinner. Given increased scrutiny over such activities and serious limitations in both Washington and most states, interest groups have looked for alternative ways to make these connections, such as hiring former legislators, who can build on their previous relationships to make their case. In the end, most important interests do get the chance to make their case, although the delivery of a message does not ensure that it will sway those in power.

The public generally envisions lobbyists as acting on behalf of the most powerful societal interests. There's no denying that major economic interests are often well represented, but this is a superficial observation in at least two ways. First, even among powerful interests there are great differences of opinion over preferred policies. For example, textile manufacturers have consistently fought for restrictions on importation of cheap foreign goods that result from the low wages paid in Asia or Latin America. In contrast, Nike lobbies for reduced trade restrictions, as it both manufactures its shoes abroad and sells many of its products around the globe. Labor unions often desire protection for their members' jobs while their members, as consumers, buy a wide range of imported products from retailers like Wal-Mart that lobby for policies to reduce tariffs and trade barriers.

Second, many of the most powerful interest groups represent large numbers of citizens who do not share a single set of beliefs. For example, the conservative-leaning National Federation of Independent Business represents hundreds of thousands of small firms that have both many similarities and many differences. The U.S. Chamber of Commerce finds it even more difficult to represent its broad mix of large business interests. In addition, many organizations with large numbers of highly committed members represent noneconomic interests, such as the Sierra Club or the Christian Coalition.

To illustrate the range of interests that are viewed as especially powerful, Table 6-1 lists the twenty-five most powerful groups within the states and in Washington, D.C. Such rankings should be taken with a grain of salt, but they indicate both the breadth and dispersion of influence.

At the national level, many of the usual suspects appear, including the AARP, the NRA and the U.S. Chamber of Commerce. Still, there is no evidence for an established "power elite" of top interests that dominate American politics. For example, the Chamber of Commerce and the Trial Lawyers have long been bitter enemies over the incidence and impact of high-cost liability litigation. Some groups, like the American Israel Public Affairs Committee (AIPAC) or the National Right to Life Committee, attempt to exercise a great deal of influence but only over a limited slice of

Table 6-1 The Twenty-five Most Influential Interests

Rank	Influential interests in the states	Influential interests in Washington, D.C.
1	Schoolteachers' organizations (NEA)	AARP
2	General business organizations (chambers of commerce, etc.)	National Rifle Association of America
3	Utility companies and associations (electric, gas, water, etc.)	National Federation of Independent Business
4	Lawyers (state bar associations and trial lawyers)	American Israel Public Affairs Committee
5	Traditional labor groups (AFL-CIO)	AFL-CIO
6	Physicians and state medical associations	Association of Trial Lawyers of America
7	Insurance companies: general and medical	Chamber of Commerce
8	Manufacturers (companies and associations)	National Right to Life Committee
9	Health care organizations (hospital associations)	National Education Association
10	Bankers' associations	National Restaurant Association
11	Local government organizations (municipal and county leagues)	National Bankers' Association
12	State and local government employees (other than teachers)	National Governors' Association
13	Farm organizations (state farm bureaus)	American Medical Association
14	Individual banks and financial institutions	National Association of Manufacturers
15	Environmentalists	National Association of Realtors
16	Universities and colleges	National Association of Home Builders
17	Realtors' associations	Motion Picture Association of America
18	Individual cities and towns	Credit Union National Association
19	Gaming interests (casinos, racetracks, and lotteries)	National Beer Wholesalers Association
20	Contractors, builders, and developers	National Association of Broadcasters
21	Liquor, wine, and beer interests and K–12 education interests (other than teachers) [a]	American Farm Bureau Federation
22	Retailers (companies and trade associations)	American Federation of State, County, and Municipal Employees
23	Senior citizens	International Brotherhood of Teamsters
24	Mining companies and associations	United Auto Workers Union
25	Truckers and private transport interests (excluding railroads)	Health Insurance Association of America

Sources: Fortune, December 1999; Ronald Hrebenar, Interest Group Politics (Armonk, N.Y.: M. E. Sharpe, 1997).

[a] Tied.

policy. Although environmental groups are notably absent from the national top twenty-five (the Sierra Club ranked forty-third), they are scarcely without power. More important, perhaps, the overall balance of interests is remarkable, with the elderly, gun enthusiasts, small business owners, supporters of Israel, and big labor constituting the top five groups. Furthermore, the variety of interests continues as one moves down the list to the governors' association, credit unions, and beer wholesalers.

Turning to the states, a similar range of interests appears. It's no surprise that education associations lead the list, given their large memberships and wide geographic base. A host of business interests are well established, as we might assume, but many of the most influential groups are frequently at odds with each other (for example, trial lawyers and physicians, labor and the chamber of commerce).

In addition, the most influential groups in Washington often do not have similar clout in the states, and vice versa. The AARP is far more respected or feared on Capitol Hill than in most state legislatures; likewise AIPAC has little influence in the states because of its focus on foreign policy and military affairs. The National Education Association, although a real force in Washington, does not come close to exercising the clout there that it does in the states, where education funding usually consumes about one-third of every state's budget and attracts the unwavering attention of the teachers' organizations. More generally, the large membership groups such as the AARP and the NRA appear less influential in the states than in Washington. Again, the framers of the Constitution got it right: a republic, with its dispersion of authority, has been protected against the concentration of power among a few interests.

Driving this point home all the more firmly is the growth in the number of interests, both in Washington and in the states. One recent study plots the growth of organized interests in the nation's capital and finds a rise from about 2,000 groups in 1970 to almost 16,000 thirty years later. Moreover, as Jeffrey Berry has demonstrated, citizens' groups (such as Common Cause, campaign finance reformers, and environmentalists) have expanded even more rapidly than interest groups as a whole. Indeed, the number of Washington-based citizens' groups has risen from fewer than 100 in the 1970s to more than 2,400 in the late 1990s.

Although the framers could not have imagined how professional lobbying would become, they understood that interests would—and should—seek to influence lawmakers. Taken together, the rights of petition and free speech represent an invitation for groups to make their case before the legislature. Ultimately, this protects us all. In other words, the so-called "special interests" are not the enemy, they are us.

In Sum

Although most Americans don't hold lobbyists in high regard, they simultaneously want their own interests to be represented on Capitol Hill and in the fifty state houses. Such desires are guaranteed by the First Amendment rights of free speech, association, and petition that give groups and lobbyists a constitutionally protected position. In addition, legislators need the kinds of information that lobbyists typically provide: timely, useful, and politically relevant. And in electoral politics, lobbyists and their groups provide a lot of the campaign funding that many lawmakers need under our current campaign finance system.

In all legislatures, there are many more registered lobbyists than there are legislators. In Kansas, for example, 500 or so lobbyists who represent approximately 700 separate groups lobby 165 lawmakers. On Capitol Hill, the 535 legislators face a legion of lobbyists, of whom the 5,000 who are registered constitute the tip of the interest group iceberg. This makes sense, in that so many interests have a major stake in what government does at both the state and national levels. Since the legislative branch is far more accessible than either the executive or the judicial branch, it makes good sense for organized interests to devote much of their attention to making sure their messages get across to senators and representatives. Indeed, for all the attention paid to campaign contributions or lobbying expenses, the core relationship between lobbyists and legislators depends on a mutually beneficial exchange of information.

In the end, legislatures work better because of lobbying, especially when all major interests can participate in policy discussions. The process is scarcely perfect, and moneyed interests sometimes have real advantages, both in contributing to campaigns and in generating and distributing favorable information. Still, a lot of effective lobbying is done by organized interests that possess relatively few resources but good arguments, especially when such groups represent a large number of members. When confronted with reasonable arguments, legislators will usually find time to listen. That is one of their jobs within a representative democracy. In turn, the legislature as a whole will become better informed than it would be otherwise. All in all, a pretty reasonable bargain.

Sources and Suggested Reading

James Madison's *Federalist* No. 10 may be the best single starting point in examining the role of interests within representative democracy. For a broad interest group interpretation of American politics, David Truman's *The Governmental Process* (New York: Knopf, 1971) remains a classic statement. Several of Jeffrey M. Berry's books make important contributions; these include *The Interest Group Society*, 3d ed. (New York: Longman, 1997) and *The New Liberalism* (Washington, D.C.: Brookings Institution Press, 1999). And E. E. Schattschneider's *The Semi-Sovereign People* (Hinsdale, Ill.: Dryden, 1975) remains a useful critique of pluralism.

John Mark Hansen's *Gaining Access* (Chicago: University of Chicago Press, 1991) offers excellent historical and theoretical insights into the group-legislator relationship. And William Browne's *Cultivating Congress* (Lawrence: University Press of Kansas, 1995) nicely complements Hansen's work. *Interest Group Politics*, 6th ed. (Washington, D.C.: CQ Press, 2002), a collection of readings edited by Allan Cigler and Burdett Loomis, offers a variety of views on contemporary groups, as does Mark Petracca's edited volume, *The Politics of Interests* (Boulder: Westview Press, 1992). For a broad overview of the group literature, see Frank R. Baumgartner and Beth L. Leech, *Basic Interests* (Princeton: Princeton University Press, 1998).

At the state level, Alan Rosenthal's *The Third House* (Washington, D.C.: CQ Press, 2001) offers a comprehensive view of lobbying in the fifty states. Clive Thomas and Ronald Hrebenar's four edited books on interest groups in each of the fifty states provide substantial detail on a state-by-state basis; these include *Interest Groups in the American West* (Salt Lake City: University of Utah Press, 1987), *Interest Groups in the Midwestern States* (Ames: Iowa State University Press, 1993), *Interest Groups in the Northeastern States* (University Park: Pennsylvania State University Press, 1993), and *Interest Groups in the Southern States* (Tuscaloosa: University of Alabama Press, 1992).

On the relative importance of business, see David Vogel, *Fluctuating Fortunes* (New York: Basic Books, 1989), and Darrell West and Burdett Loomis, *The Sound of Money* (New York: Norton, 1998). Elizabeth Drew presents a highly negative view of the role of money in politics in *The Corruption of American Politics* (New York: Times Books, 1996); Bradley Smith makes an opposite case in *Unfree Speech: The Folly of Campaign Finance Reform* (Princeton: Princeton University Press, 2001).

7

Why Is the Political Process Contentious?

THE FRAMERS OF THE Constitution believed that in representative democracy conflict is necessary to avoid the concentration of power in any one place in the government. Modern research shows that conflict strengthens representative democracy by producing better decisions. Recognizing these points, the internal rules of all American legislatures take pains to protect conflict and thereby protect the rights of the people. In the face of this conflict, compromise is the mechanism necessary to reach mutually acceptable solutions.

The challenge here, somewhat different from that of previous chapters of this book, is not to show that these conditions of representative democracy exist, for undoubtedly they do. Americans see and hear political conflict every day. The problem is that the public is turned off by the conflicts they observe, so our task in this chapter is to understand better the necessity and desirability of conflict in a representative democracy.

Who can blame the American people for not liking political conflict? Conflict prolongs the political process, is usually unpleasant to watch, and makes it seem as though nothing is being accomplished. Yet, whatever people might think of political conflict, it is an utterly unavoidable component of democratic government. In any free society, intense political differences will exist, and, as we described in Chapter 3, the United States is no exception. In light of these differences among ordinary people, the one way for political decision makers to avoid contention is to empower a dictator or some other nondemocratic decision-making entity to formulate policy without regard for the varying views to which different citizens adhere. Even as much as Americans dislike political conflict, few would go so far as to give up on democracy in order to remove contention. The reality is that, if the American government is to be a representative democracy, conflict among decision makers must exist. Since the people have differences and decision makers represent the people, then decision makers will also have differences. It is their job as representatives. If they were in complete accord with all other representatives, then some constituents would not be receiving representation.

But is the public really that put off by political conflict? After all, Americans seem to love other types of conflict, notably that undertaken by athletic teams. In the next section, we turn our attention to the specifics of Americans' attitude toward political conflict. It will soon be apparent that, their enthusiasm for athletic conflict notwithstanding, people have a deep-seated aversion to political conflict—primarily because they believe such conflict is a sign that ordinary people are being taken advantage of by special interests and selfish decision makers.

How the People View Conflict in the Political Process

What is the evidence that people believe conflict is not useful and is even counterproductive? For starters, when survey respondents report their perceptions, preferences, and attitudes, unfavorable views toward conflict are readily apparent. In Table 7-1 we present the public's answers to several questions dealing with political disagreement and conflict. These results show that a substantial portion of the adult population harbors serious reservations regarding various aspects of political conflict. This survey was conducted in 1998 as part of a study by John R. Hibbing and Elizabeth Theiss-Morse and included a national random sample of 1,266 respondents.

Some people simply feel uncomfortable in the presence of political conflict—and probably other forms of conflict, too. The first row of results in

Table 7-1 Public Attitudes toward Conflict and Democratic Procedures (in percent)

Question	Strongly agree	Agree	Disagree	Strongly disagree	Total
Political arguments cause personal unease and discomfort	2.7%	31.6%	57.9%	7.8%	100.0%
Elected officials should stop talking and just take action	22.8	62.0	14.5	0.7	100.0
Officials should debate more so as not to rush into action	5.2	49.3	41.9	3.5	99.9
Compromise is just selling out on principles	7.5	49.0	40.9	2.6	100.0
It is best to seek the advice of people who share our opinions and values	2.1	43.8	50.8	3.3	100.0

Source: 1998 Gallup Survey on Political Processes, conducted for John R. Hibbing and Elizabeth Theiss-Morse with support from the National Science Foundation (SRB-97-09934) and reported in their *Stealth Democracy: Americans' Beliefs about How Government Should Work* (Cambridge: Cambridge University Press, 2002).

the table reports the extent to which respondents agreed or disagreed that they felt "uneasy and uncomfortable when people argue about political issues." Most people disagreed with this statement, thereby indicating that they are reasonably comfortable when they witness political conflict. It is nonetheless noteworthy that better than one-third of all respondents either agreed or strongly agreed that political disagreements made them uncomfortable.

Although political conflict makes more than one out of three Americans distinctly uncomfortable, far more view conflict as simply not useful and probably unnecessary. Large numbers of respondents voiced reservations about the usefulness of standard components of political conflict such as debate and compromise. Nearly 85 percent agreed that "elected officials would help the country more if they would stop talking and just take action on important issues." The people apparently believe things would be better if elected officials would just take action—any action—rather than spend time discussing which particular action might be the wisest. Even when the people are reminded of the potential problems of acting without discussing, a sizeable number still sees little value in debate, as is apparent in the third row of the table. It reports results generated by the following state-ment: "Government officials should debate more because they are too likely to rush into action without discussing all sides." The item includes reference to a clear danger of skipping debate (rushing to judgment), but antipathy toward political discussion is so strong that 45.4 percent of all respondents still disagreed with the statement.

Compromise is another crucial aspect of coming to a solution in the face of diverse opinions; yet, as with debate, the public seems to have little use for compromise. When people were asked whether or not they agree that "compromise in politics is really just selling out on one's principles," 56.5 percent either agreed or strongly agreed. If compromise is seen in such a pejorative light, the question becomes how decision makers can be expected to resolve the deep political differences present in American soci-ety. In this sense, the public's harsh view of compromise is surprising, but the final row in Table 7-1 may shed some light on why the people feel as they do about compromise. Respondents were asked whether or not they agreed that "when you get right down to it, it's best to seek the advice of people who share your own opinions and values." Somewhat disconcert-ingly, 45.9 percent of all respondents agreed that this statement was true, thus suggesting that even when the issue is not exclusively political, people are unconvinced of the need to solicit and then consider dissenting points of view.

Given the public's hostility toward contentious procedures like debate and working toward compromise, it should not be surprising that they also dislike any aspect of the political system that is involved with conflict. Wherever they see debates, wherever they see compromises undertaken or deals being made, and wherever they see competing interests arguing, they see a problem. With an occasional exception, such as the events following the disputed 2000 presidential election, the courts hide conflict expertly. As a result they traditionally receive much higher approval ratings by the peo-ple. But the role of legislatures is quite different from that of the courts. Leg-islatures serve as forums for members to speak on behalf of the widely varying views of constituents, so they don't hide conflict; they put a spot-light on it. Consequently, legislatures are consistently the least liked formal government structure.

Similar to legislators, political parties and interest groups speak for subsets of the American people and, since various subsets are bound to think differently, engage in conflict with other parties and groups. Parties speak for their identifiers; and interest groups speak for their members. Although representing these diverse interests would seem to be the duty of legislators, parties, and interest groups, many ordinary people deeply resent them for doing it. This is apparent in the remarks made when focus group participants are asked to specify what bothers them most about American government.

> *John:* [I most dislike] all the energy wasted on just the constant fighting between parties. . . . I think government would be much more effective if there wasn't that constant fighting.
>
> *Linda:* [A]nd even in . . . their own parties they sometimes can't come to a good answer and, you know . . . they bicker between, you know, their own party.
>
> *Ben:* I'll tell you just right off the bat the thing that I don't like, or maybe I just don't understand it, is . . . where it seems like you have someone over here and someone over here. And they're always fighting, although they're both supposed to be working for this common good. You know they're always, "well he said this and you said that"; you know, bickering, and it doesn't seem like there's so much concern about where we're going.

So the people are very displeased with political conflict. They wish that legislators would quit bickering among themselves and just take a course of action without bothering to debate options. They view compromise as selling out, confrontational political parties as an affront to the people, and special interests as an abomination because by definition the goal of a special interest is to benefit a group and not the country as a whole. The prevalence of conflict in the political arena indicates to most people that current government procedures are not just a colossal waste of time but are extraordinarily counterproductive.

The Actual Role of Political Conflict in a Healthy Democracy

This highly negative view of conflict and any part of the political system that might foster conflict is quite inaccurate. Conflict is actually a great asset for a democratic polity, and the founders missed few opportunities to inject conflict into American political structures. They saw conflict as a way to ensure that no single locus of power became too influential and as a way to disperse authority widely. If it seemed to them as though highly populous states might be too influential in one chamber of Congress, what did they do? They created a second legislative chamber, the Senate, which gave greater weight to lightly populated states and placed it in conflict with the first chamber, the House. If they worried that the legislative branch as a whole would become too powerful, they designed a vibrant executive branch and counted on the inevitable conflict between the two branches to check legislative power. If they worried that the entire central government would become too dominant, they reserved substantial powers to the state governments in hopes that constant tension between Washington and the states would achieve a proper balance between the center and the periphery. All this is why the Constitution has been referred to as an "invitation to struggle." Americans should be thankful when this struggle occurs because it is a sign that power has not become too concentrated. Political conflict was the primary weapon of the founders in their battle against concentrations of power.

Not only does conflict prevent concentration of power, it may lead to better decisions. Conflict can be a powerful clarifying force in politics and elsewhere. People quite rightly dislike so-called comparative campaign advertisements because they invariably include negative charges being levied against the opposing candidate. Still, the scholarly research is clear in showing that people learn more about the candidates when they watch comparative ads than when they watch ads that focus solely on the person whose campaign paid for the ads. For whatever reason, comparisons seem to heighten our ability to learn. We see issues more clearly when we view them in the context of competing sides. A member of Congress once explained how he took advantage of conflict among interest groups to help him decide how to cast a roll call vote: "If there was going to be a labor bill on the floor, I would write to the AFL-CIO and ask why I should vote labor on the issue. Then I would send their response to the National Association of Manufacturers and ask them to rebut the arguments of the AFL-CIO. It saved work for my staff and it was an effective way of separating the wheat from the chaff in the respective arguments." Whether the choice is between policy options, candidates, or bars of soap, conflict helps to inform decisions.

The legal system in the United States is adversarial because it is thought that justice is more likely to result from conflict. Both sides make their pitch so that an impartial observer—either a judge or a jury—will be better placed to see the strength of each position prior to making the decision. Conflict could be minimized by having the independent observers merely conduct a comprehensive investigation and report the decision, but the belief is that the back and forth of defense and prosecution as each side argues and rebuts, challenges and responds, will delineate the relevant issues and points more usefully.

More specifically, the nature of the American jury system invites conflict. In Brazil, juries hear the evidence and then, without any interaction among the jurors, each individual casts a secret vote. The votes are tabulated and if more votes favor acquittal, that is the jury's verdict; if more favor conviction, the accused is doomed. The process is quick and conflict among jurors is nonexistent. But in the United States we believe that encouraging jurors to discuss the case with other jurors will lead to a better decision. There is even a theory behind this belief. Something called Condorcet's Jury Theorem maintains that through deliberation a jury will become more informed, more thoughtful, and more complete than if the decision had been achieved as in Brazil. The logic of the theorem holds that each juror has "private" information, information that he or she picked up during the trial that may have been missed or forgotten by other jurors. Through the process of deliberation, this information is shared with other jurors. Consequently, as anyone who has been on a jury is likely to know all too well, jury deliberations can be laden with conflict, but the thinking is that all the deliberation and conflict is worth it because the result is likely to be a more enlightened decision. Much the same idea is summed up more colloquially by the old saw that "two heads are better than one."

The logic behind legislatures is similar. Theoretically, it would be possible to assign a single individual to make political decisions without any legislative involvement. In other words, we could leave decisions solely to the president or to a governor. Such an arrangement would result in much less political conflict than we have today because the decision maker would merely act, possibly after attempting to divine the feelings of people across the country. But the founders wisely recognized the danger of such an arrangement and the value of having separate representatives assigned to speak for distinct interests and parts of the country. Just as attorneys speak for their clients in confrontational processes, so legislators speak for their constituents in capitols around the country. They inevitably clash with legislators whose constituents have different preferences, but the conflict is good and should make it more likely that the ultimate decision is thoroughly considered and is sensitive to the concerns of all.

The people seem to think that political conflict is a mistake, but as we have seen, it is actually designed into our political system at virtually every stage. Consequently, the authors of the Constitution spoke about political conflict in terms that are quite different from those used by ordinary people. What the founders called a separation of powers, the people now call gridlock. What the founders called deliberation, the people now call bickering. And what the founders called compromise, the people now call "selling out." Somehow, the value of political conflict has been forgotten and people typically conclude that conflict is an evil that must be eradicated at all costs.

Political Conflict as the Essence of a Healthy Legislature

Just as controlled conflict is written into the Constitution, so has conflict been embedded in the rules and organization of all legislatures in the country. In legislatures, members are given rights to speak, to introduce bills, to amend the bills of others, to offer input. These rights apply even if a particular member holds beliefs that are not shared by any other member of the legislature. Without these rights, there would be no assurance that the views of all sides had a chance of being heard—and the American public would be understandably upset by such a limitation. Yet, as we have seen, the American public is also upset by the commotion that naturally results from the existence of these rights. For it is this very right of each of our representatives to speak for the unique views of their constituents that leads to a slow and fractious legislative process. The protection of rights for all legislators and, indirectly, all constituents to be heard is best seen in provisions dealing with the three fundamental organizing aspects of legislatures: bill introduction, committee activity, and floor debate.

Bill Introduction

Although some legislatures place limits on the number of bills each member can introduce, all members have the right to introduce legislation. Where this right is not limited, the number of bills introduced can be astronomical, as we saw in Chapter 4. Members see their ability to introduce legislation as an important, fundamental right, and they use it often. They may use it to introduce a bill that no other legislator supports. They may use it just to make a point. They may use it to please a constituent. But they use it. In doing so, however, legislators make it necessary for the legislative process to take a surfeit of sometimes bizarre bills and reduce it to a manageable number of bills that actually have the breadth of support to become law. The fact that there are so many bills that are important to a single member but don't command the interest or support of a sufficient number of members to become law is testament to the incredible diversity of interests of representatives and their constituencies. Some members and constituents will be pained by the failure of their pet cause to advance, but they should be consoled that when this happens the legislative process is working as it should.

Committee Activity

Both state legislators and members of Congress need to make informed decisions on an incredible range of complicated topics. A sensible way of dealing with this complexity is to create subgroups that can specialize in certain topics. Thus, the U.S. House of Representatives breaks itself into nineteen standing committees, and the smaller U.S. Senate into sixteen. State legislative bodies follow a similar pattern, usually dividing into somewhere between ten and twenty committees that have jurisdiction over such matters as education, agriculture, social services, the judiciary, and the tax code. These committees have powerful gatekeeping and agenda-setting abilities. Typically, they engage in a form of triage, deciding which of the many specific bills referred to them deserve further attention and preliminary care.

The relevant point for the current discussion is that great effort is made to ensure that diverse views will be heard at the committee stage. Each committee is headed by a chairperson, and in Congress and most state legislatures the party with the most members is granted the prerogative of holding all committee chairs. But although the minority party in the legislature may not get to lead the committees, it is granted substantial membership on the committees and usually the right to decide which of their members will be on each committee. Every member of Congress, for example, will be on at least one committee and typically two or three, not to mention several additional subcommittees. However off-beat a member's views might be, committee assignments will not be denied.

Once on the committee, legislators with dissenting views will probably be given access to committee staff services as well as the ability to call witnesses during committee hearings, to ask questions of witnesses, to make points for "the record," to offer input and amendments to legislation, and generally be heard. Obviously, each legislator cannot win on all, or even most, committee issues, but for the most part American legislative committees create remarkable rights for the expression of minority sentiments.

Floor Debate

The ability to be heard certainly continues once a bill leaves committee and advances to the legislative floor, where all members will have the chance to be involved. The extreme case of legislator rights on the floor is the U.S. Senate. The Senate fancies itself as "the greatest deliberative body in the world." While modern-day observers of Senate debate may quite rightly question this label, the point remains that Senate rules make it very difficult to keep anyone from speaking on any topic at any time. Senate rules generally operate on the basis of unanimous consent. If Senate leaders wish to cease debate and move to a vote on a given topic, they must seek unanimous consent from all senators. Should a single senator desire to speak further, that senator will be able to do so, even to the point of filibustering, unless special and rare steps are taken to remove that honored right temporarily. As might be imagined, the Senate is notoriously difficult to lead— partially as a consequence of rules that grant each individual senator tremendous powers to delay action.

To be sure, most other legislatures have more restrictions on individual members than does the U.S. Senate. Nonetheless, provisions are usually in place that allow those with dissenting views, often members of the minority party in the legislature, to publicize those views, perhaps to the point of forcing a vote on an issue even when defeat is almost certain. Typically, for example, the minority is provided the opportunity to introduce amendments to, or even a substitute for, a bill. These key amendments or substitutes offer the minority's solution to a problem. They usually fail to secure the needed support, but they permit minority members an important opportunity to indicate what would have happened if they were in charge. When the majority takes steps to deny this opportunity, the minority usually claims that norms of the institution or perhaps even norms of democracy have been violated.

If citizens were asked whether they approved or disapproved of giving all members of a legislature equal opportunity to speak and to offer amendments, they would resoundingly approve. In fact, one of the reasons people don't like legislative committees and parties is that they seem to confer more power to some members than to others. What these same citizens apparently do not understand is that, by conferring meaningful rights on all members, the legislature cannot help but acquire many of the political traits people claim to despise. And when every unique member from every distinct constituency is given the ability to speak out, there will be disagreements, even ones that may become shrill on occasion. When every unique member from every distinct constituency is given the ability to offer amendments in committee or on the floor, the governing process is bound to be slow and confusing.

By advocating full and equal rights for all legislators and then simultaneously disparaging legislatures that are contentious and ponderous because members have full and equal rights, the American people are being logically inconsistent. It is impossible to have one without the other—except in a fairy tale world in which all legislators and all constituencies want exactly the same legislative outcomes. By allowing every member to introduce bills, to serve on committees, and to participate meaningfully in floor debate, legislatures work hard to make conflict possible. But the people seem to dislike political conflict. It is important to investigate the reasons more deeply.

Conflict Comes from the People, Not from Parties and Special Interests

The key to understanding the demonization of political conflict begins with recognition of people's belief that down deep, Americans, for all their apparent differences, are actually in accord on important political matters. But since, as we have seen, political consensus among the people of the United States is a myth, the only choice is for the people to face up to the necessity of conflict and join with Madison in trying to make the best of the situation.

How can the political system arrive at a decision in the face of extensive diversity? First, there must be a mechanism for hearing from all the different people with all their different views; otherwise, all people's views would never be known. This mechanism could provide for the people voicing their views directly or for these views to be voiced indirectly by a representative of the people. Either way, some voices will differ from and even contradict other voices. In light of these different expressed preferences, what should be done next? The most logical step after initial debate is to see if there are solutions that might be more or less acceptable to a variety of viewpoints. This stage of negotiating, bargaining, and compromising will be filled with conflict but is in many respects the most crucial. Sometimes, the very nature of an issue makes compromise impossible—and these are the issues that cause democratic government the most difficulty. But more often than not, with enough time and effort, a middle ground can be located that would be at least tolerable to all. People, of course, tend to want something much more than a "tolerable" outcome, but the curse of making collective decisions amid political divergence is that "half a loaf" is the most we deserve to get. Otherwise, the preferences of those who disagree with us would have been quite inappropriately ignored.

Far from being an unnecessary hindrance to getting things done, debate is a vital way of learning everyone's preferences. Far from being an indication that someone is guilty of "selling out on principle," compromise is the way we arrive at a mutually acceptable solution in the face of diverse preferences. Only through a process that appears contentious can diverse preferences be known and then factored into a solution. Ideally, the solution will be the equivalent of a vector; that is, a combining of many disparate forces into the best single representation of those forces. But even if all contending preferences are perfectly captured in the solution, participants will still be disgruntled because they believe themselves to be correct and deserving, not half correct and half deserving. This frustration is natural, but the important point is that it should *not* lead people to assume there is an alternative that would make everybody happy.

The public is not mistaken about the extent to which conflict exists in the political system; there is a lot of it. But the public *is* mistaken about the necessity and desirability of that conflict. Too many people believe the governing process is contentious because elected officials are not listening to the people; in truth, the process is contentious because elected officials *are* listening to the people. People need to be less willing to place all the problems of the political system at the doorstep of the parties, special interests, and legislators, because in point of fact the problems actually stem from people's own inability to agree with their fellow citizens. We provide two examples of conflict existing even when the usual elements of the political process are not present: New England town meetings and a nonpartisan legislature.

Consider the following quotes from five different people:

> "I get sick of it, sick. . . . I listen to 'em argue and wrangle and it goes on for hours."
> "It's just bickering back and forth."
> " . . . nothing but a big fight."
> "There are too damn many arguments."
> "You get quarreling and a big hubbub."

It would be reasonable to assume that these comments were directed at a government institution such as Congress that is infested with special interests, political parties, and self-serving politicians. But in actuality these comments and many more like them were made to researcher Jane Mansbridge by people who had just participated in a New England town meeting. Town meetings are a form of direct government in which people sit down with their neighbors to make key decisions. The central point is that these meetings involve no political parties, special interests, or elected officials. Instead, they consist of several dozen ordinary people working through issues that directly affect their lives—from potholes to school budgets. The meeting that generated such negative reactions from participants was typical of these town meetings, and that is what makes it so important.

The strong inclination of participants to be put off by political conflict at regular town meetings needs to be noticed by all those who believe that if we could just paint parties, special interests, and politicians out of the picture then conflict would be gone too. In their reaction, these town meeting participants make it clear that nothing could be further from the truth. People are just as turned off by dissension and debate when they are involved in it themselves as when they observe it in Congress, in a state legislature, or in other parts of the system. Parties, interest groups, and elected representatives do not cause conflict but rather are ways of dealing with conflict. As is indicated by the experiences with town meetings, political processes could exclude these contentious components but that would not diminish the amount of conflict present.

Besides New England town meetings, another easy place to find evidence of conflict's pervasiveness is the Nebraska State Legislature. Although better known for being a unicameral legislature, an equally interesting feature is that it is officially nonpartisan. Other state legislatures have experimented with nonpartisanship in the past, for better or worse, but the Nebraska Legislature is the only one that currently bans parties. The key question for our purposes becomes what happens to the level of legislative conflict when parties cannot operate in the normal fashion. Studies of roll call voting in the Nebraska Unicameral confirm that patterns do not follow party lines but that they still reflect substantial conflict. Parties may not be present but variation across constituencies remains, debate still occurs, and compromised solutions still result. Nebraska's experience indicates that parties are not the source of conflict. If anything, they serve as a useful way of organizing conflict, thereby facilitating solutions.

The simple fact is that in the context of diverse preferences there is no way to make collective decisions democratically without conflict. With more than a quarter of a billion people of all colors, backgrounds, traits, experiences, abilities, talents, and exposures, and with all parts of this menagerie afforded the opportunity for political input, how *could* there be no conflict? And if all parts were not given input, how could there be a democracy?

In Sum

Invariably, when political theorists list the conditions necessary for a political system to be considered a democracy, one of those conditions is the existence of a "legitimate opposition"; that is, somebody or something that disagrees with the current decision makers. This opposition is necessary to keep those in power on their toes, to force them to be sensitive to ordinary people (or the opposition will), and to make sure that the people have a choice. If there is no opposition or if the opposition does not take issue with those in power, there will be no conflict, and one of the key criteria for a government to be democratic would be missing. It is crucial, therefore, to have a place where this legitimate opposition can create the conflict that is at the core of democratic government. That place is the legislature.

Legislatures attempt to find solutions to difficult societal issues. They do so by analyzing and debating competing proposals and then by compromising among them. They do so by giving all members of the body a broad array of rights that make it possible for the expression and promotion of disparate views. Members of legislatures introduce all kinds of bills, legislative committees listen to all types of witnesses, and floor debates contain all manner of disputes. When they see this happening, the citizens complain that legislators are just wasting time, talking instead of acting. They don't adequately recognize that the marketplace of ideas that legislatures embody is the goal of democratic government—not the enemy of it.

The truth of the matter is that ordinary people have a surprisingly different view of governing from that of politicians and pundits. The latter typically believe that government works best when there is an excited commotion of ideas. Choices among these ideas are then facilitated by conflict and competition in the open marketplace. Ideas garnering the most support will get more attention and will stand the best chance of being adopted into law. Various parties and interest groups champion the cause of particular ideas, and voters know enough about the competing proposals to support the candidates they believe to be on "their side." Elite political observers are bothered if candidates are not busy staking out distinct issue positions that then make it possible for the people to choose.

But the people themselves have a completely different view of politics. The people would rather that contests be left to the field of sports, not politics; they do not like endless campaigns; they do not like policy wonks; they do not like political entities that seem to exacerbate disputes; and they are not eager for issues to be "clarified" by competing solutions. In short, most people do not find politics intrinsically interesting and want the political system to take issues off their personal radar screens, not put more issues on those screens. The people would much prefer to see politicians quietly solving problems.

Indeed, this is what appeared to happen in the wake of the terrorist attacks on New York's World Trade Center and the Pentagon in September 2001. Democrats and Republicans alike took to the microphones and pledged their support to President George W. Bush. Congress immediately and with virtually no dissent appropriated $20 billion for disaster relief and made it clear there was more where that came from. Members on both sides of the aisle said they wanted to punish those responsible, presumably Osama bin Laden and his network. All members advocated increased support for defense and security. This show of remarkable unity, combined with the closely related "rally-around-the-flag" effect, drove support for the president, for Congress, and for government in general to some of their highest marks ever. Bush's popularity topped out at over 90 percent, and trust in government matched levels not seen since the mid-1960s. The public absolutely loves it when those in government seem to be united, when conflict among politicians is not visible.

Americans naturally wonder why the political arena cannot always be so agreeable. Why does it take a major national crisis to drive conflict out of representative government? The answer is simple. Democracy is in many respects a luxury. When a situation demands quick decisions, when life or death matters are at hand, complex democratic decision procedures will not work. This is why every military that has ever existed has been arranged in a hierarchical fashion, with ascending ranks and descending chains-of-command. Can you imagine a military in which all soldiers have an equal vote on strategy and actions? As it is, some soldiers may not think the general's decision is the best one, but they go along with it because dissension among the ranks would quite likely be deadly. For this same reason, politicians tend to unite behind the president (the commander in chief) when crisis times afflict us. We would not want it any other way.

But would we really want this deferential, "whatever-the-leader-says" type of decision making to be present even in normal, noncrisis times? Despite the attraction such a tidy process might hold for some, upon reflection it is obvious that far too many of the requisites of democracy would have been sacrificed. Democratic leaders need to be challenged whenever challenges are appropriate. Conflict could be removed from our political system, but it could not be removed without making our government much less democratic than it is now. We need an out-group that believes it has a better way, and that out-group needs to have a real chance of becoming the in-group. This situation will inevitably entail conflict between the two groups, but it will also inevitably entail democracy.

Thus, although many people have an understandable desire for conflict-free government, it is an impossibility if the system is also to be democratic. There will be times when representative institutions and mechanisms such as legislatures, political parties, and interest groups are not serving the people well. At these times, by all means the people should strive to reform the system so that it performs better. But we should never labor under the misconception that these reforms could somehow eliminate political conflict. Not only is this impossible but, even if it could be made to happen, we would see that Madison was correct in calling the elimination of conflict a cure worse than the disease. It may seem to the public as though representative government is about tearing down consensus, but it is actually about building consensus—and the best and most democratic way to do this, whether we like it or not, involves conflict in an open political body such as a legislature.

Sources and Suggested Reading

For a brilliant discussion of the inevitability of disagreement and, relatedly, conflict in the political arena, see James Madison's famous *Federalist* No. 10. For an equally brilliant treatment of the superiority of indirect as opposed to direct democracy, see the works of Edmund Burke, especially his famous "Speech to the Electors of Bristol." Many of his speeches and writings can be found in *Burke's Politics*, ed. Ross J. S. Hoffman and Paul Levack (New York: Knopf, 1949).

For other and more modern treatments of the advantages of representative democracy in dealing with conflict, see Alan Rosenthal, *The Decline of Representative Democracy* (Washington, D.C.: CQ Press, 1998), and Donald Wolfensberger, *Congress and the People: Deliberative Democracy on Trial* (Baltimore: Johns Hopkins University Press, 1999). Burke's views have been a staple in political theory for quite some time. Rosenthal's book deals primarily with state legislatures and Wolfensberger's with Congress, but they share a strong concern that the health of representative democracy could be threatened if people continue to believe that conflict somehow is not necessary and that legislative institutions are failing if they engage in conflict. For a very useful earlier work with a similar theme, see former senator Fred Harris's *In Defense of Congress* (New York: St. Martin's Press, 1995). Finally, on the general theme of public misunderstandings of legislatures, see the essay by former U.S. representative Lee Hamilton entitled "What I Wish Political Scientists Would Teach about Congress," *PS* 33 (December 2000): 757–765.

Bernard Crick has written eloquently about politics as a clash of competing opinions and interests in *In Defense of Politics*, 4th ed. (Chicago: University of Chicago Press, 1992). People's aversion to political conflict is detailed in several different ways and by several different works. In *Beyond Adversarial Democracy* (Chicago: University of Chicago Press, 1983), Jane Mansbridge provides a riveting firsthand account of people's strong negative reaction to conflict even when it occurs in town meetings with their friends and neighbors. In *Avoiding Politics*

(Cambridge: Cambridge University Press, 1998), Nina Eliasoph details the efforts of volunteer organizations to steer clear of any issue that may inspire conflict out of fear that such conflict could have deleterious consequences for the group. And in *Stealth Democracy: Americans' Beliefs about How Government Should Work* (Cambridge: Cambridge University Press, 2002), John R. Hibbing and Elizabeth Theiss-Morse provide evidence that people would prefer that their government operate without any conflict or even debate even if this means the mechanisms of government would be less visible and accountable.

Perhaps the best treatment of minority rights in legislatures, especially Congress, is found in Sarah Binder, *Minority Rights, Majority Rule* (Cambridge: Cambridge University Press, 1997). Also relevant is Barbara Sinclair's *Unorthodox Lawmaking,* 2d ed. (Washington, D.C.: CQ Press, 2000). For general treatments of legislative rules, see the relevant chapters in Roger H. Davidson and Walter J. Oleszek, *Congress and Its Members,* 8th ed. (Washington, D.C.: CQ Press, 2002), and Steven S. Smith, *The American Congress* (Boston: Houghton Mifflin, 1999). On state legislative rules, see Alan Rosenthal, *Legislative Life* (New York: Harper and Row, 1981). The quote from the member of Congress on the utility of interest groups can be found in John R. Hibbing, *Choosing to Leave* (Washington, D.C.: University Press of America, 1982).

8

What Makes Legislators and Legislatures Accountable?

In 1994 DEMOCRATIC Speaker of the House Thomas S. Foley found himself challenged by Republican neophyte George R. Nethercutt Jr. in his eastern Washington congressional district, where he had won fifteen consecutive elections. No Speaker had lost an election since 1862, and Foley spent $2.1 million on his campaign to the challenger's

$1.1 million. Yet Foley lost by 4,000 votes, of 216,000 cast. By denying him reelection, the voters of Washington's Fifth Congressional District had held him accountable for his actions both as their member of Congress and as the Speaker of the House. What were Foley's transgressions? In part, he suffered from being a tough partisan in the House, where he used the rules aggressively to benefit the Democratic majority. He filed suit at home against a term limit law passed by a voter initiative, voted in Congress against district opinion that supported a flag-burning constitutional amendment, and publicly questioned the Persian Gulf War. Foley's constituents could cast a ballot that would punish both Foley and the entire Democratic Party in the House; enough of them did so that he lost. His district had held him accountable for his actions, as well as the actions of the Democratic majority and the entire House, which had experienced internal scandals caused in part by lax management of the institution.

In addition, Foley's defeat came as part of a national trend that swept Democrats out of control of the House for the first time in forty years. Republicans picked up fifty-two seats in the House of Representatives, in large part because the voters held Democrats responsible for a legislature they distrusted and a Clinton administration whose priorities they questioned. Given their loss of the Senate as well, it is fair to say that congressional Democrats were blamed for the perceived sins of both the legislative and executive branches.

And what of Rep. George Nethercutt? Speaker Newt Gingrich rewarded him with a seat on the powerful Appropriations Committee, and he won two more elections before being confronted with the choice of whether to run or not in 2000. For most incumbents, this would have been an easy decision, but Nethercutt had campaigned hard in 1994 as a firm advocate of term limits. Although he pledged to stay only six years, almost immediately he began to retreat from this position. Despite vigorous opposition from term limit advocates, including $300,000 in advertisements against him, Nethercutt won reelection handily in 2000 by emphasizing his service to his Fifth District constituents. By returning him to Congress, these voters held Nethercutt accountable for his actions, much as they had previously with Foley. But in 2000 their judgment was different as they endorsed Nethercutt's assessment that six years was not long enough to become truly effective as a member of Congress. The thirty-year veteran of Congress, Tom Foley, would have agreed with him.

For representative democracy to work, legislators must be held accountable at the next election. There must be meaningful competition for office, and electoral defeat must be at least potentially a threat to incumbents. If retribution at the polls is to work at all, legislators' actions must be held up for examination. Legislative processes and decisions need to be transparent, or largely so. This means that votes, especially on the floor, but also in committee, must be recorded, so that journalists, interest groups, and opposing parties can publicize them.

Many critics argue that both national and state lawmakers have become almost immune to electoral defeat. In 1998 and 2000, for example, more than 98 percent of House incumbents who sought reelection were successful. State reelection rates are not quite as high, but the vast majority of sitting legislators win reelection. Moreover, many challenges are extremely weak, and lots of lawmakers, especially at the state level, run unopposed. In addition, incumbents can raise campaign funds much more easily than can most challengers, so even potentially endangered legislators may escape a strong challenge by scaring off opponents.

Those who claim that legislators are not accountable for their actions point to the fact that the legislative process is complex and resistant to easy understanding. Assigning responsibility to individual lawmakers, beyond their recorded votes, may be difficult. And even with votes, lawmakers can frequently structure decisions so that they can avoid tough choices, at least in public. Interest groups, opposing parties, and the press often try to hold legislators accountable for their actions, but public attention to legislative bodies has declined substantially over the past twenty to thirty years.

In short, critics look at incumbency, campaign financing, and legislative coverage and can argue that accountability—both for individual members and the legislature itself—is difficult to exercise. In this chapter we will explore how the electorate, legislators' personal ambitions, the media, interest groups, political parties, and financial disclosure laws promote legislative accountability and how state term limit laws have affected legislative performance.

The Legislature: Insular or Accountable?

Every two years we elect all our U.S. House members, one-third of our U.S. senators, and more than two-thirds of all our state legislators. Of the almost eight thousand state and national legislators, *more than two-thirds serve two-year terms.* Such frequent elections demonstrate how formally accountable our lawmakers are. Yet they are often viewed as distant and non-responsive, cut off from their home folks.

A visit to almost any capitol can illuminate why legislators often seem less than responsive. The most dramatic architectural feature of the U.S. Capitol and most statehouses is a large dome. State legislators and capitol journalists often use the phrase "under the dome" to distinguish their insider political games from the public's view of the legislature. To be sure, the "under the dome" culture is real. Like other large institutions, such as universities, high-tech companies, or auto assembly plants, legislatures have their own organizational cultures, language, and labyrinths. Yet, legislatures are different from corporations or universities, because the public can hold their members accountable for their actions through regular, frequent elections.

Generally, lawmakers are accountable for their actions, their public pronouncements, the bills they introduce, and, most important, the hundreds of votes that most of them cast each legislative session. Most votes do not mean life or death for most legislators. After all, many legislative issues do not matter that much to a great majority of their constituents. But every once in a while, a key issue becomes the center of attention, and one vote might cost a few lawmakers their seats. It could be on water quality, handgun restrictions, tax cuts, or school funding. Legislators must consider the views of their constituents, their own ambitions, what they see as the best policy, what their party leaders and the chief executive want. Then they must vote: yea or nay. Abstaining is not really an option in most cases, save for the occasional instance when a legislator declares a conflict of interest. So lawmakers vote and await the consequences.

In addition to the critics' point that legislators are not accountable because incumbents usually win, another concern is that the public knows little about what happens in Congress or in their state legislature. Reporting on legislative bodies, especially in the states, has become less thorough over the past twenty years, as television stations and even newspapers have reduced their coverage of legislatures. In legislative chambers dramatic scenes are few and far between, in contrast to reporting on auto accidents, criminal activities, and human interest stories. The news that does come out of Congress and state legislatures emphasizes conflicts and posturing. Especially in the states, little seems to occur for most of a legislative session, and then there is a burst of activity at the end of the 60 or 90 or 120 days allocated for legislators to meet. Outside observers have a difficult time understanding that the legislative process usually works slowly, as majorities are built, member by member. And the session's end is often the only time that

Table 8-1 Length of Legislative Terms

Chamber years	States
House 2, Senate 2	Arizona, Connecticut, Georgia, Idaho, Maine, Massachusetts, New Hampshire, New York, North Carolina, Rhode Island, South Dakota, Vermont
House 2, Senate 4	Alaska, Arkansas, California, Colorado, Delaware, Florida, Hawaii, Illinois, Indiana, Iowa, Kansas, Kentucky, Michigan, Minnesota, Missouri, Montana, Nevada, New Jersey, New Mexico, Ohio, Oklahoma, Oregon, Pennsylvania, South Carolina, Tennessee, Texas, Utah, Virginia, Washington, West Virginia, Wisconsin, Wyoming
House 4, Senate 4	Alabama, Louisiana, Maryland, Mississippi, North Dakota, Puerto Rico
Senate 4	Nebraska

Source: *The Book of the States, 2000–01* (Lexington, Ky.: Council of State Governments, 2000).

leaders can coordinate negotiations across issues—negotiations leading to packages that can command majorities in two houses and win the governor's signature.

If news coverage of the legislative process is often scanty, newspaper editorials exacerbate problems by questioning the "efficiency" of legislatures and the ethics of individual legislators. Editorial writers regularly assume that legislators' votes are for sale to the interests that contribute to their campaigns. They make it seem that legislators are somehow betraying the public trust and need to be more responsive to the public. The fact of the matter is, however, that state legislators and members of Congress are highly accountable for their actions. Strangely enough, lawmakers may be too accountable for their actions, too responsive to their constituents, too concerned about the next election that is right around the corner.

More than anything else, the desire to win reelection constrains lawmakers. All legislative terms in the United States except for the U.S. Senate (six years) are relatively short. Legislators have two-year terms in fifty-eight chambers and four-year terms in forty-one chambers (Table 8-1). This means that the next election is never far away and therefore a constant source of concern for legislators who want to keep their jobs.

Especially if they come from competitive districts, incumbents cannot afford to relax their reelection efforts, if they want to return. Depending on the state, anywhere from 14 percent (Arizona) to 58 percent (New York) of the districts are competitive, as shown in Figure 8-1. In Congress there is

Figure 8-1 Competitive Seats: Average Percentage of Legislative Seats Won by Less than 60 Percent of the Vote, 1992–1996

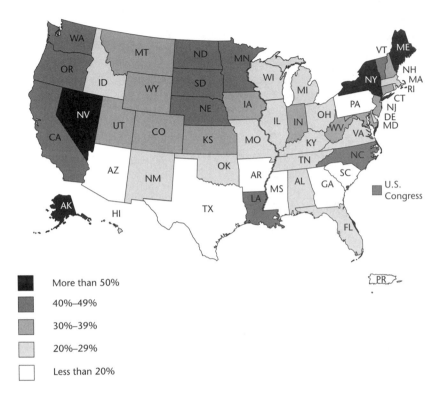

More than 50%

40%–49%

30%–39%

20%–29%

Less than 20%

Source: National Conference of State Legislatures, 1999.

considerable difference between the two chambers. The House of Representatives is like the Arizona Legislature, with only 15 percent of the seats won by close margins. In the more visible U.S. Senate races, 25 percent of the seats are marginal.

Even though most legislators win their seats by fairly large margins, incumbency scarcely ensures reelection, as Speaker Foley and his Democratic colleagues rudely discovered in 1994. In every electoral cycle, there are at least a few legislators who either lose unexpectedly or have "near death" experiences in which they narrowly retain their seats. As one scholar put it, members of Congress feel "unsafe at any margin," although no single vote would ordinarily place them in jeopardy. As one representative put it, "I don't think any one vote would defeat any congressman anywhere. I hear some of my colleagues say that, but I don't believe it. If you get too far away from your district, you'll lose it. But on any one vote, the important thing is that you be able to explain why you did it." This assessment makes sense, but on occasion a single vote does make all the difference. In 1957 Rep. Brooks Hays, D-Ark., voted courageously to support a modest civil rights bill and subsequently lost his seat to a last-minute, write-in segregationist candidate. More recently, Rep. Marjorie Margolies-Mezvinsky, D-Pa., cast the decisive vote to support President Clinton's 1993 budget, which included a tax increase that she had promised to oppose. Like Hays, her choice received lavish attention in the press and placed her political career in jeopardy. In the end, she narrowly lost her reelection bid in the Republican sweep of 1994. We previously mentioned that several Democratic state legislators in Vermont lost their 2000 elections in part because of votes they had cast on the issue of civil unions for gay people. Even legislators in so-called safe seats can have electoral worries, because they can be challenged in primary elections by members of their own party.

Despite understanding how little attention voters pay to their activities, legislators must anticipate the possible reactions of their constituents to any given vote. They know that individual votes can be taken out of context and aggressively publicized by an opponent, a political party, or an interest group. Through continuing contact with the voters in their districts, lawmakers generally get a good sense of what their constituents will and won't support. In addition, lawmakers have built-in advantages in explaining their votes both to the press and directly to the public.

For legislators who aspire to higher office, their ambitions themselves are another source of accountability. State representatives who want to become state senators or state senators who eye a U.S. House seat tend to think carefully about how they would appeal to their future constituents. Ambition, strangely enough, may well foster higher levels of accountability, as lawmakers gauge how two overlapping but distinct sets of constituents may react to their actions. More generally, considerable accountability comes through legislators' *anticipation* of what their constituents will think. As congressional scholars like Richard F. Fenno and Douglas Arnold have demonstrated, legislators ordinarily have a keen sense of their districts' wishes.

The Agents of Accountability

Citizens may not know it, but legislatures regularly consider bills that affect every individual in some way. So citizens need help in monitoring legislative activity, and a lot is available from two major sources. First, various institutions monitor what legislatures do and alert citizens to the policy implications of pending actions. The media, interest groups, and political parties all commit substantial resources to informing voters about the activities of both legislatures as a whole and individual legislators. Although the media ordinarily claim to have no ax to grind (which may or may not be true), political parties and most interest groups do have their own agendas and perspectives. Whatever their motivations, these institutions combine to alert citizens to what the legislature is cooking up.

Second, legislators participate in a process that has become increasingly transparent. This means that legislators' actions are open to scrutiny in both legislative and electoral politics. Floor proceedings in the Congress and many state legislatures are televised, and almost all significant electoral contributions must be reported. If citizens and their surrogates—parties, groups, and the press—want to learn about their lawmakers' records, they can do so, especially in the Internet age.

The Media: Ups and Downs in Legislative Reporting

Covering the legislature—either in Washington, D.C., or in state capitals—constitutes a real dilemma for reporters. Given the number of issues and members, many of whom crave publicity, legislatures offer a rich array of opportunities for stories. Yet, as noted earlier, the coverage of legislative activity has declined over the past three decades. For reporters to hold lawmakers accountable, they must be able to get their stories into print or on the air. In the states, this can be an especially formidable task, in that readers often express little interest, and local television coverage of many state legislatures is almost nil. Although the congressional press corps has grown steadily over the last thirty years, statehouse reporting has declined. Television journalism has fallen away almost completely in many states. Two *American Journalism Review* studies in the late 1990s documented the fall-off in state legislative media coverage, just at the time that increasing responsibilities devolved to the states. A grand total of 513 full-time reporters covered all American state capitols. Considering that individual state budgets regularly run into the tens of billions of dollars, an average of ten reporters per legislature is woefully inadequate. As veteran reporter David Broder notes,

> When I began covering national politics in the 1960s, almost every state capitol boasted a cadre of resident reporters who had been in the pressroom for years, who knew how issues had been handled, had sources throughout the building, and knew where all the bodies were buried. They were not hero-worshippers by any means, but they loved the beat they covered and were eager to explain what was going on there. Sadly, that is a rarity now and the coverage of legislatures is often compressed to the point of being unintelligible and is rarely informed by any historic perspective.

Nevertheless, many state and national reporters can and do hold legislators accountable for their actions, in terms of both policies and ethics. In fact, the post-Watergate era has produced new relationships between reporters and legislators. Historically, journalists and lawmakers both benefited from a symbiotic relationship in which reporters got access and information but often did not print everything they knew in deference to the legislators, who could shut off the information at any time. Moreover, reporters regularly ignored the personal foibles of legislators, especially when it came to excessive drinking or extramarital affairs.

Watergate, along with a major congressional sting operation (Abscam) in 1980 and various major scandals in several states, produced a generation of reporters, especially at the national level, who have sought to expose impropriety or the appearance of wrongdoing. This has produced a dualistic approach to reporting on legislators. Reporters are more aggressive and skeptical than in the past, yet they still need to maintain reasonably good relationships with most lawmakers. Walking this fine line has led reporters and legislators to "negotiate coverage," as political scientist Timothy Cook has put it.

That is, both reporters and legislators have something that the other desires. Reporters can provide coverage of lawmakers and their pet projects.

In turn, senators and representatives often possess information that will allow reporters to generate a newsworthy story, which can command substantial newspaper space or television time. At the same time, an ambitious reporter may have little need or desire to form working relationships with lawmakers and may choose to write stories that make state legislators, and by extension the legislature, look bad. In the end, even though legislators may distrust reporters, they need them and vice-versa.

Does such negotiated coverage act to hold lawmakers accountable for their actions? The media as a single, if multifaceted, institution probably cannot do the job on its own. But, combined with interest groups and parties, the various components of the media—newspapers, magazines, television, radio, and Internet—can provide much of the material that voters need to enforce some kind of rough accountability among members of the legislative branch.

Interest Groups: Countervailing Power

Hundreds of organized interests cluster around legislators, from their initial campaign to their last days of service. Given groups' campaign contributions and their extensive lobbying efforts, it is tempting to view interests as reducing the accountability of the legislative process. After all, if one believes that legislators' votes are "for sale" or that high-priced lobbying dominates decision making, then it makes sense to think that ordinary constituents are left out of the process. Many public interest groups, like Common Cause, explicitly make these arguments, going so far as to label the legislative process as corrupt.

But there is another, entirely reasonable perspective on the role of interest groups. Consider a lawmaker who is undecided on proposed finance legislation that would benefit bankers at the expense of the insurance industry. The banking association makes a sizeable contribution to her campaign, and its lobbyists visit her on numerous occasions, armed with a well-conceived set of arguments in favor of their position.

The insurance industry has not made any major contributions to the legislator, but its lobbyists mount an intensive grassroots lobbying campaign to convince her that their point of view is correct. Every insurance agent in her district receives information about the pending legislation, and they are urged to contact their lawmaker. In addition, several major national insurance firms make sure that their local affiliates get in touch with the legislator. Since the insurance industry sees the banking legislation as hurting the average citizen, it works with consumers' groups to rally support against the banking bill. No one can predict accurately how the legislator will eventually come down on this legislation, but she will certainly understand that her actions are being watched.

In short, the pluralist notion of "countervailing power" often proves to be more than a theoretical concept. Even a powerful interest, such as the banking industry, may find itself opposed by an equally potent lobby. What does this mean for state legislators or members of Congress? They know that they will be held accountable for whatever actions they take on a piece of legislation. The groups are watching, waiting to see if they need to make an issue of a legislator's vote in the next election.

Given the proliferation of organized interests, it is rare for an important issue not to generate lobbying from a wide range of groups, many of whom will eagerly report back to the lawmaker's constituents. Granted, the monitoring of legislative activities can be difficult, but, as noted, the legislative processes at both the state and national levels have become increasingly transparent over the past thirty or forty years. Although there are still last-minute deals and obscure provisions hidden in large legislative packages, on most important issues organized interests have the opportunity to make their case—not just to lawmakers, but to their constituents as well.

Many groups issue report cards or ratings that judge lawmakers' records; legislators often think twice about opposing a major interest like labor or the Christian right on an important vote, knowing that their position will affect their score. Organized interests have also become increasingly active in electoral campaigns by spending millions of dollars across the nation to help elect or defeat candidates with whom they disagree. In the 2000 congressional elections, group expenditures on their own candidate-related advertising hit $95 million, with virtually all of these funds being directed toward thirty to forty highly competitive campaigns. Whatever we might think of these independent expenditure tactics, groups do seek to hold candidates directly accountable for their views. Moreover, groups like labor unions and the Christian Coalition combine with the Democratic and the Republican Parties, respectively, to hold legislators accountable.

Political Parties: Elections and Beyond

Although elections constitute the framework of accountability for American legislators, political parties provide the substance. That is, an overwhelming number of state and national legislators identify with one of the two major parties. As of 2001, exclusive of nonpartisan Nebraska, fewer than fifty seats in Congress and the other forty-nine state legislatures were held by independents or partisans not identifying with either the Republican or the Democratic Party. For lawmakers to be held accountable, the opposing political party must offer a viable choice to the electorate. We have seen that legislators do take elections seriously, even when they hold a substantial advantage. Still, only the threat offered by real competition can produce continuing legislative accountability. Overall, the levels of competition in both Congress and the statehouses across the country should hearten us. The narrow Republican margin in the House (222–210, with 2 independents) and the even slimmer Democratic Senate advantage (50–49, with 1 independent) have been thoroughly analyzed, but similar numbers also exist in the states.

Although serious partisan competition may not be a sufficient condition to guarantee accountability, it is sobering for a legislative majority to know that it can be replaced in the next election. In 1994, congressional Republicans succeeded in holding Democrats responsible for both unpopular policies, such as the Clinton health care proposal, and the internal House banking and post office scandals. Even when voters know relatively little about specific issues they can use the party label as a shorthand way to hold a majority party responsible for its record.

In 2001 Democrats held 3,819 state legislative seats, nationwide, in contrast to the 3,531 that were in Republican hands. As has the U.S Congress, most state legislatures have grown increasingly competitive during the 1990s. One immediate implication is that the legislative parties have a large stake in protecting (or capturing) the majority, precisely because the divisions are so narrow. This means that both major parties eagerly hold each other accountable for their actions. Even when legislation is difficult to enact, legislative parties often force votes that require opposing partisans to take public positions on issues they may wish to avoid. For example, pro-life legislators frequently add amendments to bills that will require more moderate lawmakers to take a stand on an abortion-related provision. The same is true in regard to tax cuts, gun laws, education spending, and a dozen other issues. In many instances, lawmakers are held accountable for positions they take, even though there is little likelihood that a bill will be passed.

In addition, narrow partisan majorities require legislators to take care in assessing their positions on dozens of pieces of legislation. They know that if they are not accountable to their constituents, their party could lose a seat in the next election. They are thus even more highly motivated to take their constituents' wishes into account; ironically, such an approach may well make their party less unified and less powerful in the statehouse.

Fostering Accountability: Disclosure

If legislators are to be held accountable for their actions, voters must have adequate information. Roll call votes allow the electorate to assess their representatives' positions on a wide range of issues. But almost all states have gone considerably farther by making important information available to voters through the media, political parties, and interest groups. As of 2001 only three states don't require some basic financial disclosure from lawmakers. In addition, most legislatures require disclosure from lobbyists and interest groups as to how much they have spent on their attempts to influence legislative outcomes. And many states demand that groups and lobbyists identify which legislators receive benefits from lobbyists.

One unintended consequence of disclosure is that it sometimes creates the appearance of impropriety where none exists. It may appear as if the votes of lawmakers who accept a couple of lobbyists' dinner invitations to fairly expensive restaurants are available for $150 or so. This is misleading in the extreme. Still, disclosure generally allows voters to assess if they think financial interests, campaign contributions, and lobbying expenditures have unduly affected their representatives' votes.

Table 8-2 Term Limits in State Legislatures

State	Year enacted	Yes votes (%)	House limit[a]	House year of impact	Senate limit[a]	Senate year of impact
Arizona	1992	74	8	2000	8	2000
Arkansas	1992	60	6	1998	8	2000
California	1990	52	6	1996	8	1998
Colorado	1990	71	8	1996	8	1998
Florida	1992	76	8	2000	8	2000
Louisiana	1995	76	12	2007	12	2007
Maine	1993	68	8	1996	8	1996
Michigan	1992	59	6	1998	8	1998
Missouri	1992	75	8	2000	8	2002
Montana	1992	67	8	2000	8	2000
Nebraska	2000	56	Unicameral		8	2008
Nevada	1996	70	12	2008	12	2008
Ohio	1992	68	8	2000	8	2000
Oklahoma	1990	67	12	2004	12	2004
South Dakota	1992	64	8	2000	8	2000
Utah	1994	b	12	2006	12	2006
Wyoming	1992	77	12	2006	12	2006

Source: National Conference of State Legislatures, www.ncsl.org.

a Length of term limit in years.
b Enacted by legislature.

Increasing disclosure to increase the transparency of legislative actions and campaign funds may not satisfy all critics of the process, but it does provide a baseline of information that allows reporters, opposing candidates, parties, and interest groups to hold up an incumbent's record to a reasonable amount of scrutiny.

Term Limits: Can Accountability Be Mandated?

Responding to the idea that lawmakers had become insulated from electoral pressures, in the 1980s and early 1990s various groups and individual advocates (for example, author George Will) backed term limits for both state legislators and members of the U.S. Congress. In the states this movement has had a major impact: as of 2002 seventeen states had imposed term

Table 8-3 Consecutive versus Lifetime Term Limits

Limit in years	Consecutive	Lifetime ban
6 house, 8 senate	—	Arkansas, California, Michigan
8 total	Nebraska	—
8 house, 8 senate	Arizona, Colorado, Florida, Maine, Montana, Ohio, South Dakota	Missouri
12 total	—	Oklahoma
12 house, 12 senate	Louisiana, Utah, Wyoming	Nevada

Source: National Conference of State Legislatures, www.ncsl.org.

Note: Dashes indicate that no state has this qualification.

limits on their state legislators, almost all by voter initiative. Several states also passed term limits for members of Congress, but the courts have ruled that the states don't have the power to impose term limits on federal officials. Such a step would have to begin with Congress either in the form of a law or, more likely, a proposal for a constitutional amendment.

Term limits vary substantially from state to state as to when they first take effect and how restrictive they are. By 2000, term limits had taken effect in eleven states. In these states, 369 of 1,541 members were unable to run for reelection (the remaining members had not served long enough). As time passes, increasing numbers of states and lawmakers will be affected—just as the advocates of restrictions had hoped (see Table 8-2).

More important than when limits actually affect legislators is how restrictive they are. California, once the epitome of legislative professionalism, stands at one end of the spectrum: lifetime limits of two four-year terms for senators and three two-year terms for House members. The least restrictive states—Louisiana, Nevada, Oklahoma, and Utah—mandate twelve-year maximums for each chamber. In addition, states vary as to whether their limits apply only to consecutive terms or to lifetime eligibility (see Table 8-3).

Critics of term limits have voiced numerous objections to this mechanical means of ensuring that a fresh supply of legislators will enter the legislature. First, there is a serious question as to whether this policy addresses an actual problem. Between 1987 and 1997, 72 percent of all state senate seats turned over, as did 79 percent of state lower-house seats. With an overall turnover of almost 78 percent, the idea of a permanent class of lawmakers is difficult to maintain. Although some states do keep legislative leaders for fairly long periods, most chambers experience substantial turnover among leaders, further undercutting the notion of entrenched lawmakers.

In California, where many careerist legislators were forced out of office by term limits, legislative careers are short, even if political careers are not. Thus, legislators are continually considering where their next office may be. Within the legislature, the learning curve is steep. Second-year assemblyman Darrell Steinberg notes, "It's not as if members can afford to sit on the back bench and wait their turn. They're expected to get right on in there. My advice is focus, focus, focus. The key is to find issues that have not received real political prominence, but need leadership. That's where you can really make an impact."

Such an approach may serve the individual legislator, but the institution as a whole is likely to suffer. Under term limits the individual legislators are often not held accountable for their actions, in that it's easier to wait for an open seat election than to mount a campaign against an incumbent. If individual lawmakers are difficult to hold accountable, so too is the legislature itself, because the members do not have to suffer the consequences of their actions.

There are other problems of institutional accountability in term-limited states. In Maine, for example, legislative committees have struggled to process bills in a timely and coherent manner. With less accumulated experience and expertise, the most important committees faced a surge in the number of bill introductions, many from inexperienced legislators. The legislative leadership responded by instituting various structural and procedural changes that have placed limits on members' abilities to introduce bills and by allowing committees to meet monthly while the legislature is out of session. Ironically, this latter change may make the legislature more of a full-time job than it was previously.

In a similar vein, Michigan legislators in the post–term limit era looked a lot like their counterparts before tenure was restricted. They remained solicitous of their constituents, even when they knew that their length of service was limited. At the same time, term-limited Michigan legislators appear to have increased their reliance on partisan and staff-based sources of information.

The effects of term limits on state legislatures varied from state to state in the 1990s. Under the most severe restrictions (for example, California's six years in the assembly, eight years in the senate), lawmakers are often thrust into leadership roles before they "learn the ropes" of the legislative process. In states with longer time frames, such as twelve years in both upper and lower chambers, term limits may well have little impact on either legislative performance or accountability.

In Sum

Strangely enough, both Congress and the state legislatures may have become overly oriented toward responsiveness in this age of instant communication and speedy travel. Legislators may well assume that their every move will be reported back to their constituents, who might—conceivably—hold them accountable for any objectionable decision. In an era of a "permanent campaign" in which every policy issue is framed and debated in relation to its potential effects on the next election, legislative leaders frequently must decide between reaching policy compromises on thorny problems and fanning the fires of electoral politics by framing issues in confrontational ways.

If every legislator worries continually about being held accountable for every action by his or her constituents, the legislature as a whole might well grind to a halt—and thus act collectively in an irresponsible manner. As representative assemblies, legislatures must have the capacity to discuss and deliberate the major issues of the day and ultimately make policies that address these issues. Then the electorate can hold the legislature (and its majority party) accountable for its actions.

How do contemporary legislatures stack up? Overall, we see legislatures that encourage party competition, a reasonable amount of disclosure, extensive openness, and the close monitoring by interest groups. Many legislators run unopposed or without strong opposition, but most lawmakers still fret about being accountable to their constituents. Most legislative scholars see the early stages of term limits as an unfortunate "fix" that does not enhance accountability, but so far the effects of term limits on state legislatures have been modest in most states.

In the end, the ballot box remains our most important tool in enforcing accountability, and anyone who spends much time around legislatures will find their members heavily influenced by the thinking, real or perceived, of the folks at home.

Sources and Suggested Reading

On the accountability of individual members of Congress, one must first look at many of Richard F. Fenno's writings as well as David Mayhew's classic *Congress: The Electoral Connection* (New Haven: Yale University Press, 1974). Fenno's *Home Style* (Boston: Little, Brown, 1978) may be the most important book on this topic. His case studies of several senators are also worth reading, especially *When Incumbency Fails: The Senate Career of Mark Andrews* (Washington, D.C.: CQ Press, 1992) and *Senators on the Campaign Trail* (Norman: University of Oklahoma Press, 1996). Finally, Fenno's *Congress at the Grassroots* (Chapel Hill: University of North Carolina Press, 2000) helps us understand how accountability operates over the course of an extended political career, especially as a legislator's district changes.

Douglas Arnold's *The Logic of Congressional Action* (New Haven: Yale University Press, 1990) gives us a sense of how legislators anticipate their constituents' reactions—and how both legislators and the legislature can change positions on a major issue. John Kingdon's *Congressmen's Voting Decisions,* 3d ed. (Ann Arbor: University of Michigan Press, 1989), places constituency in the context of other influences on legislators' voting behavior.

The literature on responsible party government also relates to accountability. A good overview comes in Austin Ranney's *The Doctrine of Responsible Party Government* (Urbana: University of Illinois Press, 1954), and the most forceful argument on its behalf is E. E. Schattschneider, *Party Government* (New York: Farrar and Rinehart, 1942). On interest groups as agents of accountability, see the references in chap. 6 of this volume. David Magleby's *Election Advocacy* (Salt Lake City: Brigham Young University, 2001) and *Outside Money* (Lanham, Md.: Rowman and Littlefield, 2000) detail the independent expenditures of interest groups in 1998 and 2000.

At the state level, see Gary Moncrief, Peverill Squire, and Malcolm Jewell, *Who Runs for the Legislature?* (New York: Prentice-Hall, 2001), as well as Alan Rosenthal, *The Decline of Representative Democracy* (Washington, D.C.: CQ Press,

1998). And on the role of the press in accountability, a good starting place is Timothy Cook, *Governing with the News* (Washington, D.C.: Brookings Institution Press, 1997).

On term limits, see *Term Limits in State Legislatures,* by John M. Carey, Richard G. Niemi, and Lynda W. Powell (Ann Arbor: University of Michigan Press, 2000), as well as tracking by the National Conference of State Legislatures (www.ncsl.org). George Will presents one case for legislative term limits in *Restoration* (New York: Simon and Schuster, 1995).

9

How Well Have Legislatures Been Working?

IN JUDGING REPRESENTATIVE democracy, people have to assess just how the system works and how well legislatures perform. Earlier chapters have suggested that misunderstanding and misperception, brought about by a negative environment, accounts for much discontent. How much can be attributed to the poor performance of legislatures themselves?

How, in fact, have the U.S. Congress and state legislatures been performing, and has their performance improved in recent years? It is not easy to measure the performance of legislatures or even to agree on just what dimensions ought to be assessed. The focus here is on how the institution and the process work, not on what policies are produced. Policies are certainly important, but in a democracy policies depend largely on what a majority of Americans want. Legislative institutions and legislative processes are not only the means of arriving at public policy but also an end in themselves. In a democracy the machinery of government is as important as its products. Therefore, we will look at the representativeness, capacity, integrity, openness, competitiveness, participation, internal democracy, and responsiveness of legislatures. According to these values, as will be shown below, at both the national and state levels, legislative performance is better than it was twenty-five years ago, although it looks worse than it used to look. Progress has surely been made, but that does not mean there are no problems. To the contrary, there are quite a few problems, as we would expect in a democratic system.

Representativeness

Since the U.S. Supreme Court decisions on reapportionment in the 1960s, legislatures have become more politically representative than before. Rural districts used to be overrepresented and urban and suburban districts underrepresented in the U.S. House and state legislatures. Thus, the votes of some citizens counted more than the votes of others. Today every person has an equally weighted vote in the election of members of the U.S. House and of both chambers of the legislatures in the states. Except for the U.S. Senate, where the smallest states have representation equal to the largest, "one person, one vote" is truly the national standard.

Not everyone is satisfied with the current system, however. Some Republicans in largely Democratic districts and some Democrats in largely Republican districts feel disenfranchised. From a practical point of view, they may be, since they seldom can elect one of their own to represent them. Supporters of third parties rarely win, so they too have to look to others for representation. A political minority, and especially one in a district dominated by the opposition, has cause for discontent. But short of a change to a system of proportional representation, whereby a multimember district elects representatives in proportion to the votes cast by each party, no solution is in sight. Political gerrymandering, the drawing of districts to favor one party or the other, has some bearing on these problems, but the major reason for one-party dominant districts is that Democrats and Republicans tend to reside in different locations. Decennial redistricting reinforces this. That is why only about one out of ten seats in the U.S. House is truly competitive and why competitive districts in the states range from about 15 percent to slightly more than 50 percent. The only way to achieve competitiveness district by district would be to gerrymander in order to equalize Republican and Democratic voters, a very unlikely political prospect, or to resettle populations, an even unlikelier one.

Descriptively, as well as politically, legislatures today are more representative. The demographic characteristics of lawmakers in Congress and state legislatures still do not mirror the publics they represent. They are more elitist in several important respects, such as educational level attained, occupational status, and income. But contemporary legislative bodies come closer to resembling the publics they represent than in earlier years. Occupationally, legislators have a greater variety of backgrounds. For example, lawyers once were the largest occupational grouping, but they no longer dominate the way they did. Although they still constitute over half the members of the U.S. Senate, their percentage in the U.S. House is down to 37 (from 57 in 1953). In state legislatures on average only about one out of six members is an attorney instead of one out of four as was formerly the case.

Racial minorities have increased their representation at both the national and state levels. In 1953 only two African Americans served in the U.S. House and none in the U.S. Senate; in 2001 forty-one were members of the House, but there were no African American senators. Only two African Americans have served as senators in more than one hundred years, and as of 2001, racial minorities in the Senate included only one Japanese American, one person of Hawaiian descent, and one Native American. Hispanics have also gained representation in the House, increasing from one in 1953 to nineteen in 2001. At the state level minorities have gained a larger foothold, particularly African Americans in southern legislatures and Hispanics in Arizona, California, Florida, New Mexico, and Texas. In the early 1970s the percentage of blacks in state legislatures was 3 percent. Thirty years later that percentage had doubled, to 6 percent. As of 2001 there were approximately 600 African American and 200 Hispanic state legislators.

The most substantial change in the composition of legislative bodies has been the increase in the number of women. As of 2001, thirteen women were U.S. senators (including both senators from California, Maine, and Washington), and sixty were members of the House, instead of one and twelve, respectively, in 1953. Women constitute 22 percent of the 7,424 senators and representatives in the fifty states, whereas in 1969–1970 they made up only 4 percent of the total. Today, women total one-third or more of the members of legislatures in Arizona, Colorado, Nevada, Oregon, and Washington and from one-quarter to one-third in California, Connecticut, Delaware, Hawaii, Illinois, Kansas, Maine, Maryland, Minnesota, New Hampshire, New Mexico, and Vermont.

Without question, the growth in the number of women and minority members has changed legislative agendas and has resulted in new blocs and coalitions advancing different ideas.

Capacity

For some time now Congress has had the capacity or wherewithal to do its job. For a half century Congress has been a full-time, professional legislature that is in session year-round. Members have access to information, staff resources (totaling more than 23,000 people), special agencies and support facilities, and the latest in computer technology. State legislatures, however, did not develop their capacity until the 1970s and 1980s, during a national modernization movement. Some states—such as California, Michigan, New York, and Pennsylvania—added substantial capacity; others—such as Delaware, New Hampshire, South Dakota, Vermont, and Wyoming—added capacity in more modest increments. But gains were made just about everywhere:

1. Legislatures and their members increased the amount of time they devoted to the job of lawmaking, including constituent outreach and service. Some removed constitutional provisions that restricted the length of their sessions; others extended their regular sessions; many went from biennial to annual sessions; and nearly all those that were in session for only two, three, or four months a year increased the amount of work they did during interim periods, as we reported in Chapter 4. By the 1990s, even in states with citizen legislatures, the average member was devoting one-quarter to one-third of his or her time to legislative work, and in states with professional legislatures, the average member was spending two-thirds to full time on such work.

2. Legislatures provided for adequate space and facilities for committees, individual members, and staff. Capitol buildings were renovated, legislative office buildings were constructed, electronic data processing was installed. In the 1960s offices for rank-and-file legislators were rare; today, except in a handful of states where space is still extraordinarily limited, members have their own office or share one in the capitol. A fair number have offices in their districts. Even more important, rooms have been set aside for standing committees to hold hearings, meet, and vote on bills.

3. Legislatures made improvements in their operations. Management committees were established, bill deadlines were instituted, and consent calendars were adopted for noncontroversial bills. Efficiency was enhanced, at least to some degree, in an institution that can never be fully efficient because it has to resolve conflict.

4. Legislatures strengthened their standing committees by reducing their numbers, defining their jurisdictions, and refashioning their procedures. Committee assignments became more limited, so that members could focus on and develop expertise in one or a few areas. In one form or another, committees continued exploring policy issues during periods between legislative sessions.

5. Probably most important to capacity building, legislatures increased the number and competence of legislative staff. Staff were assigned to leaders, party caucuses, standing committees, and in some states to individual members. In the 1960s and 1970s the expansion of staff was marked; it slowed in the 1980s; and the growth ceased in the 1990s. Legislatures today vary greatly in the size and allocation of professional staff (see Table 9-1), but everywhere the fiscal, policy, legal, and bill-drafting assistance that staff professionals provide is indispensable to the operations of the legislature.

The question is often asked if more professionalized legislatures, that is, those with greater capacity, are better than legislatures with fewer resources. It is a question that is difficult to answer. Usually people want to know if the professionalized legislatures produce better policy, but as we have already pointed out that is impossible to judge and not our focus here. From the standpoint of the legislative institution, all we can say in answer to this

Table 9-1 Permanent Staff of U.S. Congress and State Legislatures, 1979–1996

State	1979	1988	1996
Alabama	200	339	316
Alaska	116	251	237
Arizona	280	323	472
Arkansas	230	250	292
California	1,760	2,865	2,506
Colorado	173	189	213
Connecticut	225	400	446
Delaware	32	49	58
Florida	1,095	1,581	1,896
Georgia	275	466	511
Hawaii	150	151	256
Idaho	55	51	61
Illinois	984	1,066	969
Indiana	138	171	183
Iowa	93	163	180
Kansas	126	117	121
Kentucky	135	216	317
Louisiana	327	360	419
Maine	46	138	133
Maryland	328	447	505
Massachusetts	595	782	—
Michigan	1,047	1,287	1,359
Minnesota	420	602	638
Mississippi	130	124	132
Missouri	212	368	476
Montana	108	128	119
Nebraska	182	199	202
Nevada	85	115	170
New Hampshire	84	120	139
New Jersey	492	780	1,465
New Mexico	40	49	49
New York	1,600	3,580	3,461
North Carolina	90	118	168
North Dakota	26	31	31
Ohio	390	524	552
Oklahoma	101	171	260
Oregon	173	288	240
Pennsylvania	1,430	1,984	2,682

(Table continues)

Table 9-1 (continued)

State	1979	1988	1996
Rhode Island	81	153	216
South Carolina	146	251	269
South Dakota	75	67	60
Tennessee	270	175	213
Texas	986	1,460	1,964
Utah	71	86	111
Vermont	34	34	35
Virginia	306	191	468
Washington	370	582	535
West Virginia	124	126	158
Wisconsin	476	568	691
Wyoming	18	19	18
50 State Totals	16,930	24,555	26,972
U.S. Congress	26,768	28,031	24,713

Sources: National Conference of State Legislatures, www.ncsl.org; Norman J. Ornstein, Thomas E. Mann, and Michael J. Malbin, *Vital Statistics on Congress, 1999–2000* (Washington, D.C.: AEI Press, 2000).

question is that legislatures in larger population, socially complex, high-government service, and large budget states need greater resources if they are to compete as coequal branches of government. The legislative capacity needed by Congress or states like California and New York is different from what is required by New Hampshire or North Dakota. For the most part the levels of capacity and professionalization chosen by the various state legislatures match the size and complexity of their populations and governments.

Ironically, perhaps, the very capacity of Congress and state legislatures poses problems. Legislators may be superb policy wonks, political operatives, and constituency ombudsmen, but many are not trained as managers. Consequently, some don't adequately concern themselves with management issues like structure, facilities, or staff. Management problems occur, conveying to the public images of mismanagement, waste, and inefficiencies. Accurate or not, the images persist. The American public's regard for professional legislatures, one of the products of capacity building, is not positive. Indeed, the 1992 initiative in California that imposed term limits also forced the legislature to cut back on its expenditures, and the result was a downsizing of staff.

Expertise that is encouraged by the continuity of a legislator's service and specialization on standing committees also poses a challenge for contemporary legislatures. Congressional committees no longer have the clout they once did, and the current Republican majority in the House has limited committee chairs to six years. Both senators and representatives are somewhat less likely to specialize nowadays than before. At the state level, specialization was seldom as finely honed as in the U.S. House, and in term-limited states substantial expertise in particular policy areas is unlikely to develop. Members will serve for shorter periods of time and will be more inclined to move from one position to another, as they try to achieve leadership positions before their terms expire.

Staffing also poses problems. Staffing patterns vary among the states. A few legislatures may have enough staff; the majority are still probably understaffed. Some legislatures rely most heavily on partisan staffs, others on nonpartisan staffs. Some staff organizations are relatively centralized, others relatively decentralized. Each staffing pattern has its limitations. But perhaps the major problem is that the recruitment and retention of able professionals—whether partisan or nonpartisan—is seldom easy.

Integrity

Despite what Americans tend to believe, the integrity of members of Congress and state legislatures is higher today than it used to be. The overwhelming majority of members are honest and public spirited. This is largely because behavior that once was tolerated in American politics is no longer condoned. We expect more of our elected political officials, have set high standards for their ethical behavior, and keep raising the bar that they have to jump over in order to pass ethical muster.

Since Watergate, congressional scandals have occurred regularly, albeit perhaps on a diminishing basis. The banner year was 1976. Rep. Robert L. F. Sikes and Wayne Hays were rebuked for their behavior. Then in the so-called Koreagate scandal, accusations were many but convictions and reprimands were few. In 1980 and 1981 six House members and one senator were convicted of accepting bribes in an FBI sting operation known as Abscam. In 1989 Speaker Jim Wright had to resign from the House under a cloud and in 1991, in the case of the so-called Keating Five, five senators were investigated and then cleared by the Senate Ethics Committee, although they were taken to task for poor judgment or, in one case, improper conduct. Since then, members of both the House and the Senate have been investigated and charged with improprieties.

State legislative ethics cases were also prominent in the 1970s and 1980s, with FBI stings in California, Kentucky, and South Carolina and an undercover operation by local authorities in Arizona. Since then Florida, Massachusetts, Michigan, Minnesota, New Jersey, New Mexico, Ohio, Pennsylvania, and Wisconsin also have had to deal with legislative scandals.

At both the congressional and state levels, the ethics of members today are highly regulated. Nearly everywhere, in addition to laws prohibiting bribery and extortion, legislators are required to file a financial disclosure statement that details their investments and the sources of their income. Although members of Congress are not permitted to earn outside income, legislators in all fifty states are able to supplement their public salaries with outside earnings. Neither members of Congress nor legislators in about one-third of the states are permitted to accept honoraria for speeches to private groups on matters pertaining to their public office. Depending on the particular state, legislators must disclose gifts they receive or are limited as to the dollar value of gifts they can accept. Some states have a "no cup of coffee" law, which bars legislators from accepting anything at all.

Conflict-of-interest regulations also shape the lives of state legislators. Because most members have outside employment, the danger exists that their private occupations will conflict with their public duties. They have to be eternally careful, not only of conflicts but of the appearance of conflict. In most places they may recuse themselves from voting on an issue, if they feel conflicted. Since people just about everywhere prefer citizen legislators to full-time, professional ones, there is probably no way to eliminate entirely the possibility of conflict of interest in the states.

Ethics problems are endemic in legislative bodies, as they are elsewhere. Legislatures have devised ways designed to raise the consciousness of members on questions involving ethics. In Congress and the states, codes of ethics set general standards. Some states offer ethics training for members, and a few states even require it. Maryland provides private counseling in which members review their outside involvements with a staff attorney on a confidential basis. Nowadays, when ethical complaints are filed against members, legislatures undertake serious investigations, hold hearings, decide on the allegations, and mete out punishment. In recent years legislative ethics committees in Congress and the states have done yeoman service in assessing the behavior of members. In a number of instances, these committees have recommended sanctions—even expulsion—that have been adopted by the full bodies. Members have not been soft in judging their colleagues.

Probably the most serious contemporary challenge to the integrity of legislators and legislatures is campaign finance. Americans distrust a system in which elected officials and political parties accept campaign contributions, especially large ones. They feel that contributors get special treatment in return for their money. The media, public interest groups like Common Cause, and outcries by elected public officials themselves feed this distrust. Everyone points a finger at the "corrupt" system and speculates on the intentions of contributors. But there are few accusations that specific individuals gave their votes or rendered other favors in return for contributions. There are very few indictments and even fewer convictions. Research by political scientists, moreover, has not established a causal relationship between contributor money and legislator behavior. Indeed, it would be exceedingly difficult to do so.

Whatever campaign finance laws are devised, money will continue to play a role in elections—and so will those who fund and otherwise support campaigns. Individuals and groups that make campaign contributions usually give to legislators who are already on their side. Labor tends to support Democratic candidates; business, Republican candidates. Their messages and the messages of the candidates they support are not terribly different. And they ought to be heard by the public. Campaign contributions enable the debate to take place, and where a contest exists both sides get heard.

Even if money were totally removed from the system, members of Congress and state legislators would still be under pressures of all types and from every kind of source. How they balance these pressures is a continuing issue—and an ethical issue—for them.

Transparency

Congress and state legislatures are more transparent than ever. In fact, they are among the most open institutions in American society, much more so than the executive, the courts, organized religion, business, or labor. Citizens today have access to enormous amounts of information about both their legislators and their legislatures.

Probably most important, the positions legislators take on issues are recorded and available to the public. Years ago many of the critical votes in the U.S. Senate and House, as well as in state legislatures, were nonrecord votes. That is, they were voice or division votes that were totaled but not recorded by member. The public had no information as to how each member voted. Today the votes that senators, representatives, and state legislators cast in committee or on the floor on issues of any substance are on the record. In 1998, for example, U.S. senators voted 318 times and U.S. representatives voted 547 times on final passage of bills, not to mention being recorded on many committee votes. State legislators, too, go on record each year hundreds of times, on both major and minor issues. Members of legislative bodies cannot escape their voting records, which naturally become ammunition for opponents who want to replace them in public office.

People have access not only to information on where their legislators stand on issues but also on how they earn their living, which lobbyists entertain them, and what individuals and groups contribute to their election campaigns. As far as incumbents are concerned, voters have far more information available to them than they can ever use in making their choices.

Legislatures themselves are also open, not entirely but to a considerable extent. Citizens can find agendas, calendars, bill status, and analyses on legislative Web pages. They can view C-Span coverage of proceedings on the floor and in selected committees in the Congress, and for about one-third of the legislatures they can take in parts of the process on similar channels. They can observe much of the process firsthand, from the senate or house gallery or in a committee room. In some places they are even welcome to sessions of the legislative party caucuses.

Despite "sunshine" or open meetings laws, however, key aspects of the legislative process still take place outside of public view and outside of the press's view. That is because so much of the legislative process goes on outside of committee rooms and legislative chambers, as members deal with one another informally and on the run. Moreover, getting support for measures and building consensus on the one hand, or organizing opposition on the other, involves deliberation, negotiation, and strategizing that are unlikely to proceed in public view. Straight talk and bargaining require some wiggle room for participants; it is too politically perilous for legislators to compromise when they are fully exposed and can have their bargaining positions taken out of context and used in a campaign against them. But working things out, shielded from public view, tends to feed suspicions that ordinary citizens are being sold out behind closed doors. The truth is that nobody is being sold out, and the results of negotiations are always made public for everybody to see.

Demands for more openness and more information are unrelenting, although they are far more likely to be made by the media than by the average voter. The irony is that people currently have much more information available to them than they will ever use. They have what ought to be most important for their voting decision: the party of the incumbents; their voting records on significant issues; and the endorsements of key interest groups.

Competitiveness

If competitive politics—in which each side has a reasonable chance to win—are of value, as political scientists and political commentators believe, then legislative systems have made enormous progress. Competitiveness may not be a principal characteristic of politics at the level of individual candidacies, but it certainly dominates at the national and state levels, as has already been shown in Chapters 1 and 8.

For the large majority of incumbents who run, the competitive aspect of their elections is the possibility (however remote) that they could lose. Psychologically, incumbents feel unsafe whatever their previous margins of electoral victory. Individual candidates naturally want to win their elections, and they want their parties to win too so that they can be part of the majority rather than part of the minority. The majority party organizes the chambers, holds all or most of the committee chair positions, sets the agenda, and has a better chance than the minority of having its proposals enacted into law.

Thus, each party wants to win a majority and thereby control the senate or the house. With control goes the power to get things done, and the two parties want to do different things. They no longer offer the choice between Tweedledum and Tweedledee (if, indeed, they ever did), which is not much of a choice at all. Generally speaking, Democrats and Republicans differ philosophically and support contrasting policy positions. The Democrats are for more government, the Republicans are for less; Republicans want to return tax revenue to the taxpayers, Democrats want to spend some of the money; Republicans would let the market operate freely, Democrats are less reluctant to guide the market with regulation; Republicans are friendlier to business, Democrats are friendlier to labor. The differences are consequential, not simply "political." As liberal representative Barney Frank, D-Mass., portrayed the division in a 2001 *New York Times* story: "This is about real stuff. This isn't about personalities. This isn't some high school dance."

The parties, moreover, represent distinct bases of interest group support and distinct ideological advocates on the right and left, all of whom tend to push for harder and clearer lines between the two sides. Although ordinary voters are not nearly as politicized as the Democratic and Republican core constituencies, they too identify with one of the two parties and they too cast partisan votes in elections for Congress and state legislatures. The *National Journal* in 2001 called the United States "the 49 percent nation," since in the past three presidential elections and last three House elections each party has won 48 or 49 percent of the vote, with neither winning 50 percent or over.

The tendency has been for the two parties to become more ideologically distinct. At the national level, the Democrats still have conservatives and the

Republicans still have moderates, but in many places the centers of gravity are more distant from one another than earlier. Finding consensus within each party and dissensus between the two is easier today.

The large majority of issues with which any legislative body deals do not cause partisan division. Democrats and Republicans are apt to join together in support or opposition, and partisans may be found in both camps on legislation. But on major issues—especially taxes and appropriations and those relating to the role of government versus that of the marketplace—party voting is becoming more common, having risen in the past twenty years and peaking in the Gingrich Congress of 1995. By the 1990s, for instance, from half to two-thirds of roll calls in the U.S. Senate were party-line votes, with a majority of Democrats opposing a majority of Republicans. Nearly all the votes since 1994 on the adoption of the budget resolution in the Senate have found virtually all Democratic senators opposing virtually all the Republican senators. The same has been true on U.S. House votes on adoption of the budget resolution. The notable exception was in 1998 when President Clinton was able to put together a bipartisan deal.

Partisan division appears to be increasing at the state legislative level as well. Omnibus budget and tax bills find the parties opposed to one another in many places. Ohio provides an example. For years the majority party in the Ohio senate and house was able to get at least some minority votes for its budget bill. In 2001 the Republican majorities could not get a single Democrat to vote for the budget.

Competitiveness is highly regarded in America, partisanship is not. Partisanship, however, is an almost inevitable by-product of competitiveness, especially if differences are profound and the stakes are high. Partisanship permeates the legislative process. Obstruction and incivility become more common, as in the contemporary U.S. Senate and U.S. House. Each side appeals beyond the body to the public in order to gain partisan advantage. Message politics is not simply posturing and publicity. As described by congressional scholar Lawrence C. Evans, it is a method by which "[c]ongressional leaders seek to integrate the legislative agenda, party communications and campaign tactics, and the grassroots endeavors of key advocacy groups into a single broad strategy aimed at influencing the policy debate and increasing voter support for their respective parties." Senators, like House members, use message politics to gain partisan advantage on the big issues for both policy and reelection reasons.

The election campaign and legislative policymaking are also linked in the competitive states of the nation. The legislature, as well as the terrain outside, is now an arena for contesting elections. An increasing amount of what the legislative parties do in senates and houses is governed by the upcoming election. During the legislative process itself each party attempts to put the other on the wrong side of a vote on a popular issue. The minority, in particular, raises issues and introduces amendments with electoral fallout in mind. Indeed, the principal role of the minority, in many legislative bodies today, is to "throw bombs" in the hope of destroying the majority's prospect of winning the next election.

Congressional and presidential scholars have dubbed the constant calculation of political advantage in every policy decision the "permanent campaign." The transformation of legislative parties and legislative leaders into campaign organizations and campaign managers has had negative consequences for representative democracy. People feel that the system has become too politicized. Perhaps it has. Nonpartisan motivations are not trusted; bipartisanship is more difficult to achieve; and civility, as well as collegiality, suffers. But competition is intense and battles are waged. Voters can choose between the two sides.

Participation

Participation encompasses not only voting but also working on campaigns, giving money to candidates, and acting as an advocate for an interest or idea. Perhaps ironically, although voting in elections has declined, other types of participation by groups and their members in the legislative process have increased. The involvement of interest groups in lawmaking in Congress and the states continues to be a vital part of the process. The difference today is that the number and diversity of groups trying to affect public policy have expanded. There are so many special interests, covering every conceivable issue, that the explosion of advocacy, in the language of Jonathan Rauch, has led to a system of "hyperpluralism," and not just pluralism as in the past.

No longer do a few groups dominate, as earlier; now many groups share power. Teachers today are influential in nearly all the states. But although they can derail many measures that threaten their interests, they are still not able to advance their agendas as far as they would like. In part, that is because teachers like other groups have opposition. The fact is that few issues are advanced by one group that are not opposed by another group. Not infrequently, impressive coalitions form on both sides. So today, participation, like electoral politics, is a highly competitive enterprise.

The resource base of participating groups has also expanded. Money, of course, counts, because it helps build capacity. Political, organizational, and managerial skills promote effectiveness. Size and geographical dispersion are probably as important as anything else. Large numbers of members in every state and congressional and legislative district are impossible to ignore. A group's image or standing with the press or public counts. If it is critical to the national or state economy, it will have an advantage. Also important are the cohesiveness of a group's membership, its dedication to a cause, its ability to form coalitions, and the specificity of its agenda. In addition, the nature of the issue, the composition of the legislature, and the offensive or defensive posture of the group come into play. Some groups enjoy some of these resources; other groups enjoy others. Some are very well endowed; others are not so well endowed.

The ways in which interest groups exploit their resources also vary. No longer is advocacy or lobbying primarily an inside game based on social or political relationships or who has contributed to whom. Recently, lobbying has evolved into something of an outside game, employing grassroots techniques, drawing on organizational memberships, and engaging in public relations and media appeals. Actively or passively, more people are involved in advocacy than ever before. And there are many, many people for groups to draw on, since the large majority of Americans belong to one or another special interest group and many belong to more than one.

Participation by so many groups has helped open up the system. Yet, interest group participation is problematic in several respects. First, people have the impression that "special interests" are those other interests, not their own. They feel shut out, although they are not. Perhaps this is partly because more extreme groups and more extreme views seem to dominate the debate within the parties and on the legislative stage. Second, in a system of "hyperpluralism," the chances of stalemate are heightened, especially if opposing views are rigidly held. Third, the opposite of sharp disagreement and stalemate can also raise concern. Suppose two sides get together and agree on a measure. Often legislatures will defer to compromises worked out by all the involved groups; yet the larger public's interest—albeit a less direct interest—may not seem to be well served. Fourth, despite the pluralism of the system, not all groups are equal and some are more powerful than others. Large stakeholders usually have more to say about public policy than do small stakeholders. There is always something about which to be concerned in a democratic system. Such concern is constantly expressed, and whether the system is working well or not it is almost constantly undergoing reform.

Internal Democracy

Most people believe that a legislature ought to be a democratic institution, composed of members with an equal say over matters. Indeed, legislative bodies have always been relatively democratic. Every member has a vote in the chamber and an electoral constituency outside. But lately, legislatures have become even more democratic, in that internal power is more dispersed than it once was.

Take the U.S. Senate, which in the 1950s was a clubby, inward-looking body. Power was unequally distributed, concentrated in the committee leaders. It became dispersed in the mid-1960s, with subcommittee leaders sharing in power, and by the 1970s the Senate was an individualistic body. Today any member can bring the Senate to a halt by denying a request for "unanimous consent." The use of extended debate has always been a threat, but the actual use of the filibuster has been relatively rare. In the 1950s about one filibuster occurred in each Congress; in the 1990s the average was twenty-eight. Individual senators, moreover, can offer many nongermane amendments on the floor and can force the body to take up hot-button issues. Leaders serve the members, and not the other way around.

The U.S. House has also witnessed a dispersal of internal power. The so-called barons—the chairs of the standing committees—dominated in the 1950s and 1960s, but the Democratic caucus in the mid-1970s pushed through a series of democratizing reforms: committee chairs had to be nominated by a steering and policy committee, led by the Speaker; a secret ballot would be cast by members of the caucus; and a series of measures ensured the power of subcommittees while distributing chairmanships widely among Democratic members. For a brief period, following the 1994 elections, with the Republican majority and the Gingrich speakership, strong leadership returned to the House. It did not last long, however.

The dispersion of power in state legislatures is just as noteworthy. Newer generations of members are far more independent than older ones. Connected as they are to their constituencies, members maintain independence of leadership. Each has his or her own career and personal agenda, which leaders are obliged to respect. Nowadays the rank and file, as well as leaders, have information and staff assistance to call upon. Every majority-party legislator can expect a meaningful committee assignment, and in many states appropriations committees have been enlarged so that more legislators now have some say on the budget. In Utah, for instance, every legislator serves on the committee that oversees the budget.

The presiding officers can no longer depend on their followers. Too many times, leaders have been ousted by members of their own party or by a bipartisan coalition. Even the legendary Willie Brown, the former Speaker of the California Assembly, never forgot that he served at the pleasure of the Democratic caucus. His biographer, James Richardson, recounts the many times Brown would assert he had forty-one votes (out of eighty in the assembly), and with forty-one he could continue as Speaker. But he wouldn't have the forty-one unless his Democratic colleagues were satisfied with his leadership.

The tenure of today's leaders—whether at the national or state level—will be shorter than that of past leaders. Members want to move up the ladder and are unlikely to reelect a leader for twenty, fifteen, or even ten years. In term-limited states, moreover, no one serves in the senate or house longer than twelve, eight, or in a few cases six years. That means that the term of leaders in these states will probably run no longer than four years and possibly only two.

Internal democracy offers greater opportunity for members, at least for majority-party members. Some would still argue that leadership in states like Georgia, New York, and Texas is too strong and power is too centralized. No doubt negotiations in many states on major issues, such as the budget, are conducted among top legislative leaders and the governor. Nevertheless, the real problem may be that leaders are too weak to do their job. The challenges they face are weighty. They have to oversee the management of the house in which they serve and advocate the interests of the legislature as the principal institution of representative democracy. Not least among their jobs is that of finding common ground, facilitating compromise, forging consensus, and enabling the legislature to locate and work its will (whether that will is partisan or bipartisan). Without reasonably strong leadership all this is extremely difficult to do. It is difficult enough to do with strong leadership.

Responsiveness

Legislative bodies today are taking on issues that were rarely addressed before. Many of these issues—for example, abortion and gun control—are very contentious. But they are tougher to duck now than in the past. Even after settlements are reached, these issues will not go away. They persist year after year, as each side renews the battle on legislative terrain.

Not only do legislative bodies face up to tough issues, they are also expected to solve them—that is, "they should pass laws," according to political scientist Barbara Sinclair, "that deal promptly and effectively with pressing national problems" and at the same time they should reflect the will of the people. Americans insist that their legislatures should get something done, but what they mean by that is something they favor. Alas, the problem is that people are divided in what they favor.

It is impossible, of course, for legislatures to please everyone, however responsive legislatures try to be. They respond to the needs of interest groups. They respond to the pleas of ordinary citizens. They respond to what appear to be national problems. Yet, different legislators, belonging to different parties and with different core constituencies, respond differently. Agreement simply cannot be taken for granted.

Joseph Cooper points out how the framers saw the need in a representative democracy for a balance between independence and responsiveness. That balance has shifted heavily to the responsiveness side. Along with partisanship and divided government, according to Cooper, this makes the passage of landmark legislation that attempts to resolve tough problems even more difficult than it was earlier. Although action will take place, he grants, it "will be watered down and tied more closely than in the past to sheerly political determinations of whether cooperation for the purpose of winning favor with the public or intransigence for the purpose of casting blame on opponents best serves to maximize partisan advantage." As a result, the effectiveness of both bargaining and deliberation as a means of resolving conflict declines, all of which militates against the success of representative government.

Most Americans think that Congress and state legislatures are still too closed, too autocratic, too unresponsive. They certainly would endorse the increased openness, internal democracy, and responsiveness of Congress and state legislatures that have already taken place. Yet, as the system has been changing, it may have changed too much; it may no longer be in balance.

The idea of representative democracy, according to the constitutional framers, was to balance the need for consent with the need for deliberation. They believed, writes Cooper, that "consent should be based on reason and deliberation, not merely the summation of wills, and that a legislature was essential to attain the levels of consent and deliberation necessary for government in the public interest." In order to fulfill their responsibilities, legislatures require some measure of autonomy, that is, room in which to do their job. Boundaries used to separate legislatures from their environments, even though the demands of constituents and groups always made their way across the border. But the distance between legislatures and their publics has narrowed, so that little space currently separates them. The press is more intrusive than it used to be, and directly or indirectly, people are in the legislature's face. Electronic democracy and teledemocracy are at hand. Legislative autonomy is minimal.

Today, Morris P. Fiorina writes, "the Congress is less insulated, and the boundary between the environment and the institution has grown fuzzy." The same applies to the states. The environment exercises far greater pressure on legislators than the norms and the practices of their institutions. The legislature as an institution is weaker than it used to be, and that itself may help erode representative democracy.

In Sum

Problems associated with the legislative process continue. In a democratic system such as ours, that can be anticipated. Problems simply have to be worked on constantly. Campaign finance and ethical conduct always require attention and tinkering. Fair and adequate representation has to be assured. Opportunities for participation need broadening. Sometimes partisan politics have to be contained. The list of problems goes on. Despite the imperfection of the system, Congress and state legislatures have improved over the past fifty years. They have gotten better, not worse.

Given the performance of Congress and state legislatures, it would seem timely to take stock of what we have and how it measures up in fact, not merely in the rhetoric of reform, media, or campaigns. In any case, what are the alternatives?

Sources and Suggested Reading

This chapter draws on several works, all of which provide penetrating analyses of Congress and state legislatures. On Congress, see especially *Congress Reconsidered*, 7th ed., ed. Lawrence C. Dodd and Bruce I. Oppenheimer (Washington, D.C.: CQ Press, 2001). In this volume are chapters by Barbara Sinclair, "The New World of U.S. Senators"; Dodd and Oppenheimer, "A House Divided: The Struggle for Partisan Control, 1994–2000"; Morris P. Fiorina, "*Keystone* Reconsidered"; Lawrence C. Evans, "Committees, Leaders, and Message Politics"; and Joseph Cooper, "The Twentieth-Century Congress." Also important is Barbara Sinclair's

Unorthodox Lawmaking: New Legislative Processes in the U.S. Congress, 2d ed. (Washington, D.C.: CQ Press, 2000). On state legislatures, the most comprehensive coverage of their changing nature since the 1960s is in Alan Rosenthal's *The Decline of Representative Democracy* (Washington, D.C.: CQ Press, 1998).

The opening reference in the chapter to "disaffected democracies" is from Robert D. Putnam, ed., *Disaffected Democracies: What's Troubling the Trilateral Countries?* (Princeton: Princeton University Press, 2000). The best theoretical treatment of representation is by Hanna Fenichel Pitkin, *The Concept of Representation* (Berkeley and Los Angeles: University of California Press, 1967).

Congressional ethics are dealt with in Michael J. Malbin, "Legislative Ethics," in *Encyclopedia of the American Legislative System,* ed. Joel H. Silbey (New York: Scribner's, 1994), and in Dennis F. Thompson, *Ethics in Congress: From Individual to Institutional Corruption* (Washington, D.C.: Brookings Institution, 1995). Alan Rosenthal covers state legislative ethics in *Drawing the Line: Legislative Ethics in the States* (Lincoln: University of Nebraska Press, 1996) and *The Ethics Process in State Legislatures: Disciplining Members in a Public Forum* (Denver: National Conference of State Legislatures and State Legislative Leaders Foundation, April 1999). Another important work is Jonathan Rauch's *Demosclerosis: The Silent Killer of American Government* (New York: Times Books, 1994).

The quotation on message politics in the House is from the Evans chapter in Dodd and Oppenheimer, *Congress Reconsidered.* The quotations in the section "Responsibility and Responsiveness" are from Sinclair's *Unorthodox Lawmaking* and Joseph Cooper's chapter in Dodd and Oppenheimer, *Congress Reconsidered.*

10

Representative Democracy Does Work

WE HAVE EXPLORED JUST how Americans regard representative democracy, how the framers of the U.S. Constitution intended it, and how Congress and state legislatures manifest it. The question that now needs to be addressed is, Does representative democracy work? The answer (no secret here) is yes, it works. But whether it works or not depends on the standards by which we assess it.

What Standards Should We Use?

If the standard is citizen satisfaction, the answer is that representative democracy does not work very well nowadays. As we have seen in Chapter 1 and throughout this book, Americans take a dim view of the politicians, politics, and processes that drive the political system in the nation and the states. As the aftermath of the terrorist attacks on America reveals, people love their country. In a time of national crisis they are positively disposed toward government. And they love democracy—but democracy as an abstraction, not as a concrete reality. That's because the actual practices of democracy involve conflict, proceed slowly, and require debate and compromise— none of which people appreciate. Most important, Americans believe politicians are self-serving; they don't trust them; they believe that politicians and special interests take advantage of them. Therefore, according to John R. Hibbing and Elizabeth Theiss-Morse in *Stealth Democracy*, Americans want democracy but do not want to have to put up with it.

Another standard might be how representative democracy in the United States compares with democratic systems in other places. The publics in advanced industrial democracies are no more positive about their systems than are Americans. In ten out of thirteen countries for which survey data are available confidence in parliament has declined, and in several cases the drop is pronounced. Concurrently, there is evidence of some decline in confidence in politicians. Institutions in a separation-of-powers system such as ours cannot easily be compared with institutions in a parliamentary system found in other democratic regimes. Nonetheless, it can be said that many of the developing democracies in Africa, Asia, Europe, and Latin America regard American legislatures with admiration. Parliamentarians from abroad are frequent visitors to Congress and state legislatures and try to model their institutions and processes after ours. They look to Congress and the states for technical assistance, and the United States has sent missions to many developing democracies. If emulation counts, then our system is doing pretty well.

Another standard that can be employed in assessing the U.S. Congress and state legislatures today is how they compare with those of the past. As we showed in Chapter 9, since the mid-1960s, immediately after the reapportionment revolution and at the beginning of the legislative modernization movement—legislatures have generally improved as political institutions in at least eight ways.

1. They are more representative, with substantially more women and racial minority members.
2. They have greater capacity—the wherewithal in staff and information—to do the job.
3. They have greater integrity and behave more ethically.

4. They are more transparent and open to public scrutiny.
5. They are more competitive, with either political party having the ability to win.
6. They are arenas for more widespread participation by groups and individuals.
7. They are more democratic internally, with opportunity and power dispersed among the members.
8. They are more responsive to the public.

Ironically, the success of legislatures may be inversely related to the way the public sees them. Legislatures may indeed be better, but they may look—or be made to look—worse.

Still another standard for assessment would be an absolute one. How well does the system work compared with an ideal system? The problem here, of course, is that not everyone would agree on what the ideal is. What, in short, is a *good* legislature? Democrats regard the good legislature as one controlled by Democrats; Republicans regard it as one controlled by Republicans. For advocates and interests the good legislature is one that satisfies—or comes close to satisfying—group demands. Political science has not really addressed the issue, but some students of the subject would insist that a legislature, in order to be effective, has to perform successfully certain requisite functions. If we could agree on these functions and find ways to evaluate them, it might be possible to make a reasonable judgment as to how good a legislature is. But, thus far, no such agreement exists.

What Are the Alternatives?

Representative democracy and state legislatures, as was pointed out in earlier chapters, do have problems. The system is flawed, imperfect. It is constantly changing. But as Winston Churchill commented about democracy in general, "It has been said that democracy is the worst form of government except all those other forms that have been tried from time to time." Accordingly, we might judge representative democracy, not only according to the standards mentioned above, but also as it compares with likely alternatives. In choosing between representative democracy on the one hand

and executive dominance or direct democracy on the other, which system do we prefer?

Executive Dominance

One alternative is executive dominance. Let the president or governor and the departments and agencies of the executive branch make, as well as administer, law. After all, presidents and governors are democratically elected either by the entire nation or the entire state and are easier to hold accountable than are legislatures. According to proponents of executive dominance, legislatures only get in the way of the good policy that emanates from the office of the chief executive.

Executive dominance is certainly not what the framers of state and federal constitutions had in mind. The system that they desired is based on a fear of concentrated power in any one place. It adheres to the principle of separated powers, whereby the executive, legislative, and judiciary are restricted in the power they can exercise independently of the other branches of government.

The weakening of executive power and the granting of power to the legislature and the people characterized the framing of the state constitutions in the 1776–1787 period. Typically, under the state constitutions that predated the U.S. Constitution, legislatures selected governors, who were limited to one term and denied veto power. Soon after, however, state constitutional framers changed direction, concluding that in a republican form of government the legislative branch had a natural tendency to exert control over other departments. The U.S. Constitution created an executive that could hold its own with the legislative branch. After the framing of the U.S. Constitution, the executive branch in the states, specifically governors, began to act as a check on legislative power.

In the nineteenth century, the executive gained power in relation to the legislature and by the twentieth century had carved out a distinct advantage. Since the 1950s Congress has been reasonably coequal to the president—sometimes somewhat more, sometimes somewhat less. But today the seesaw tilts to the president in the executive-legislative relationship. The very expansion of government has vested more decision making in the president and bureaucracy. As a consequence, according to Joseph Cooper, "Congress's role and power in relation to the presidency have declined." Certainly in times of crisis, whether military or economic, the president has been ascendant and Congress has followed his leadership.

State legislatures were generally subordinate to executives until the legislative modernization movement of the late 1960s and 1970s. The co-equality of the legislative branch was an assumed value of the modernization movement; greater legislative strength in relation to the executive was an objective. Building capacity—in time, staff, information, and facilities—was the means. The attainment of increased capacity probably fed the collective ego of the legislative institution. Because they had the wherewithal to do the job, legislators began to feel that they were up to the job. And the rhetoric of legislative independence encouraged them to act as if they were actually independent. Strengthened egos combined with legislative assertiveness and capacity made for a more balanced relationship between the two branches of government at the state level.

But even with the resurgence of legislatures, governors still have an advantage. The choice is theirs whether to use it or not. The bases of gubernatorial advantage over the legislature, as in the relationship of president to Congress, combine constitutional, statutory, institutional, and political elements and are manifested in the following ways.

Chief executives have the power to initiate policy. They do so through the state of the union (or state) message and special messages. Although Congress and state legislatures initiate policy on their own, they almost always deal with the president's or governor's agenda. The president formulates the nation's budget, and in most states the governor prepares the budget for the state. Congress and the state legislatures work from or proceed from the executive plan.

Chief executives are not only initiators, they are also rejecters. They can veto any bill the legislature passes, and in Congress and all but six states it takes an extraordinary majority to override such a veto. In forty-three states governors (but not the president) have authority to veto sections or items of appropriation bills, and in fifteen states they have a potent weapon in the conditional veto—a type of "if-then" statement that significantly limits legislative authority.

Chief executives have a strong hand in negotiating with the legislature. They can fulfill the needs of individual members, or they can deny individual members the appointments, projects, or pet bills they desire. They may also convey recognition, something prized by all legislators. Presidents and governors, as leaders of their political parties, command a degree of loyalty from legislators of their partisan persuasion. Legislative leaders serve, in part, as lieutenants to their party's executive leader. And if the president or governor plans to run for reelection at the head of the ticket, legislators have further incentive to make their party leader look good.

Presidents and governors have the advantage of unity. This unity, or even relative unity, as compared with the legislature, gives executives more power than perhaps anything else. There is one chief executive who speaks for the state (although in twenty states lieutenant governors are elected separately from governors and in most states the attorney general, secretary of state, and one or two other officials are also elected statewide, which gives them a constituency that matches the governor's in size). The president is the only official, other than the vice president whom he chooses for the ticket, who runs for office nationwide. Thus, the executive speaks with one voice. By contrast, the legislature speaks with a multiplicity of voices: Congress has 535 members and a legislature may have 100, 200, or more members (divided by party and chamber), each of whom speaks for his or her district. Because the chief executive is a single person, elected by all the people of the nation or state, and the legislature is a collection of individuals, each elected from a smaller district, executives are the ones who command the attention of the media. The availability of the electronic and print media affords the president and governors a "bully pulpit," which they can use to drum up public support for what they want to achieve in the legislature. The legislature is no match whatsoever for the chief executive in a battle, not if the media are the principal communicators of what is going on.

The president presumably represents the citizens of the entire nation. So too the governor responds to the needs of the state as a whole. But Republicans may not feel well represented by a Democratic president or governor, and Democrats may not feel well represented by a Republican chief executive. Those who voted for the losing candidate may also suffer from a sense of underrepresentation. The legislature offers alternatives for citizens who are not reconciled to an incumbent president or governor. It offers alternatives to minorities of all sorts. Moreover, lawmakers, unlike chief executives, provide access to government for citizens who want it. Imagine an ordinary citizen lining up an appointment with the president or even a governor. It does not take a leap of faith to realize how manageable it is for ordinary citizens to see their member of Congress or state legislator, either in the district or in the federal or state capitol.

Chief executives are already powerful figures. Congress is always engaged in an uphill battle for coequality, because of the dominant position of the modern presidency. Governors, too, have substantial power—more in some states than in others, as Table 10-1 indicates. The scores, compiled by Thad Beyle, are based on six measures of institutional power: tenure; appointment authority; number of other statewide elected officials; budget; veto authority; and party control. Surely, governors in Maryland, West Virginia, New York, Pennsylvania, and New Jersey are well positioned in regard to their legislatures. So are governors in most of the other states. Perhaps, governors in states such as Texas, North Carolina, and Rhode Island operate—at least comparatively speaking—at a slight disadvantage.

For those who prefer action to deliberation, negotiation, and compromise, enhanced executive power may be attractive. The executive can act more quickly and usually more decisively. After all, it is much easier for one individual to make a decision than it is for a whole group of individuals in the nation's senates and houses. For those who would rather see diverse values and interests taken into account, even if action is more labored, the legislature is a healthy check and balance. If deliberation, negotiation, and compromise are desired, legislatures are practically indispensable. Also, if consensus for a particular policy or outcome is to be forged, legislatures are much more effective than executives. Finally, as the constitutional framers pointed out, citizens who are wary of concentrated power in a democracy have strong reason to maintain an independent legislature. Executive dominance is by no means the preferred choice.

At the national level the president plays an even greater role than governors under normal conditions. On matters of foreign and defense policy, but not on matters of domestic policy, Congress nearly always operates in the shadow of the executive. And in a time of national crisis or emergency,

Table 10-1 The Power of Governors, 2001

State	Power rating	Rank	Rank in order by rating	
Alabama	3.2	36	1	Maryland
Alaska	3.8	11	1	West Virginia
Arizona	3.6	21	3	New York
Arkansas	3.1	39	4	Pennsylvania
California	3.5	28	4	Utah
Colorado	3.8	11	6	Hawaii
Connecticut	3.6	21	6	Michigan
Delaware	3.5	28	6	New Jersey
Florida	3.6	21	6	North Dakota
Georgia	3.2	36	6	Ohio
Hawaii	3.9	6	11	Alaska
Idaho	3.5	28	11	Colorado
Illinois	3.7	16	11	Iowa
Indiana	2.9	44	11	Nebraska
Iowa	3.8	11	11	South Dakota
Kansas	3.7	16	16	Illinois
Kentucky	3.7	16	16	Kansas
Louisiana	3.1	39	16	Kentucky
Maine	3.1	39	16	Montana
Maryland	4.3	1	16	Wisconsin
Massachusetts	3.6	21	21	Arizona
Michigan	3.9	6	21	Connecticut
Minnesota	3.4	31	21	Florida
Mississippi	3.3	33	21	Massachusetts
Missouri	3.4	31	21	Tennessee
Montana	3.7	16	21	Washington
Nebraska	3.8	11	21	Wyoming
Nevada	3.0	42	28	California
New Hampshire	2.8	46	28	Delaware
New Jersey	3.9	6	28	Idaho
New Mexico	3.3	33	31	Minnesota
New York	4.1	3	31	Missouri
North Carolina	2.9	44	33	Mississippi
North Dakota	3.9	6	33	New Mexico
Ohio	3.9	6	33	Virginia
Oklahoma	2.7	48	36	Alabama
Oregon	3.2	36	36	Georgia
Pennsylvania	4.0	4	36	Oregon

(Table continues)

Table 10-1 (continued)

State	Power rating	Rank	Rank in order by rating	
Rhode Island	2.6	50	39	Arkansas
South Carolina	2.8	46	39	Louisiana
South Dakota	3.8	11	39	Maine
Tennessee	3.6	21	42	Nevada
Texas	3.0	42	42	Texas
Utah	4.0	4	44	Indiana
Vermont	2.7	48	44	North Carolina
Virginia	3.3	33	46	New Hampshire
Washington	3.6	21	46	South Carolina
West Virginia	4.3	1	48	Oklahoma
Wisconsin	3.7	16	48	Vermont
Wyoming	3.6	21	50	Rhode Island
50 states	3.5			

Source: Thad Beyle, in Kendra A. Hovey and Harold A. Hovey, *CQ's State Finder, 2002* (Washington, D.C.: CQ Press, 2002).

Note: Ties in ranking reflect ties in actual values.

such as the war on terrorism, the power of the presidency expands further. In such circumstances collective leadership, such as the legislative branch can provide, is insufficient. As of this writing, in 2002, President George W. Bush leads the nation, and Congress reviews and supports administration proposals for conducting the war on terrorism, securing the homeland, and funding the enterprise. Congress is participating in the wartime agenda, albeit as a junior partner, but is ready to resume its more conventional role as a coequal branch when the emergency subsides.

Direct Democracy

Another alternative to representative democracy is direct democracy, a system that would allow people to vote directly on issues without the need for representatives to decide for them. Advocates of direct democracy want the people directly to exercise as much power in the government as possible.

Over the years a variety of proposals have been advanced to promote increased citizen participation and greater citizen deliberation, including national issue forums, policy juries, deliberative polls, public opinion polls and focus groups, and even choosing public officials by lot from the ranks of citizens.

More recently, technology in the form of electronic media is bringing the United States closer to direct democracy. In his 1992 presidential campaign, Ross Perot advanced the idea of electronic plebiscites on important issues. With instantaneous reporting of electronic referendums of voters in their districts and the likelihood that the results would be reported in the press, many representatives would be hard-pressed to ignore whatever the predominant opinion happens to be that day. An election opponent could make a lot out of a representative's defiance of a majority in the district. Some representatives would be happy to be taken off the hook. "You can ask them," one Florida house member said facetiously, " 'I have to vote on Thursday, what would you like me to do?' " Under such a scenario, legislators would become agents of their constituency, and the legislature would become the reactor to successive public opinion majorities.

Dick Morris, in his book *Vote.com,* regards direct democracy as both inevitable and desirable. It is his view that even though people are too turned-off to vote to elect public officials, they will happily vote to tell public officials what to do. "We are going to take to this Internet and tell our representative what to do whenever we damn well feel like it," Morris predicts. Not everyone, of course, has equal access to the Internet. The affluent and the young are much more likely to be connected than the poor and the old.

The nation has been "moving away from a reliance on the collective judgment of its elected representatives toward letting the voters assert their sovereignty directly," observes a reporter for the *National Journal.* The losers in this movement are the traditional institutions that have been the main intermediaries between the government and its citizens. These include political parties, unions, and civic associations. The techies refer to this phenomenon as "disintermediation," the cutting out of the middleman, as has happened in e-commerce. It is these intermediaries, however, that afford citizens opportunities to join with like-minded others and participate in the political enterprise.

Table 10-2 Initiative States Ranked in Order of Use, 1990–2001

State	Year initiative adopted	Number on ballot 1990–2001
Oregon	1902	75
California	1911	66
Colorado	1910	44
Washington	1912	39
Arizona	1910	28
Massachusetts	1918	24
North Dakota	1914	19
Nevada	1904	17
Alaska	1959	16
Maine	1908	14
Missouri	1906	13
South Dakota	1898	13
Montana	1904	12
Nebraska	1912	12
Florida	1972	10
Arkansas	1909	8
Idaho	1912	8
Michigan	1908	8
Ohio	1912	8
Oklahoma	1907	8
Wyoming	1968	8
Utah	1900	5
Mississippi	1992	2
Illinois	1970	0

Source: National Conference of State Legislatures, www.ncsl.org.

The initiative, a reform introduced in the Progressive era early in the twentieth century, illustrates how direct democracy can work in practice. Currently, twenty-four states permit citizens to vote on a proposition through an initiative process that bypasses the legislative process. The states have varying requirements for initiatives, such as the number of voters' signatures that have to be collected to put the issue on the ballot and the percentage of this vote needed for adoption. The initiative has been used extensively in Arizona, California, Colorado, Oregon, and Washington (see Table 10-2), and its use overall has been increasing.

The initiative that gave rise to the modern era was Proposition 13, adopted by the voters of California in 1978. In limiting the extent to which property taxes could be raised, the initiative had a profound impact on the revenue structure of the state. Since then, California has been the country's most visible battleground for initiative campaigns, sometimes with one coalition of interests battling another. In 1988, for example, on one side the insurance industry had three initiatives on the ballot and on the other side lawyers had one. Between them the antagonists spent more than $82 million on the campaign. In 1996 the same groups clashed again, at a cost of $25 million, but all three measures that were sponsored in that battle failed. Other California initiatives have dealt with more ideological matters, such as an anti-immigration initiative and an anti–affirmative action initiative, both of which passed.

Or take Oregon, for instance. In the period from 1978 to 1998, ninety-seven initiatives were on the ballot, an average of nine per election. In the 2000 general election, Oregon citizens had to decide on twenty-six ballot measures (more than they voted on in the entire 1956–1975 period), including several antitax measures that called for the state to cut billions of dollars from its budget and an item that would require a vote on any proposed tax or fee increase of any kind. Hans Linde, a former justice of the Oregon Supreme Court, refers to the initiative as "lawmaking without government."

Proponents of the initiative offer a number of points in its favor. First, the initiative is important as a last resort, when a legislature has refused to act; further, because the initiative presents a threat, often it is able to spur legislative action. Second, the initiative allows all issues, not just special-interest concerns, to be included on the public agenda. Third, it expresses the popular will directly, without the filtering or distortion introduced by the representational process. Fourth, it reduces alienation toward government because voters who express themselves directly on issues can see government as their own and not someone else's. Fifth, the initiative maximizes the full human potential of citizens as they engage in democracy. Sixth, it results in more informed constituents. Seventh, it reduces the incidence of abuse and corruption endemic to the legislative process. Eighth, it lessens the protection of turf by various interests and encourages change.

Almost all these arguments in favor are rebuttable. First, if the legislature refuses to act on an issue, it is nearly always because the public as well as legislators themselves are sharply divided. Second, nearly all initiative issues are proposed by special interests or by political leaders of one sort or another. For the most part, legislators who are the elected representatives of their constituencies are shut out. Third, the popular will is reflected in the initiative, but usually it is a will crafted by issue campaigns and media advertising, not by deliberation, negotiation, and compromise (what critics call the "distortion" of the legislative process). Fourth, there is no evidence that the initiative reduces alienation; the likelihood is that it increases it, at least among the many people on the losing side. Fifth, engagement is a good idea in theory, but fewer people vote on most initiatives than vote for candidates. Sixth, any issue campaign can provide additional information to citizens, including issue campaigns designed to affect the legislative process. Seventh, it is true that voters, unlike legislators, will not be accused of bartering their votes for campaign contributions. But, unlike legislators, they are not accountable for outcomes. Legislators have to run at the next elections; voters simply go on with their everyday concerns.

In states where the initiative is most frequently used to amend the constitution or make law there is talk of tightening up the process. But hardly anyone—and certainly not any elected politician—advocates doing away with the initiative. Where they have it, citizens overwhelmingly want to keep it. A 1997 Field Poll in California, for example, found that 77 percent thought the initiative was a good thing, whereas only 7 percent thought it was a bad thing. In a national survey, Hibbing and Theiss-Morse came up with a similar finding: 84 percent either strongly agreed or agreed that it was a good idea to "use ballot initiatives more."

The experience of town meetings in New England, as political scientist Jane J. Mansbridge shows, is a far cry from the myth with which Americans are familiar. The myth is that of citizens deriving satisfaction from participating in local decision making. In reality, participation is limited, and for participants "the fears of making a fool of oneself, of losing control, of criticism, and of making enemies" all create tensions that result in the repression of conflict by stifling the discussion of differences. Not surprisingly, even in the framework of town meetings ordinary people do not like conflict. Indeed, Hibbing and Theiss-Morse point out that their focus groups have shown that although Americans do not want to make political decisions themselves, they do want to restrain and weaken elected officials and political institutions like legislatures that make decisions on their behalf. Morris P. Fiorina concludes that "[i]t is time to abandon the notion of political participation as part of human nature. It is not; it is an unnatural act. . . . Contrary to the suggestions of pundits and philosophers, there is nothing wrong with those who do not participate; rather, there is something unusual about those who do."

Although Americans in general favor the idea of the popular initiative, the initiative process clearly benefits some people more than others. Political entrepreneurs with a cause can win more through an initiative than through the legislature. Legislators, themselves, resort to the initiative sometimes even before they attempt to move a measure through the legislative process. That way they need not settle for half a loaf; it's all or nothing. Those who want to run statewide and those who have been elected statewide make use of the initiative to advance their political careers. Since Jerry Brown's governorship, which ended in 1983, every governor of California has sponsored or cosponsored a ballot initiative. In Oregon, Bill Sizemore, an unsuccessful candidate for governor in 1998, has since then made the promotion of initiatives a full-time enterprise. He was responsible for six antitax propositions on the 2000 ballot. In a cartoon in the *Oregonian,* the state's largest newspaper, a teacher diagrams the three branches of state government on the class chalkboard: "Executive, Legislative, Sizemore." Wealthy individuals like George Soros, whose objective is to legalize marijuana for medical use, can exert enormous influence through the initiative process. All they have to do is to identify a promising state by polling, then hire signature collectors, and finally underwrite an expensive campaign. For example, Ron Unz has sponsored bilingual education prohibition initiatives in California, Colorado, and New Mexico.

Most ballot propositions are the product of organized interests, many of which are well funded and all of which employ whatever means necessary to win. Direct democracy, thus, does not limit the power of organized interests, as those who favor the initiative process claim. In the words of Joseph Cooper, "It only changes the ground rules of politics in favor of interest groups that are adept at arousing and exploiting those sweeping and momentary public passions that Madison and the framers were so anxious to contain." Indeed, money is probably more important in initiative campaigns than in candidate elections, although citizen groups with relatively little money to spend can also be successful in initiative elections if they have the right issue. The conclusion that Richard J. Ellis reaches in his book *Democratic Delusions* is that initiatives "typically reveal more about the ideology and preoccupations of those who supply the initiatives than they do about the priorities and values of voters."

Advantages of Representative Democracy

Representative democracy allows opportunities for judgment and skill on the parts of those elected by voters. On their parts, voters ordinarily have little concern for matters of public policy. Even if they did have to decide, in a very general way, on an initiative proposition, they would tend to do so on the basis of a campaign's emotional appeals. For the representative in a legislature, it is not just a matter of deciding yes or no on issues, but of settling on the specific provisions and language of law. In legislation, the devil is in the details. Many initiatives show little knowledge of existing law or of drafting laws, and courts overrule many that they find unconstitutional. Over the long run, this puts the courts in a difficult position. In the legislative process bills are more likely to be modified and clarified on their way to enactment. Some enacted bills may be technically deficient and some simply do not work in practice. But, for the most part, legislatures get done what they aim to do. Those engaged in the process, particularly those who have been at it for a while, are far more skilled at lawmaking than citizens. Indeed, they ought to be. Thus, respected political philosophers and political scientists—people such as Walter Lippmann, E. E. Schattschneider, Joseph Schumpeter, and V. O. Key—evinced a strong belief in a division of labor, with those elected to govern allowed to govern but held accountable by the electorate for how they governed.

Linkage is an essential component of the legislative process but is totally absent from the initiative process. Legislators decide on proposals in context, whereas voters face measures that are disconnected from one another. In a legislature measures introduced today are related to measures introduced in the past. The electorate does not have the memory that the legislature does (nor should it be expected to). Just as the public sees no linkage vertically, it also fails to see it horizontally. In a legislature there are connections among bills. Citizens deciding on an initiative, however, do not have to confront trade-offs. They need not take into account the balance sheet of desirable programs on one side of the ledger and the undesirable need for raising revenues to pay for them on the other side. Nor do voters have to consider priorities as do legislators. A Florida legislator put the dilemma simply: "Do you want to spend $1 billion on prisons? The answer is yes. But if you knew you had to take $1 billion away from education, would you say yes?" Legislators usually do not have the luxury of having their cake and eating it too. Constitutionally or statutorily, state budgets must be balanced. Legislators have to balance them and have to make hard choices in order to do so.

In the initiative process few citizens have a very good idea of the provisions on which they are voting. They depend on information from issue campaigns conducted by means of television, radio, and direct mail. The information they receive tends to be couched in emotional terms and intended to win. Unlike direct democracy, representative democracy allows for deliberation. Citizens are constrained by time, competing interests for whatever leisure hours they have, and an inability to interact on a face-to-face basis. The initiative process is done largely in isolation, without human contact. "There is a real price to public policy," explains David Magleby, an expert on initiative and referendum, "when a chat room substitutes for a committee process or what happens in hallway conversations."

The deliberation that takes place in a representative assembly, as defined by political scientist Joseph M. Bessette, is essentially "reasoning on the merits of public policy." It is a process in which participants seriously consider substantive information and arguments and try to persuade each other as to what constitutes good public policy. Deliberation deals with the merits of an issue and not the politics or the tactics. The process involves three elements: first, the communication of information, including facts and reasons; second, arguments that connect facts to desirable goals; and, third, persuasion leading a policymaker to take action based on the information and arguments. In a deliberative process at least some participants are open to information and arguments that are brought to their attention and are willing to learn from colleagues, lobbyists, and others.

Deliberation is only one element in the legislative process, because the "merits" of an issue, as far as elected public officials are concerned, are not only substantive but also political. That is to say, how constituents, interest groups, political parties, and others feel about issues count as well as do substantive provisions. Nor can reasoning alone ordinarily reconcile opposing interests and views. Bargaining and compromise of one sort or another are used extensively, particularly on those measures that affect the public less directly or little at all. Many of the issues that affect economic interests are of this variety. To get what they want, proponents have to negotiate with the opposition, giving on one point in order to gain on another. The two sides may "logroll," trading one issue in return for another or agreeing to an increase for a budgetary item here if there is also an increase there. Sometimes, the two sides on an issue conflict head on, with a floor vote settling the issue. More often, a compromise, which pleases neither side but is acceptable to both, resolves the issue. In either case, in order to reach a majority, legislators must negotiate, bargain, and compromise along the way.

In the initiative process, compromise does not come into play. "If you win, you get it all," in the words of Magleby. Citizens are used to making decisions individually in terms of either yes or no, this candidate or that candidate, up or down. They do not vote on alternative bills and they cannot amend a proposal to make it more acceptable. All they can do is vote affirmatively, negatively, or abstain. Representative democracy, however, requires thoughtful consideration, give and take, and continuing efforts to forge majorities. Anticipating the impact of electronic democracy, Lawrence K. Grossman writes: "Whenever the public becomes directly engaged in a major controversial issue, the process of negotiation, compromise, and deliberation—the essence of effective policy making—becomes difficult, if not impossible."

Yet, democracy requires compromise by elected public officials and a disposition to accept compromise on the part of the public. That disposition may be somewhat tenuous, because many Americans regard compromise as selling out one's principles. But the disposition is even more tenuous in nondemocratic societies, as is recounted by Jean Bethke Elshtain, a political philosopher. In her book *Democracy on Trial* she repeats a conversation she had in Prague in the summer of 1990 with a former dissident who was elected to Parliament in the aftermath of the democratization of Czechoslovakia. He explained that the Czechs had a real problem because they were not used to democracy and it would be difficult to build democratic dispositions. It would take time, because "the democratic ideal is a very difficult ideal." For him, the democratic ideal had at its heart the idea of compromise, "because you have to accept that people are going to have different views, especially on the most volatile matters and important issues." In Elshtain's judgment, "Western democracies are not presently doing a good job of nurturing these democratic dispositions that encourage people to accept that they can't always get what they want."

Responsibility for one's decisions is another aspect of representative democracy missing from a process dominated by citizens. In a legislature, every member, or practically every member, takes a stand on just about every issue, with the exception of the very few matters that are intentionally swept under the rug rather than voted on in public. Whatever passes into law does so by the vote of a majority or near majority. In contrast, most ballot measures that pass do so with substantially less than a majority of eligible voters in support. Voters, of course, do not have to explain their votes, or defend them. Indeed, no one knows how or whether a particular citizen voted. Legislators are on record, not for everything they do, but for quite a lot. They have to defend their records, justify their decisions to their constituencies, and fend off attack if their election is contested.

Representative democracy tends, more than popular democracy, to take into consideration long-term interests. Legislatures can be faulted for not looking ahead, at least not ahead beyond the next election. As present-oriented as they may be, legislators are still less likely than citizens to sacrifice the intermediate term for more immediate gratification.

Representative democracy, furthermore, takes some of the direct confrontation and conflict out of the policymaking process. Consensus for policy outcomes is built through negotiation, bargaining, and compromise. Such consensus building tends to dilute policy, so that neither side gets quite what it wants. Occasionally, the result is an awkward contraption that can command a majority in the process but does not work very well in practice. More often, if both sides agree to it, a compromise will prove quite workable. In the alternative offered by a parliamentary form of government cohesive party majorities would simply enact their own policies, outvoting their opponents rather than compromising with them. Even if legislative parties were that cohesive, in two-party states such an arrangement would lead to policy by fits and starts. The party in power would enact its programs, but the opposition would repeal them when it won power. Policy would zig and zag. Could such programs be administered? Could bureaucrats cope? What could citizens expect? Under conditions of direct democracy, this could also be the situation, with different people voting and some people changing their minds and altering direction from referendum to referendum. When policy changes rapidly, implementation becomes almost impossible.

In Sum

As compared with executive dominance and direct democracy, the legislative process has much to recommend it. The legislature was intended by the framers of the Constitution to act as a middleman, mediating between the public and policy. In *Federalist* No. 10, Madison conceived of representative democracy as a way to add reason to the popular will. His idea was that voters would elect people who were wise, virtuous, competent, and experienced. Together, such representatives would deliberate before deciding. The process would "refine and enlarge" public views by "passing them through the medium of a chosen body of citizens," who would be able to express "the cool and deliberate sense of the community," not just peoples' transient impulses or passions. *The Federalist Papers* are replete with references, not to the specific interests of the district or state, but to "the permanent and aggregate interests of the community," "the public good," "the good of the whole," "the public weal," "the common interest," and the like. All were to be arrived at by a process engaged in by representatives elected by the people.

Probably no legislative body can be expected to live up to the ideal set forth in the writings of Alexander Hamilton, John Jay, and James Madison. Few contemporary legislators will stand in the way of a strong popular will, even if they believe that it may be in the best interests of the nation or state to oppose their constituency. Few will risk opposing "factions" or interests that are aroused and have strong support in their districts. Few have a notion of a public interest independent of their own views, their party's views, and their constituency's views.

The Federalist ideal has been modified by other currents in the development of the American political system, currents that have enlarged the role of the people and restructured that of the people's representatives. Today the system of representative democracy provides a reasonable balance between the power of the public on the one hand and the power of the office-holder on the other.

Representative democracy does work—by no means perfectly, but reasonably well. It allows for the interplay of self-interest, group interest, and the public interest. Precisely how representative democracy works is difficult to nail down. It varies, depending on the time, the place, and the issue. Although the representatives whom citizens elect to Congress and state legislatures are not quite the people of "virtue" Madison envisaged, the overwhelming majority of them are impelled by public service motivations. They desire to do good, and they also want to be reelected. The first motivation causes them to want to stay in office, and the second causes them to heed their constituents' wishes. Their constituency is probably more important to them than any other single factor, with the possible exception of their own beliefs. On the relatively few issues of widespread concern in the district, more likely than not constituents are divided; some feel one way, some the other. But on most issues that legislators address, only a small proportion of constituents have much of a feeling at all. Those that do are likely to be members of interest groups that are taking a leading role on the issue in question. The legislative process is one in which people are represented, not only by those they elect to office, but also by groups to which they belong or that represent their values, interests, and opinions, whether they are members or not. Constituency, interest group, and political party all are brought to bear on legislators as they engage in the lawmaking process.

The processes of representative democracy are conditioned by the diversity of the nation and states. The public's values, priorities, interests, and opinions differ and sometimes conflict. Such differences and conflicts are expressed through three principal channels, each of which overlaps the others. The first channel is the elected representatives, the people selected to speak in the legislature on behalf of the electorate. The second channel is the political parties, the organizations with which most Americans affiliate and for whose candidates most Americans regularly vote. The parties represent different constituencies and provide alternative policy agendas on the major policy issues before the legislature. The third channel is the interest groups, many of which align themselves with either the Democrats or the Republicans. These groups are narrower than parties or representatives in their representation and more focused in their policy objectives.

The concerns of the electorate, political parties, and interest groups all come to bear on the lawmaking process in a complex interaction depicted in Figure 10-1. Debate, deliberation, negotiation, conflict, and compromise are all crucial elements of this majoritarian process. Not every issue has an equal chance of receiving a succession of majority endorsements. It depends on the merits of the case, the amount and intensity of political support and opposition, the strategies and tactics employed, and the circumstances at the time. Some issues manage to navigate the process with little or no opposition. Others, however, make little headway. Relatively few are fought out; a large number are worked out.

The system requires constant adaptation and tinkering. As Joseph Cooper writes, "Democratic government is always a work in progress with no guarantees of success and no easy formula to direct or confirm results." Improvements have to be made continuously, albeit not the same ones in Washington, D.C., and in each and every state. In addition to the need for improvement, which it does get, representative democracy requires understanding and support, which it does not get nowadays. Many Americans have an illusory notion of what democracy entails and are turned off both by its actual practice and how the media portray that practice. That illusory notion, as described by John Mueller, is "one which suggests that lawmaking under democracy . . . should be characterized by careful deliberation and consensual resolution in which the views of honest and naive little peo-

Figure 10-1 The System of Representative Democracy

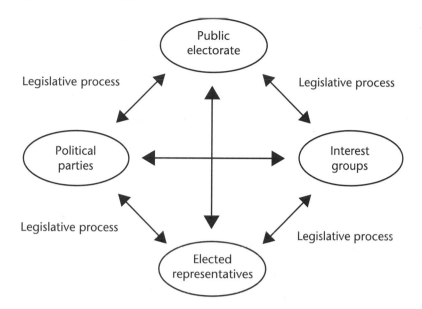

ple . . . should eventually prevail." But democracy does not work that way, nor should it. Democracy is far more complicated, conflictual, and disorderly.

At a time when the nation itself is threatened, it behooves us to take stock of just what Americans are defending. Americans are defending their country, their flag, and their free and democratic way of life. Part of that democratic way of life is the political system that serves them far better than they believe and pretty well over all. The future of their political system is by no means assured. The preservation of representative democracy depends on acknowledgment, appreciation, and support, none of which is in sufficient supply. We have no problem subscribing to the abstract principles of democracy; it's the messy practices that we are not prepared to accept.

The alternatives are unappealing—executive dominance or direct democracy or some combination of both. Cooper's warning with respect to Congress merits our concern. "When cynicism abounds," he writes, "declining confidence in congressional performance fosters continuing reductions in congressional power and the gradual transformation of the decentralized form of deliberative democracy intended by the Framers into a centralized forum of plebiscitary democracy, based on presidential and bureaucratic power." Does it make sense to jettison a system that has worked so well for so long? And to put what in its place?

Sources and Suggested Reading

The section on executive dominance draws on pp. 293–324 and that on direct democracy and representative democracy on pp. 27–48 of Alan Rosenthal, *The Decline of Representative Democracy* (Washington, D.C.: CQ Press, 1998). For the effect of modern technology on representative democracy, see Lawrence K. Grossman, *The Electronic Republic* (New York: Viking, 1995), and John G. Geer, *From Tea Leaves to Opinion Polls* (New York: Columbia University Press, 1996). From another point of view, see Dick Morris, *Vote.com* (Los Angeles: Renaissance Books, 1999). The *National Journal* article referred to in the discussion of direct democracy is by Burt Solomon, "We the Mob," July 1, 2000, 2140–2143.

John R. Hibbing and Elizabeth Theiss-Morse's analysis of citizen attitudes toward democracy and participation is reported in their *Congress as Public Enemy* (Cambridge: Cambridge University Press, 1995) and in their *Stealth Democracy* (Cambridge: Cambridge University Press, 2002). The New England town meeting is explored by Jane J. Mansbridge in *Beyond Adversarial Democracy* (Chicago: University of Chicago Press, 1983). An important argument is advanced by Morris P. Fiorina in his chapter, "Extreme Voices: A Dark Side of Civic Engagement," in *Civic Engagement in American Democracy,* ed. Theda Skocpol and Morris P. Fiorina (Washington, D.C.: Brookings Institution Press, 1999).

Still the most informative work on the initiative and referendum is David B. Magleby, *Direct Legislation: Voting on Ballot Propositions in the United States* (Baltimore: Johns Hopkins University Press, 1984). We draw on Magleby's recent comments, which are in CSG West, *Western Initiatives: A Challenge to Representative Democracy,* excerpts from CSG-West Committee on the Future of Western Legislatures (July 1999). Also important is Richard J. Ellis, *Democratic Delusions: The Initiative Process in America* (Lawrence: University Press of Kansas, 2002). For further reading on the initiative, see David S. Broder, *Democracy Derailed: Initiative Campaigns and the Power of Money* (Orlando: Harcourt Brace, 2000), and on the initiative in California, see Peter Schrag, *Paradise Lost: California's Experience and America's Future* (New York: New Press, 1998).

Joseph Cooper's chapters "The Puzzle of Distrust" and "Performance and Expectations in American Politics: The Problem of Distrust in Congress" are essential reading; they introduce and conclude his edited volume, *Congress and the Decline of Public Trust* (Boulder: Westview Press, 1999).

Strong historical and contemporary arguments are advanced in favor of representative democracy in the following: John Mueller, *Capitalism, Democracy, and Ralph's Pretty Good Grocery* (Princeton: Princeton University Press, 1999); Michael Schudson, *The Good Citizen* (New York: Free Press, 1998); Joseph M. Bessette, *The Mild Voice of Reason* (Chicago: University of Chicago Press, 1994); and Jean Bethke Elshtain, *Democracy on Trial* (New York: Basic Books, 1995).

Index